T0330352

The Value of Applied Economics

A.J. Brown as a young man

The Value of Applied Economics

Economics

The Life and Work of Arthur (A.J.) Brown

Kenneth Button

University Professor, Schar School of Policy and Government, George Mason University, USA

Edward Elgar
PUBLISHING

Cheltenham, UK • Northampton, MA, USA

Published by
Edward Elgar Publishing Limited
The Lypiatts
15 Lansdown Road
Cheltenham
Glos GL50 2JA
UK

Edward Elgar Publishing, Inc.
William Pratt House
9 Dewey Court
Northampton
Massachusetts 01060
USA

A catalogue record for this book
is available from the British Library

Library of Congress Control Number: 2017947107

This book is available electronically in the **Elgar**online
Economics subject collection
DOI 10.4337/9781786433664

ISBN 978 1 78643 365 7 (cased)
ISBN 978 1 78643 366 4 (eBook)

Typeset by Servis Filmsetting Ltd, Stockport, Cheshire
Printed and bound by CPI Group (UK) Ltd, Croydon, CR0 4YY

Contents

Preface

There are different types of biography. This one falls into the category of what are sometimes called, "intellectual biographies." It certainly covers the life of an individual, the English economist Arthur Joseph (A.J.) Brown, but it does not dwell greatly on his personal life, other than regard to how this seems to have affected his approach to economics and policy advising. What it does, however, is spend some time on the intellectual and contextual background to his work, most notably the changes in the economic climate over his lifetime and shifts in the ways economics was approached.

The book is distinguished by having a Foreword written by Arthur Brown's sons, Henry and William. This provides a very personal perspective on Brown's personality and his family life outside of academia. It enriches the volume by giving a clearer image of how this very reserved and modest man approached life, and some of the factors that influenced his attitudes over time. It becomes clear that his caring and thoughtful approach regarding his home life were entwined with the way he approached life as a professional economist.

I would like to thank Zhenhua Chen for his assistance with data analysis, and Willy Brown, John Bowers, Ali El-Agraa, Andrea Salanti, and Tony Thirlwall for useful comments contributing to this work. Additionally, Nick Brewster from the Special Collections Section of the Brotherton Library, Leeds University, provided invaluable help in guiding me through Arthur Brown's correspondence and papers, and those of the School of Economics and Commerce. The comments of three referees and the editor have been invaluable. The usual disclaimers apply.

Foreword by Henry Brown and William Brown

ARTHUR BROWN AS A PRIVATE PERSON

All children have perspectives on their parents that are unique in both strengths and weaknesses. Kenneth Button has provided a fine account of the intellectual journeys of our father which were the background to our growing up; but it was a background of which we were only casually aware. For us he was simply part of the family. It is an interesting challenge to disentangle some memories that might provide the reader of this book with a fuller picture of Arthur Brown, beyond the academic economist.

A good starting point is with our mother, Joan. A clergyman's daughter from Lancashire, she was a classics scholar at Oxford when they met. It was a reflection of her strength of mind that, despite the college rule that it would deny her a full honours degree, they married while she was still an undergraduate. Their three sons were born in Oxford during the War while he worked in London, and at its end the family moved to Richmond upon Thames. In 1947 we settled in the house in Leeds where they lived for the rest of their lives. She looked after the home and family. Building on her love of its literature, she taught herself Russian, taking a degree in 1963 and then becoming a teacher of Russian and Latin at Leeds Girls' High School. Our parents were totally devoted to each other, and she was a constant support for him. Their mutual support was especially important when, in 1959, the family was devastated by the death of our eldest brother, John, in an accident in the Swiss Alps at the age of 19.

Home was a large house built in 1912 with an acre of garden, much of it woodland, on the edge of the Meanwood Valley. Until long after we left there was no television in the house, but ever-growing shelves of books on a great variety of subjects. Our parents were both keen gardeners. For our father 'the great thing about a garden is that it is always working with you', and 'the wonderful thing about gardening is that you almost always get more done than you expected'. It was the focus of his weekends and one reason why he kept physically fit, because a large and varied garden demands constant manual work. As children, the garden gave us considerable freedom from parental supervision. We were free to climb trees and dig dens – and later learn more constructive skills such as the use of axes, bowsaws and scythes. As they grew older, our parents beat a careful strategic retreat from the garden, allowing it to become ever more jungle-like, with massive rhododendrons, climbing roses and resident foxes.

A distinctive feature of the family was that neither parent ever learned to drive. They both liked walking, and Leeds had a good public transport system. This meant we were not to become familiar with the nearby Yorkshire Dales until later in life. Having no car shaped our holidays, always reached by railway. Twice a year for as long as they were alive we would stay with our paternal grand-parents who had retired to a village near Prestatyn, Wales, wonderfully close to both the beach and hilly countryside. Each August we would go, by the memorable Settle–Carlisle line, for two weeks in a hotel near Loweswater in the north-west Lake District. There we walked the fells and messed about in rowing boats on Crummock Water. Our father greatly enjoyed making holidays creative and useful as well as fun, which ensured we became adept with maps and, for example, with drawing little graphs that plotted the distance of a walk against altitude. Even on holiday his love of back-of-envelope calculations never left him. In remote spots, in miserable weather, his 6-inch slide-rule would be brought out to resolve a debate about the weight of water passing over a weir, or the number of trees in a plantation. Loweswater became a home from home for our parents, who returned there, usually twice a year, until infirmity intervened nearly fifty years after their first visit.

In some ways our father filled the conventional paternal role of the 1950s. He would get up after we had left for school and return from work after we had finished tea. But he was not a remote parent. He took great interest in our enthusiasms and hobbies. Given the time, he would join us listening to, for example, *The Goon Show* and Tom Lehrer. His mildly bawdy sense of humour was never far away. He was an enthusiastic photographer, which in those days meant color transparencies viewed on a screen in a darkened room. These were always great family occasions, full of conversation, whether the pictures were of a recent holiday or from his own increasingly exotic trips abroad for work. Later we were sometimes to travel with him, and he delighted in sharing with us the associated sights and discoveries. On visits home, after we had left, it is the long conversations that come to mind. These were never about gossip or ephemera. He was always interested in discussing what we and he were doing and reading and thinking, and about major events in the world around us.

A soft-spoken man, he probably came over as rather shy. Perhaps he was slightly intimidating because he was not strong on small-talk and was impatient of what he perceived as folly. He was genuinely modest, and had mixed with the Great and Good sufficiently to be rarely impressed. Beyond the family, his closest friends were from among his academic acquaint-ances, past and present. His times in the States provided lasting American friends, and he remained a loyal reader of the *New Yorker* all his life. His reading was very broad. He kept his early interest in science alive with a regular subscription to the *New Scientist.* Although he did not share our mother's interest in fiction, he retained his youthful affection for Jane Austen, Conan Doyle and pre-war detective writers such as Dorothy L. Sayers. He preferred to read fact-based material – travel writing, modern history and biographies. He maintained a lively interest in the visual arts, rarely missing an exhibition in London if it could be fitted into his regular trips there.

Perhaps least evident to others was his love and knowledge of both English and German poetry. In his youth he had read a great deal and, having an extraordinarily retentive memory, he remembered a great deal. It was fascinating to watch him slowly dredge up from his memory whole verses, prompted by some passing poetic quote. Wordsworth was a favorite. When he was away from home, living in the States, he and our mother had worked their way through the Shakespeare sonnets together, week by week, by airmail letters. He returned to reading poetry after his retirement. It was partly the conciseness of good poetry that appealed to him. He was dispar-aging of grandiose waffle. He took delight in applying what he called his 'reversal test': does a given statement sound equally plausible if you insert a negative in it? His passion for evidence may lie behind his ceasing to be religious at some point in his late twenties, despite that religion remained important to our mother. It was also a reason for his never becoming politically involved, despite being politically well informed. He found the world intensely interesting, and the challenge for him was to understand it.

Henry Brown and William Brown
July 2017

1. Introduction

This book does several things, although certainly not in equal amounts. It is primarily an economic, as opposed to a personal, biography of an influential English economist, Arthur Joseph (A.J.) Brown. In this case, though, the influence was neither on the development of high theory nor on the knee-jerk reaction of public opinion that often determines subjects for biography. Rather, it examines the importance and changes in application of applied economics in public policy creation. Added to this, it is an account of how economics can usefully be applied to examining important problems of the day in a rigorous and structured way given the data and technical constraints in place. Linked to this, it implicitly examines the commonality of many economic problems across time and space. It also looks at how university-level economics education in Britain changed in the 1950s and 1960s, and the challenges of building a successful department, if not from scratch, then at least from a relative small scale.

Most academics are people of their times. Arthur Brown fits very much into that mold. He taught and researched economics from the 1930s through the 1980s at a time when many transitions in the subject were taking place; at a time when there were major shifts in the way that the role of higher education, especially in the UK, was perceived; and at a time when there were significant changes in the world economy. In particular, the period from the Great Depression to the 1960s saw the push to operationalize the ideas found in John Maynard Keynes's "book on economic theory which will largely revolutionize—not, I suppose, at once but in the course of the next ten years—the way the world thinks about economic problem."[1] But, within economics, it also saw the emergence of systematic macroeconomic data collection, the intellectual technical tools to model from it, and the "electro-engineering equipment" to analysis it.

Brown was an economist who in a way straddled this world. He went to Oxford in the mid-1930s to study "science" (these days it would be called physics), graduated in politics, philosophy, and economics (PPE), and went on to become an academic in a provisional English university and to provide a range of public services making use of largely Keynesian economic ideas but within an older tradition of applied economics that can be traced back at least to the nineteenth century. In this context, he interacted with many of the leading economic thinkers of his time, such as Roy Harrod, James Meade, Charles Hitch, Jacob Marschak, John Hicks, Henry Phelps Brown, and later Bill Phillips, Wassily Leontief, and Oscar Lange.

The challenges of economics, at least most of that which has any real-world use, was famously summed up by Keynes (1924: 333n), whom most would consider one of the more accomplished practitioners, even if not always agreeing with all his views:

> Professor [Max] Planck, of Berlin, the famous originator of the Quantum Theory, once remarked to me that in early life he had thought of studying economics, but had found it too difficult! Professor Planck could easily master the whole corpus of mathematic economics in a few days. He did not mean that! But the amalgam of logic and intuition and the wide knowledge of facts, most of which are not precise, which is required for economic interpretation in its highest form is, quite truly, overwhelmingly difficult for those whose gift mainly consists in the power to imagine and pursue to their furthest points the implications and prior conditions of comparatively simple facts which are known with a high degree of precision.

THE SHIFTING SANDS OF ECONOMICS

Defining economics beyond Jacob Viner's quip that "Economics is what economists do" or Kenneth Galbraith's more caustic "Economics is extremely useful as a form of employment for economists" is not easy. Even Joseph Schumpeter (1954: 3), in his seminal work on the history of economic analysis, does not attempt a definition. Rather, he talks about being concerned with "the history of the intellectual efforts men have made to in order to *understand* economic phenomena or, which comes to the same thing, the history of the analytic or scientific aspects of economic thought" (italics in original). But he never defines what "economic thought" is. Today's students are often left in similar murkiness surrounding more experienced scholars. Many modern textbooks do not even try to provide a definition, but simply update Viner and Galbraith's vagueness by dancing around, providing a definition using phrases such as "We let the subject matter speak for itself." In this age of dissolving disciplines and interdisciplinary analysis this is, however, perhaps less of a cop-out that it may initially appear.

This vagueness is perhaps more reasonably justified in the changing nature of economics. The modern idea of economics—compared to say chemistry or physics on the hard-physical science side, or distinct notions of literature and sculpture on the arts side—is relatively new and, importantly, far from settled.

Although Schumpeter's work on the history of economic thought extends back to classical times, economics as we now think of it is generally traced back to the second part of the eighteenth century. In the days of Adam Smith, economics was largely seen as part of a wider moral philosophy. Smith's (1776) work clearly takes this line, with his *An Inquiry into the Nature and Causes of the Wealth of Nations* dealing with what he calls "familial rights"—now generally considered the core of economics. His earlier work, *The Theory of Moral Sentiments* (1759), sets this within a broader range of subjects that also included ethics and virtue, private rights and natural liberty, and state and individual rights (what might be considered political science today). Smith's subsequent definition of economics, as the title of his famed 1776 tome highlights, places it squarely as the study of the nature and causes of nations' wealth, or simply as the study of wealth.

How this is to be done, how wealth is to be defined, or indeed what is a 'nation" in the modern world, keeps economic philosophers occupied. The subject has also increasingly been expanded in scope as these debates have taken place and a range of sub-areas, partly as a function of the need to make analysis manageable, have emerged. The long listing of "Subject Descriptors" found in the *Journal of Economic Literature* is clear testament to this.

Our interest here is in a microcosm of this world of work, and particularly in one person's contribution to our understanding of how economies function. The backdrop is not the heady days of turmoil in economic thinking at the end of the eighteenth century, not the early Industrial Revolution, not the days of Empire, and not those of the Great Depression—although the latter marginally comes into the story, when many of the better-known economists came to the fore. Rather, it is a period of consolidation of existing economic ideas and of quantification and public policy adjustments. This was the period from the very late 1930s to the late 1970s. And, while the focus is largely on the United Kingdom and economics therein, there is much wider geographical relevance to the work involved.

The period immediately after World War II saw considerable shifts in emphasis in the economics discipline. The traditional approach, with its focus on exposition and prose, was being transformed by the likes of Jan Tinbergen, pushing forward more explicit quantification, and of Paul Samuelson, bringing the language of mathematics to the core of the subject; in the pre-Samuelson era, 70 percent of articles in the *American Economic Review* in 1940 contained no mathematics. None of these changes were entirely new in themselves—Stanley Jevons, Léon Walras, and others had been involved in encouraging more explicit formalization—but the early 1950s saw a major shift in the mainstream.

As the study of the aggregate gained ground, Keynesian economics—with its novel concepts such as the consumption function, liquidity preference, and marginal efficiency of investment—cried out for more formalization and quantification. The inflations of the immediate post-World War II period highlighted a specific area where Keynesian theory was proving deficient: understanding the forces that cause rises in aggregate price levels. To help resolve this type of problem, electronic calculators, and later mainframe computers, began to provide the necessary powers of estimation, econometrics (the link between data and theory), and mathematics (the tools for formal hypothesis setting). The political desire to have more control, or at least influence, over national economies provided the stimulus for systematic data collection. Institutionally, this led to a period of shifting "power" within the academy, with an overall rise in the perceived importance of economic research and education resulting in new departments being formed, existing ones being expanded, and some established ones losing influence.

Against this background, the interests here are several. One is the nature of the transition process in economic methodology, and examining just how messy it was. It was neither a rapid change nor a very clean one, and certainly there was questioning of the speed at which some of the results thrown up was useful. Against this background, the interests here are several. One is the nature of the transition process in economic methodology, and examining just how messy it was. It was neither a rapid change nor a very clean one, and certainly there was questioning of the speed at which some of the results thrown up were useful. In this context, the role of the economist changed in terms of how and what economic advice was given to government and industry, and the sorts of information that was given. Coupled with this was the matter of what education and training economists should receive in universities, and what types of career paths would emerge. These were matters that Brown was as much engaged in as in the actual changes in economic thinking themselves. While he produced important theoretical papers Brown's main contributions were, however, on the application of economics.

THE ROLE OF THE APPLIED ECONOMIST

A reading of Adam Smith, and indeed of most subsequent works of the neo-classical economists of the nineteenth century, reveals considerable knowledge of and interest in the economic conductions of their time. Their authors did not see economics as a sort of intellectual exercise based entirely on inductive methods, but rather as one that had relevance and an understanding of actual relationships that would allow the development of economic policy. When cogitating in front of his students over the justi-fication for his 1979/80 and 1980/81 London School of Economics (LSE) course on the History of Economic thought, Lionel Robbins observed that, "It's a subject which, strange as it may seem, has the property of being described—to use the fashionable word—as relevant to your interest in the world around us" (in Robbins et al., 1998: 6).

So, what are the general skills required of an economist? Here Keynes provides the answer:

> The study of economics does not seem to require any specialized gifts of an unusually high order. Is it not, intellectually regarded, a very easy subject compared with the higher branches of philosophy or pure science? An easy subject at which few excel! The paradox finds its explanation, perhaps, in that the master-economist must possess a rare combination of gifts. He must be mathematician, historian, statesman, philosopher—in some degree. He must understand symbols and speak in words. He must contemplate the particular in terms of the general and touch abstract and concrete in the same flight of thought. He must study the present in the light of the past for the purposes of the future. No part of man's nature or his institutions must lie entirely outside his regard. He must be purposeful and disinterested in a simultaneous mood; as aloof and incorruptible as an artist, yet sometimes as near to earth as a politi-cian. (Keynes 1924: 321–2)

But, given this, the discipline of economics has fragmented over the years into schools of thought, methods of analysis, subject content, and degree of interface with other disciplines such as sociology and psychol-ogy or topic areas such as policy studies. Where economists work depends on their interests and, given notions of comparative advantage, their skills portfolio. But perhaps more importantly and, like in many other subjects, there has been something of a split between the theoretical and more abstract side of the discipline and the applied side.[2] As with physics and other disciplines where this also features, the boundaries are not firm and individuals often cross them in their work. Indeed, in the latter account of Brown's work, while much of this would fall into what most would consider the applied side of the divide, he also worked on the theoretical.

The contents of a symposium published in the *History of Political Economy* offer more detail of how applied economics has developed. In that work, Roger Backhouse and Jeff Biddle traced the history and meaning of the concept of applied economics, suggesting that "at least by the turn of the century [1900], and probably earlier, it had become common for economists to talk and think in terms of applying applied political economy/economics." They add: "In the twentieth century, the idea that there is a distinct set of activities that can be labelled *applied economics* has come to be reflected in the institutional structure of the discipline" (2000: 5, 9; italics in original).

At that time, however, there was not necessarily agreement as to what the term "applied" meant, and views on precise definitions and boundaries differed and have subsequently evolved over time. Nevertheless, Backhouse and Biddle argue, this conception of applied economics "involves a strict distinction between building theory and applying theory, with the former activity being regarded as more important from a scientific standpoint. . . . Related to this is a belief that applied economics is more ephemeral than theory" (p. 12). This was reflected in some quarters in the late nineteenth century and slightly later, when the more general use of the term applied economics was used to indicate its practical side: that is, it had some use for business or policy making.[3] This is the way John Neville Keynes (1917) defines it in *The Scope and Method of Political Economy*.

Backhouse and Biddle also suggest that any history of economic thought that focused on applied economics could lead to a very different outcome from one that did not. Moreover, it is necessary to understand the issues that are important at any time: "to neglect them is to distort the history" (2000: 13) Hence, "the notion of applied economics itself is an object of historical investigation," including "the perceived relationship between applied and non-applied economics," which has "changed significantly over the past century." Of relevance, here, it is maintained that: "It is when one reaches the 1950s that any failure to focus explicitly on applied economics can lead to a seriously distorted picture in which the bulk of the discipline is neglected" (p. 14).[4]

From different perspectives, various other economists have expressed related concerns about the focus of economics in the late twentieth century onwards. For example, Ronald Coase (2006), when considering a widely debated case of the economic implications of a hold-up of the take-over of coachbuilder Fisher Body by General Motors (GM), observed that mainstream economics is strong on theory but weak on facts, a position more recently argued by Stephen Littlechild (2008) in a lecture at Cambridge. In his view, this imbalance has led economics into error. To quote Coase (2006: 276) on the general situation:

> As I see it, progress in understanding the working of the economic system will come from an interplay between theory and empirical work. The theory suggests what empirical work might be fruitful, the subsequent empirical work suggests what modification in the theory or rethinking is needed, which in turn leads to new empirical work. If rightly done, scientific research is a never-ending process, but one that leads to greater understanding at each stage. In scientific research, we may win battles but not the war.

Another major British economist of this period, although one that stayed in the United Kingdom for his academic career, Maurice Peston (2006: 81), also bemoaned the lack of realism in much of modern analysis:

> Economics journals continue to be full of weird and wonderful theories, which are for the most part rehashes of earlier weird and wonderful theories. What has changed is that it is now absolutely necessary to formulate everything in high-powered mathematical terms. I know I should be accused of churlishness if I were to add that this is intended largely to disguise the essential triviality of what is set forth. Occasionally, something of intellectual interest emerges, and there is even the odd article that throws light on the real world. Econometrics too gets more and more sophisticated, but rarely is anything of interest discovered.

There have been concerns that the shift towards more formalization of economics from the 1950s, despite the resistance of such names as J.K. Galbraith, the move away from the historical school that had been generally dominant in Continental economic thinking, and the institutionalism of the likes of Thorstein Veblen, John R. Commons, Wesley Mitchell, and Clarence Ayres (with its pedigree largely in the US) were also distracting economists from the real world. However, the emergence of cliometrics and the New Institutional Economics—and Nobel Prizes being awarded to Robert Fogel and Douglass C. North in the former context and to Oliver Williamson and others in the latter—suggests that this situation has subsequently been at least partially reversed. Brown was certainly aware of the debates over these topics but, that at least in the 1950s, institutions were still adequately being handled in applied economic analysis, although his views on economics education at the time were somewhat different:

> It is doubtful if economists engaged in research sin very greatly by simplifying or generalizing the institutional background. It might be claimed that simplification of this kind is essential to the business of perfecting instruments of analysis and that economists are usually aware of what they are doing in this direction. But it can hardly be denied that economics is usually taught in such a way as to under emphasize the importance of the institutional background in determining what kind of theoretical analysis is applicable. (Brown, 1951c: 489)

WHERE DOES A.J. BROWN FIT INTO THIS?

By inclination, Brown was an applied economist, as can be seen from his subsequent economics textbooks (Brown, 1948; 1959a), seeing his role as applying economics to assist in the formulation and assessment of policy. The elements of his applied economics were the development of an appropriate theory for the problem and the manipulation of available statistical data to get a "feel" for the quantitative significance of the variables. Bowers (2003) outlines Brown's approach: "At meetings, having explained the economic theory, Brown would produce a small slide-rule that he carried in his top pocket and carry out rapid calculations to give some quantitative basis for argument. In his hands this simple tool kit could be devastatingly effective." By modern standards this approach would likely be considered *ad hoc*, but it was used at a time before computers and associated software were widely available, and when even electronic calculators were rare (Renfro, 2004). In practice, it provided a powerful tool for policy makers of the day.

Brown did significant work in international trade, economic development, inflation, and regional economics. His 1959 book, *Introduction to the World Economy*, was a standard text for many years, and *The Great Inflation, 1939–1951* (1955) lays claim to have presented the underlying concept of the Phillips Curve relating wage changes to unemployment some four years before Phillips himself.

Brown was the archetypical high-flying academic of his time. He graduated in 1936 with first-class honors in PPE from Oxford University and within three years, and whilst working in a Harrods research group on prices and interest (Besomi, 1998), he had published the first empirical analyses of liquidity-preference, making the first use of confluence analysis in the United Kingdom (Brown, 1938, 1939a). Meantime, he beat the future British Prime Minister, Harold Wilson, and the historian and future principal of the University College of Buckingham, Max Beloff, to a Fellowship at Oxford's All Souls College. Brown had a distinguished war service in the Foreign Research and Press Service, the Research Department of the Foreign Office, and in the Economic Section of the Cabinet Office, where he worked on German re-armament and on the creation of the Government Statistical Service. He moved to Leeds University in 1947 as Professor of Economics and head of the department at the age of 33, the youngest professor of his generation in the subject. He subsequently declined professorships at both Oxford and Cambridge.

His extensive administrative acumen, allowed Brown to build up a major academic department at the University of Leeds and to later serve as its pro-vice-chancellor. Brown was also not averse to econometrics, and was far from non-technical, having initially intended to read science at Oxford, and appointed leading quantitative economists to his department. Indeed, his DPhil supervisor was Jacob Marschak, sometimes called "the father of econometrics." Brown's contribution to public service in economics was recognized by his being President of Section F of the British Association for the Advancement of Science, an elected Fellow of the British Academy, being made a Commander of the Order of the British Empire (CBE), and receiving honorary doctorates from four universities. He was on the council of the Royal Economic Society twice and was its President from 1976 to 1978.

But Brown also had another talent, and one that was often drawn upon outside of academia. Although competent as a mathematician (and many of his papers have mathematical derivations in them), he was not in the league of John Hicks whom he thought was a mathematician in the way he thought. Most of Brown's writings were largely (and often exclusively) in prose, with a sprinkling of charts and tables. But underlying this was a solid and rigorous basis to his arguments. Indeed, it was very much of the style of Alfred Marshall, who said of presenting economics:

> [I had] a growing feeling in the later years of my work at the subject that a good mathematical theorem dealing with economic hypotheses was very unlikely to be good economics: and I went more and more on the rules—(1) Use mathematics as a shorthand language, rather than an engine of inquiry. (2) Keep to them till you have done. (3) Translate into English. (4) Then illustrate by examples that are important in real-life. (5) Burn the mathematics. (6) If you can't succeed in (4), burn (3). This last I did often.[5]

Brown's applied skills, drafting abilities, and inherent common sense made him a popular economist for government and international agencies, and whilst at Leeds he continued in part-time public service. In the 1960s he was a member of both the East Africa Economic and Fiscal Commission and the Secretary of State's Advisory Group on Central Africa (a constituent of the UN's Consultative Group that looked at the economic and social consequences of disarmament), and a member of the University Grants Committee that allocated public monies to universities. This was in addition to serving on committees responsible for establishing the Universities of Kent and Bradford. When the 1966 Wilson government launched an active regional policy, Brown was appointed to the committee considering the Intermediate Areas. He was already directing a major project on regional policy based at the National Institute of Economic and Social Research (NIESR) and thus was well prepared for the task.

What Brown was not was a "public economist" in the modern sense. Despite drafting very accessible articles during World War II, most of his research output was aimed at academics and policy makers. When it came to spreading his findings, or offering his views, he was no Maynard Keynes who wrote extensively for the *Manchester Guardian* and other newspapers and magazines between the wars, or the American economist Irvine Fisher who frequently wrote newspaper articles and circulars over the same period. Brown certainly did not produce regular contributions of the kind that Paul Samuelson and Milton Friedman did for alternative issues of *Newsweek* in the 1960s through the 1980s, or regular opinion editorials and blogs that Paul Krugman (*New York Times*) and Lawrence Summers (*Financial Times*) currently do for major newspapers; and it seems unlikely he would have become an addicted blogger even if born thirty years later! His media involved more conventional academic channels.

IS THERE STILL ROOM FOR APPLIED ECONOMICS?

The trend in economics since the mid-1960s or earlier has been one of focus on theory and abstraction, with many subject areas that were traditionally part of the economics taught at universities hived off into departments such as business schools or engineering. Indeed, the School of Economics and Commerce that Brown built up at Leeds in the 1950s is now within the Leeds Business School at the university. This trend is perhaps understandable as the market for students has shifted, with rising demand for graduates with specific skill sets rather than a more general background. Also, employers are seldom fully conversant with what is taught as part of specific degree programs and, at least in shortlisting, degree titles have relevance.

On the research side, pressure on academics has also shifted, with the "publish or perish" philosophy becoming even more pronounced, and added to this has been the widespread use of "impact factors" in assessing the quality of research. There is a degree of logic in this approach. Refereed journals (at least the more established ones), while their assessments processes are not perfect, do offer feedback from peers. The imperfections lie largely in selecting appropriate reviewers, but also in the inherent inertia in the way that peers often think.[6]

Regarding the impact factor, this is more problematic, and especially so for policy-oriented researchers. First, the medium of publication generally changes as an economist gains experience and as a wider array of opportunities emerges. As George Borts (1981: 458) put it when retiring from editing the *American Economic Review*: "Most of our authors are younger members of the profession, and most of the papers we print are distillations from doctoral theses. The older, well-established authors have many opportunities to publish outside of the realm of highly competitive refereed journals."

In Brown's case—and reflective of the publishing technologies of the time, when blogs and the like did not exist—the dissemination of ideas shifted, albeit not exclusively, to refereed articles from pamphlets, books, invited lectures, and contributions to official reports. This shift, besides the career development element, also reflected Brown's interest in economic policy; and, again referring to Borts (1981: 458), the refereeing and publication processes of journals are not ideal for this:

> There were few articles on policy issues and few expository papers. This was hardly surprising, since economists are notoriously reluctant to invest time in writing serious policy papers that will be submitted for refereeing and subject to outright rejection. For one thing, the delays required for refereeing can reduce the timeliness of a policy paper.

Second, there is the matter of the "language of economics," which has become increasingly mathematics. This has advantages of ensuring logic, although, as Thomas Piketty, author of the influential *Capital in the Twenty-First Century*, said in a 2015 *Financial Times* article: "Too often, economists build very complex mathematical models to look scientific and impress people. I have nothing against mathematics—I initially trained as a mathematician — but it's usually to hide a lack of ideas." Equally concerned is Paul Romer (who trained as an engineer) who, just prior to his appointment as Chief Economist at the World Bank, upbraided his fellow economists for their growing taste for obscure prose and "mathiness." Basically, he argues that the excessive use of arcane equations in economics papers makes them so hard to follow that they allow authors to avoid scrutiny. If economics is to benefit society, he continues, researchers need to make arguments which are clear enough to be understood, tested, and disproved.

From a publication perspective, and here again we defer to the experience of George Borts (1981: 458): "The increased use of mathematics has made life more difficult for the editor and referees." The trouble is that mathematics, while some would say it is the *lingua franca* of economists, is not the language of many of those who want to use economics in policy and other forms of decision-making. Modern technology has a way around this, and many journals have authors put their mathematics in electronic attachments, requiring a clear account of their intuition as the main text. In Brown's day, as highlighted above in the quote by Alfred Marshall, the mathematics had to essentially be there; but its translation into English was more demanding, in part because there were no electronic annexes in which to locate the mathematics, but also because the primary intended readers were often not professional economists. Economists, of course with exceptions, want to shape public and private sector decisions rather than enhance their impact factors by gaining more citations for their papers from those producing equally obscure publications.

This focus on theory can easily be tested by looking at the ways economist view their journals: the evidence is that they see many more brownie points in publishing in theoretically oriented than in applied journals and in general journals as opposed to more specialized, subject-directed journals. The h-index and others confirm this, or at least show it to be a self-fulfilling prophecy. While much of recent interest has involved factors such as citation counts, Button and Pearce (1977) surveyed UK economists and found a clear view that kudos in publication was highly correlated with outlets being perceived as more theoretically oriented.[7]

THE BOOK

At some point, it is generally useful in an Introduction to a book to provide some guidance as to its structure and approach. This book looks at the work of an important English economist from the mid-twentieth century, and does so in the context of a challenging and evolving political and social order and dynamic intellectual environment. It is not easy bringing together the work of an applied economist because of the diversity of topics that are often covered in a career. Someone involved in developing a school of thought (such as J.M. Keynes) or in stimulating a significant shift in methodology (such as Paul Samuelson, Ragnar Frisch, and Jan Tinbergen) is much easier to discuss because there is less need to provide context. Indeed, as Keynes once famously quipped in the *General Theory* (1936: 383–4):

> The ideas of economists and political philosophers, both when they are right and when they are wrong, are more powerful than is commonly understood. Indeed, the world is ruled by little else. Practical men, who believe themselves to be quite exempt from any intellectual influence, are usually the slaves of some defunct economist.

As we have seen, the applied economist essentially acts as the conduit between those generating the ideas and economic theories and their application. This involves testing and modifying concepts and, often, translating them for "practical men" when relevant to allow for public policies or private actions. It also involves debunking them in not a few cases.

Here we use the economic contributions of a major UK applied economist who was active in both academic life and as a public servant in the second half of the twentieth century to explore the types of issues that can be usefully addressed by applying appropriate economic thinking and data. The book also provides insights on how that differs from much of what is done in economics these days, where, to adopt one of the criteria of figure skating, virtually all evaluation is put on technical merit and the execution of methodology. There is inevitably judgment involved in economics, a subject that, as Keynes highlighted, often depends as much on animal spirit as it does on rational behavior. It also, despite the tendency towards abstraction, requires real-world data that models can be evaluated against. Basically, the cycle described by Coase.

Brown worked on both macroeconomics and on what may be considered mesoeconomic subjects, but his approach was essentially the same: Use the best data available and supplement it where possible; set this data in the appropriate theoretical analytical framework and use the analytical technique (quantitative assessment methodology) that fits the context. He did this in his academic papers and books, as well as in his advice to government and other official bodies. The idea of modeling for the sake of it or adopting the latest econometric technique for trendiness was never a criterion, and there seems no good reason why it ever should be.

To set things in context, the book contains a certain amount of biographical detail regarding Arthur Brown's life, which has also been supplemented in the reminiscences of two of his sons in the Foreword. After all, his wider experiences must have inevitably shaped his ideas and interests. There are also brief accounts of the lives and economic works of some of those who worked with him in a variety of ways during his life. But this is neither a strict personal biography of Brown nor that of others in the story. The book also provides quite a lot of background material about the way economics evolved over Brown's life-time, the changing questions that economists addressed, and the institutional surroundings in which they worked. This is done by way of contrasting the context of the second part of the twentieth century with the situations economists find themselves in or, and perhaps partly more accurately, have put themselves in, during the first part of the twenty-first century. In terms of exposition, the material is partly chronological, but at times is grouped together by context—people's lives and work are not always linear.

NOTES

1. Keynes' letter to Bernard Shaw, 1 January 1935.
2. Keynes' father (John Neville) seemed, however, to believe a division of labor was also needed: "theoretical and practical enquiries should not be systematically combined" (Keynes, 1917: 54).
3. Although one could question how practical economics is, as the Cambridge economist Arthur Pigou implicitly did when supposedly asking the rhetorical question: "Who would ever think of employing an economist to run a brewery?"
4. Again, in the symposium we find Christopher Dow et al. (2000) putting the case that not all economics followed this trend: "Scottish economics represented a tradition in applied economics that totally rejected such a [mainstream] view. In this tradition, the essence of

economics, as synonymous with applied economics, is remaining in close touch with the real world."

5. Alfred Marshall in a letter to A.L. Bowley, 1906 (Marshall 1925: 427).

6. For example, both the *American Economic Review* and the *Review of Economic Studies* rejected George Akerlof's 1970 paper "The market for lemons"—which essentially resulted in his being awarded the Nobel Prize in 2001—on the grounds of "triviality," while the *Journal of Political Economy* rejected it as incorrect, arguing that, if it were correct, then no goods could be traded. Only on the fourth attempt did the paper get published in *Quarterly Journal of Economics*.

7. Not only did they find, when asked how much kudos they felt publishing in particular journals conferred on them, that the academic economists sampled ranked the more theoretically oriented ones more highly, but also, when confronted with fictional titles in the list presented, many who claimed to recognize them gave a higher ranking to the fictional, theoretical-sounding ones.

2.   The development of an applied economist

THE 1930s IN THE UK

The interwar period was a challenging time to grow up in Britain. The initial euphoria that greeted the end of the "war to end all wars" that was followed by relative prosperity and then the largest economic depression in recorded history led to a loss of national confidence. At the personal level, many of the pillars of stability that formed the foundation of Victorian and Edwardian society were being questioned, and transformation was set in motion. The conventional political divisions were breaking down. This was particularly seen in the demise of the Liberal Party—which was often a natural party for many of the intellectuals of the time, including Keynes—and in the rise of the Labour Party to the point that it formed minority governments under Ramsay MacDonald in 1924 and 1929 to 1931.

Geography can also play a part in the development of a person's thinking: not just where they choose to live, which is generally something that emerges as a function of their nature and opportunities, but rather where they are brought up. Arthur Brown was born, brought up, educated for his formative years, worked for most his life, and retired in the North of England. This had been at the core of the nineteenth-century Industrial Revolution, but by the time of Brown's birth things had moved on and the region did not modernize in the 1920s and was the subject of some of the most severe consequences of the Great Depression. It was a region with many close local ties, both in the smaller communities associated with coal mining and in the larger cities and towns where whole streets of workers supplied labor to a common textile mill. The tradition in the summer, when industry was closed for maintenance, was for the same communities to travel together to seaside resorts for holidays.

Brown's upbringing was slightly peripheral to this, given his parents' occupation, and, for the same reason, he never directly felt the impacts of unemployment. But he observed, and the memories of his observations clearly stayed with him and influenced much of his later academic work, especially when he moved to the University of Leeds in the 1950s. But, equally, it was the beauty of the Yorkshire Dales in juxtaposition with the industrial cities and towns that offered mental relaxation.

It was thus in this broad, shifting environment that Brown was brought up, educated, and took up his first professional employment. Here we focus on the early years to the point that Brown graduated from the University of Oxford. In many ways, it represents a similar path to several key posts in that World War II academics from working-class backgrounds were beginning to make their way through the partly public and partly privately financed education system of the time. It also reflects the values placed on education in its broader sense by many working-class people at the time, as in the case of Brown's parents, to provide a better life for their children.

A.J. BROWN'S UPBRINGING

Arthur Brown was born in Alderley, Cheshire, in the north-west of England, but brought up in Yorkshire.[1] His grandparents had died before his birth. On the paternal side, Joseph Brown, the son of a non-conformist minister, had been a tile maker in Burslem, Staffordshire. He had died around 1880 leaving a widow and three sons—of whom James (Arthur's father), born on 7 December 1875, was the youngest—and a daughter. Brown's paternal grandmother, who he believed came from the Manchester area, was Eliza Clorley and she returned there to run an off-license in the Lower Broughton district of Salford.

Brown's uncles had something of a spirit of adventure about them, and they tried to run away to sea, only to be caught by what Brown calls "a sympathetic" captain in Liverpool who returned them to their mother. Giving way to the inevitable, Eliza arranged for places for them on the training vessel *Conway*, on the Mersey.

Brown's father only went to school part-time when he was ten, and only then for two years before beginning full-time work as a porter and handyman at a café in Manchester. He took up similar employment at the Manchester Union Club. But for most of the first quarter century Joseph Brown worked in private domestic service. The longest period (a dozen or so years) was in the service of Sir Edward Watkin, a Member of Parliament and major railway builder. He was responsible for an expansion of the Metropolitan Railway (now part of the London Underground), the construction of the Great Central Main Line, and for a failed attempt to dig a tunnel under the English Channel. Watkin's main residence was at Ross Hill near Northenden, Manchester, but Brown also accompanied him on trips involving railway business. After Sir Edward's death in 1901 Brown stayed with Lady Watkin, who moved to Kingston upon Thames.

He then took a succession of jobs in various places, ending his domestic service in the home of the Thurburns at Cransley Hall near Kettering.

Brown's maternal grandfather, Joseph Lyles, was a church schoolmaster at Cransley School in Great Budworth. Like Brown's paternal uncles, Lyles also ran away to sea, changing his name from Liles. He became a school-master in the navy, serving for a considerable time in the Mediterranean. Once out of the navy he married a woman called Wilson in about 1883 and was settled in Croydon, Cambridgeshire two years later when Brown's mother (the first of eight children) was born. In about 1886 the family moved to the Yorkshire village of Crayke for a time before finally settling down in Cransley.

Joseph Brown and Joseph Lyles seem to have had a common interest in liberal causes, a rather unusual interest among the people in Cransley. Brown waited, probably because of the need to ensure some degree of financial security before he married Lyles's daughter. By then Lyles had died and Brown had moved to Kettering. In any case, in June 1912 the Browns were appointed Steward and Stewardess of Wilmslow Golf Club.

Arthur Joseph was born in the Golf House on 8 August 1914, a location close to Manchester—some 3 miles from Wilmslow, under 3 miles from Alderley Edge, and a quarter of a mile from the hamlet of Lindow End. Because of the location, over the six years Brown was there he could never remember encountering children of his own age. His parents were busy, but his mother entertained and amused him. As he approached school age, his mother began to give him lessons, but the logistics of getting to a school were challenging to the point his father acquired a motorcycle and sidecar to ferry him if the need arose. Indeed, possibly because of his own background, his father, as did his mother, the schoolteacher's daughter, put considerable store on education as a path to success in life. The problem was resolved in 1920 when Brown's parents were appointed managers of the Bradford Liberal Club.

Brown's formal education began in 1920 in the infants' department of Carlton Street School about half a mile from the Liberal Club. This was close to where the original block of Bradford University, on which Brown had an early influence, was subsequently built. As well as formal educa-tion, the school's location, between working-class housing and a decaying area of more genteel properties, gave Brown his first contact with children of his own age; he did not apparently find the experience too "odd." What he subsequently reflected on in his unpublished reflections of his youth, and being someone who was rather shy in later life, was: "What havoc this worked with my personality I must leave others to judge." [2]

The move from the rural surrounds of the golf club to the urban envi-ronment of Bradford, coupled with entering school, brought changes to

Brown's life. As Brown puts it, while Wilmslow offered a "verandah and balcony looking south over the golf course and Mabberley Brook":

> From the windows and even from the crow's-nest housing the flagpole [of the Liberal Club], no tree or blade of grass was visible except on the horizon—a glimpse of Undercliffe Cemetery, a mile away to the north-east, the hills of Clayton and Queensbury twice as far, or more, on the other side. And, in those days, the soot deposit in Central Bradford was astonishing: black grit got in everywhere.

Bradford had been a traditional northern industrial city and, like many similar places, suffered badly after the miners' strike and subsequent General Strike of 1926. By the late 1930s, UK employment in mining had fallen by more than a third from its pre-strike peak of 1.2 million. The impact on Bradford of the decline in coal production and the incomes generated by it was largely indirect because its main industry was wool rather than coal, although there was plenty of the latter in the immediate region. The demand for textiles, however, declined sharply from the late 1920s as the Great Depression set in more generally.

Although the Great Depression was not as severe in the United Kingdom as in the US, unemployment peaked at about 15 percent compared to nearly 25 percent in America, and the duration was much shorter with significant economic growth after the UK left the gold standard in 1931, the effects were not evenly spread. Despite the paucity of regional economic data for the period, the North of England, while not the worst hit, was clearly one of the regions that suffered the most.

The city the Browns had moved to, therefore, was experiencing mass unemployment and fallen incomes, a fact that influenced Brown in much of his career. The effects of soot and grime were compounded by people out of work and with little prospect of finding employment in the immediate future, with all that entails.[3]

Brown's parents were busy managing the golf club, which had about 600 members and about 21 staff, with half a dozen living in. The main activities were providing about a hundred lunches on the two market days of the week (fewer on other days), snacks for those playing billiards, high teas, and a few drinks, and meeting the needs of occasional dinner parties. Brown usually observed, but also sometimes helped his father walk to order from the wholesale market, and regularly had lunch or tea with his parents. He would take a two-week vacation with his mother, and go to the parks in Bradford with her. His father's attempts to interest his son in golf failed badly, largely because Arthur had no aptitude for such sports. Fishing, on the other hand, proved to be conducive as a joint activity. A club member had some land a dozen miles outside of Bradford with a four-acre lake on it. He had stocked it with trout, but could not catch any and feared that pike had eaten them. Joseph Brown, a keen fly fisher, proved the landowner wrong and was granted rights to fish in the lake—this was a sport that his son did enjoy and was adept at.

As he grew, Brown became increasingly aware of the Yorkshire Dales, something that he retained for the rest of his life. Initially this involved very occasional charabanc ride on weekends, but Brown became more familiar with the area when walking there as part of his convalescence after a series of respiratory ailments and whooping cough in 1921. Later he would spend annual vacations in parts of the Dales with his mother, and subsequently, while still in Bradford, walked there with friends. Joseph Brown was less enthusiastic about the countryside than his wife and son, but the couple retired to North Wales when Joseph was 60, by which time Arthur was in this third year at Oxford.

As far as interests more germane to Brown's career go, Joseph's active involvement in politics meant that the home was well supplied with quality newspapers of the day, including the *Manchester Guardian*, as well as with the golf club's copies of weekly magazines such as *Punch* and the *Illustrated London News*. Whether this material had a greater influence on Brown than his earlier reading can be summarized from a comment in his unpublished biographical material: "I had been a reader of Arthur Mee's *Children's Newspaper*, and his *Children's Encyclopedia*, an edition of which came out in parts in the 1920s, had a great influence on my view of the world."[4]

Brown's mother, not unusually, was important in many ways. He encountered large amounts of poetry through her, as she had the view that one's head should be "well stocked" with it. Brown took this as normal, but seems to also have become increasingly interested in his mother's love of the countryside and of flowers. He became not only an enthusiastic Dales walker but also a keen gardener. Another attribute (perhaps foible might be a better choice of word) that Brown picked up was his mother's tendency to count things—sheep, cars, or whatever. Thus, he learned his basic arithmetic from her.

After three years at Carlton Street, Brown reached the age when a decision had to be made about the next step in his education. The options were to try to pass the entrance examination for the 30 percent of places at Bradford Grammar School that were reserved for city council scholars or to enter the school as fee-paying student (although this did not preclude sitting the exam). Playing safe, his parents pursued the latter course, and in September 1923 Brown had a short oral examination involving such questions as how many 1½ pence stamps could be bought for a shilling. Having passed the exam, he entered the junior section of the school, which was in a Quaker House opposite the main building.

Bradford Grammar School was founded in 1548 and granted its charter by King Charles II in 1662 that created the "free grammar school for better teaching, instruction and bringing up of children in grammar and good learning and to continue for that use forever." Indeed, by Brown's time, academically it was considered one of the UK's top secondary educational establishments. Its earliest site was next to the then parish church, and the school has always had close links with the church. During Brown's time there it was, like most public schools of the day, single sex.

Brown moved up to Bradford Grammar School a couple of years later (in 1923), having been awarded a Governor's Scholarship that halved his fees. He had attempted the examination for a City Council Scholarship but failed the intelligence test involved, later claiming that the junior section of Bradford Grammar had not, unlike city schools, involved a weekly class on "intelligence."

Brown found Bradford conducive to his interests and strengths, not least because of the limited emphasis put on organized ball games that he was neither good at nor, perhaps following from this, enjoyed. He did, however, run, and was a reasonable sprinter; he joined the Officer Training Corps (OTC), where he also shot well enough to make the school team and became company sergeant major.

More germane to his later career, Bradford Grammar at that time had gone through something of a change. Prior to World War I, under the headship of the Reverend Hulton Keeling, the school had sought to become competitive against the best public schools in the country by offering comparable salaries to its teachers, and this was mainly the staff that taught Brown. The headmaster during Brown's period there, Dr. W. Edwards, had opted in 1929 to receive direct grant funding from the Board of Education. Brown describes Edwards in his notes as "a scholarly man, shy to an almost pathological extent, dedicated to the promotion of Classical studies for the elite of the school, and to the winning of scholarships to Oxford and Cambridge." The pupils were not aware of Edwards most of the time, but his assistants made sure that there was discipline in the classroom.

Given the priorities that spilled from the top, students were separated in the third form—largely, but not entirely, by their own choice—into those focusing on classics and those on moderns, the former being somewhat superior. Brown, partly due to parental preferences, opted for the modern side. At that time, he found little interest in Latin and saw mathematics (excluding geometry) as his weakest subject, with English, history, and geography his strongest. But there was something of a change in his mathematics performance in his fourth and fifth years, when he had a new teacher and moved onto the more applied side of the subject, notably mechanics and elementary calculus. Indeed, his performance in his School Certificate examinations in 1929 saw little difference across the subjects taken, with distinctions in six.

This then posed some issues as to what to subsequently specialize in. His interest in current affairs, together with an inherent liking for the subject, meant that he had a leaning in the direction of history; but he instead opted for physical science, partly because of the influence of his chemistry teacher, W.E. Clarkson. His three remaining years at Bradford were not easy, but given that Brown was not a pure mathematician, the nature of the courses taken, with their emphasis on problem solving, equipped him for his future work in applied economics.

He spent much of his later months at Bradford working towards a university scholarship, which entailed three submissions of the Higher School Certificates examination; his third attempt failed to get him a prized state scholarship. The subjects covered in all cases were physics, chemistry, and mathematics (with German as a subsidiary subject), and he only gained a distinction in physics. In parallel with this he also sought college scholarships. In 1931, he went to Peterhouse College, Cambridge, where the Master, Field Marshall Lord Birdwood, interviewed him. The kindness and courtesy shown to the young boy by the Master influenced the way Brown later treated interview candidates in his own career. The following year he went to another Cambridge college, Queens', as part of an invited group based on their Higher Certificate performances; he then took the Hastings Scholarship examinations at Queen's College, Oxford.[5]

THE UNDERGRADUATE

In 1933, Arthur Brown obtained a scholarship at Queen's in natural sciences; the subject would today, with the focus on academic compartmentalization, be called physics. He very rapidly decided, however, to switch to politics, philosophy, and economics (PPE). In later life, he made it very clear why he decided on this course, and it was very much to do with his background and interests:

> I had been brought up very conscious of political and quasi-economic discussion. My parents were manager and manageress of the Liberal Club in Bradford, so it was that sort of atmosphere. So I got very interested in current affairs when I was in sixth form. I knew that there were one or two precedents of people going from Bradford Grammar School on science scholarships and changing to PPE. So when I got my scholarship I asked if I could change and they said, "Well come up and do an examination." So I went up and did an examination and they let me change. (Brown, 1997a: 140)

Brown had not just devoted time to his books at Bradford, or engage-ment in the OTC, but was also active as a Young Liberal in the early 1930s and was a member of the League of Nations Union. He was a regular speaker on Union matters at Sunday afternoon meetings held in non-conformist chapels. His father encouraged him, and appears to have been disappointed when Arthur did not subsequently become a major player in the Oxford Union. Whatever strengths Brown may have had at set-piece addresses such as lectures (a subject returned to later), he was too nervous to engage in interventions in public debates. This is perhaps why in his later career he proved far more effective as a "committee man" than as an orator.

Economics in Oxford at the time was in something of a flux. While it had enjoyed several eminent economic scholars over the years—especially holders of the Drummond Chair of Political Economy, such as Francis Edgeworth and James Rogers—overall it had been slower to accept economics as a subject in its own right than had been Cambridge and LSE. The subject matter of economics had been viewed by Oxford in the latter part of the nineteenth century as part of a broader approach to the empirical study of history, often associated with Arnold Toynbee, and as a practical matter there was no space to accommodate political economy in a modern history school. There was a token lecture in the *Literae Humaniores* course but this was combined with ethics.

The PPE degree had been introduced in 1921, and initially only three economics papers (plus another in economic history and half in industrial organization) were taken. This barely differed from the economics taken by the politics and philosophy specialists. Revisions followed as economists complained about their workload compared other subjects, and about its diversity. In 1931, the economics component was increased to four papers plus economic history; but, more importantly, the papers allowed for more economics in place of political economy.[6]

The overall objective of the PPE examination structure as set out in the *Economic Journal* in September 1921 was little changed by the time Brown came up:

> The examination has been arranged so that candidates may give special atten-tion *either* to Philosophy *or* to Politics *or* to Political Economy by the choice they make of prescribed books and of a further subject. The highest honours can be attained in *either* Philosophy *or* Politics *or* Political Economy, provided that adequate knowledge is shown in the other subjects of the examination.[7]

Specifically regarding political economy: "Candidates will be expected to show knowledge of economic theory, of its history and its applications to the most important aspects of modern economic conditions."

In a way, this ambition of the institution was very much in line with the prevailing view of Keynes (whose work was to subsequently influence Brown), and runs very much against what is often the approach of modern economics teaching, with its focus on mathematics and abstraction. We repeat Keynes' view, for example, writing in his obituary for Alfred Marshall in the *Economic Journal*, on the requirements of an economist:

> [T]he master-economist must possess a rare *combination* of gifts. He must reach a high standard in several different directions and must combine talents not often found together. He must be mathematician, historian, statesman, philosopher—in some degree. He must understand and speak in words. He must contemplate the particular in terms of the general, and touch abstract and concrete in the same flight of thought. He must study the present in the light of the past for the purposes of the future. No part of man's nature or his institutions must lie entirely outside his regard. (Keynes, 1924: 322; italics in the original)

The system at Oxford and Cambridge involved university-based examinations; teaching through (non-compulsory) university-wide lectures and seminars that broadly covered (although not directly) the material required for the examinations; and compulsory college-based tutorials or supervision providing individual support. Added to this, individual faculty could be lecturers or tutors, or both. Hence the number of lecture courses Brown attended is not correlated with the examinations he took. This system differed from the teaching at most other universities, including LSE, which involved more integrated practices and which influenced Brown when he later went to Leeds University as head of department.

An additional challenge in the system was the frequent vagaries of subject matter to be examined. Students today would not be very appreciative of just being given an unofficial "Select Bibliography" published by Blackwell and compiled by three academics covering, respectively, politics, philosophy, and economics.[8] The description of what was to be examined tended to be vague; for example, Brown took Currency and Credit, the rubric for which was just: "To be studied in modern textbooks and the Reports of recent public inquiries. Candidates will be expected to show a knowledge of the chief foreign systems of banking and of international aspects of currency policy" (Brown, 1988a: 29).[9]

The nature of examinations also changed over time, reflecting a shift in examiners, topics of interest, and theoretical trends (Young and Lee, 1993: 78–81). For Brown's examinations in 1936 one important new element was for students to discuss the following direct quote from the *General Theory*: "It should be obvious that the rate of interest cannot be a return to saving or waiting as such . . . The rate of interest is the reward for parting with liquidity for a specific period."

Returning to Brown's arrival at Oxford, the reforms were also market driven by the number of students interested in economics, which rose from 85 in 1923 to 142 in 1927, and to 275 by 1933 (Young and Lee, 1993). To meet the rising aggregate demand for economics, and to cover what were considered key areas, a new faculty was appointed. In 1925, G.D.H. (George) Cole had become reader in economics at University College, and then became the first Chichele Professor of Social and Political Theory. Brown (1988a: 20) subsequently judged from "a lively and wide ranging course of lectures on the current economic scene which I heard him give (as well as his numerous and famous published works)" that his ideas owed more to Karl Marx than to Alfred Marshall. Between 1927 and 1931, E.M. (Edward) Hugh-Jones, E.G. Dowdell, B.F Bretherton, L.M. Fraser, Henry Phelps Brown, James Meade, E.G. Wilson, Redvers Opie, and W.M. Allen were all appointed fellows and/or lecturers, raising the number of economists from six to 15 (Young and Lee, 1993).

Several of these people, such as Hugh-Jones, Bretherton, and Phelps Brown, taught economic history as well as economics. Some, such as Allen, were more mathematically oriented than others. The considerable majority of lecturers and tutors were Oxford graduates, with most having a PPE degree. This was probably less by design than at Cambridge, which was a logical internal recruiting ground given its more extensive involvement in economics, and Oxford had difficulty in recruiting lecturers in the late 1920s. The lecturing and tutoring responsibilities of the academics also sometimes diverged, with Henry Phelps Brown for example lecturing on statistics and data but tutoring in economic history.

As one might expect, the attributes of the Oxford economists of the period as teachers was mixed. Views also seem to vary between any individual faculty member's skills as a tutor and as a lecturer. As in major universities today, the focus in making academic appointments was on scholarship, and particularly so for fellows. They were taken in at Oxford to advance learning and knowledge. As Roy Harrod put it in a letter to James Meade in 1937, "Hertford pays you to be an economist first and foremost and not to teach undergraduates" (Young and Lee, 1993: 34). The problem for economists at Oxford was that PPE was not initially seen to be on a par with other schools in the university, and this led to difficulties in providing a critical mass of fellows for tutoring. There were thus matters of quantity as well as quality to consider.

Although one student's brilliant teacher is another's bore, Warren Young and Frederic Lee (1993: 35), making use of a diversity of sources, find that Dowdell, Fraser, Robert Hall, Harrod, Hitch, Meade, and Sayers were deemed to have "excellent teaching ability," with Allen, Cole, Hargreaves, Hugh-Jones, Opie, and Phelps Brown "only fair to good." Perhaps more useful are the attributes accredited to individuals with, on the one hand, Harrod being solid effective, inspiring and conscientious, Hitch stimulating, and Hall an excellent teacher, while Allen was considered dry, Hugh-Jones humdrum, and Opie as remarkably clever but unhelpful.

What was taught also seems to have affected things, with Phelps Brown being good in his specialized areas but otherwise austere and boring. In terms of methodology and, in particular, technical content, people like Meade, Hitch, Opie and Jacob Marschak were highly mathematically oriented, although the quality of their exposition was seen to vary. Some thought the mathematics was over their head, while others found it simple and relevant, and required no mathematical training to follow. The aptitude and backgrounds of students will have inevitably affected their views on these things.

Brown was exposed to a wide range of literature as an undergraduate at Oxford, and much of it (unlike today) was in book form.[10] But the material did not come in the organized "course outline" that dominates the demands of students today. At that time, with the Depression fresh in everyone's mind, trade-cycle theory was a core element of an economist's education and, with Harrod at Oxford, perhaps especially so there. The prevailing orthodoxy was that the Depression had been caused by structural failures, and most courses (including Brown's) focused on these and on the problems of mismatches in the various economic markets. The demand factors that are associated with economic recession as seen by Keynes were given limited time, even after the *General Theory* appeared.

Indeed, for much of his undergraduate time at Oxford, Brown seems almost oblivious to the discussions at the University of Cambridge. This may seem surprising given the engagement of people like Harrod and Meade in the debates, but undergraduate life was apparently somewhat more sheltered from this at Oxford—the cocooning of students from anything contentious seems to have existed 80 years ago, although probably much less than many want it in US universities today.

A specific, and different line, had permeated the LSE after the arrival of Friedrich Hayek in 1931. This focused on the need for neutrality of money. This neutrality had not to distort Walrasian market conditions and, for this money, expenditure had to be kept constant. If this was not so, given a constrained real output, those creating additional money could extract it for consumption, whilst others would be forced into saving. Hence, there was tension at LSE with those that blamed the Great Depression on an excess of money supply in the previous boom in the 1920s. Basically, the output produced during the boom could not be absorbed rapidly by the forced savings and in the absence of additional monetary expansion. This was often seen as an over-consumptionist argument. In later writings,

Brown (1988a: 25) said he found this illogical because, with Walrasian markets, the cost of maintenance and replacement of the capital stock would be included in the maintenance and depreciation allowances before wage earners and shareholders got any spending power.[11] But we run ahead of the story a little, and London was not Oxford.

STUDIES AT OXFORD

The Marshallian ideas of the workings of perfect markets and, once any imperfections have been dealt with, of full employment thus dominated the Oxford syllabus that confronted undergraduates in the early 1930s. The unemployment of the day was structural; and, in Brown's case, neither being tutored by Harrod nor Meade helped with any immediate shift towards a Keynesian-style approach. There were inevitable transfers of ideas and academics from Cambridge as the Oxford PPE degree was set up and more systematic thinking about economic matters emerged. Added to this, the Drummond Professor at the time was Brown's ultimate D.Phil. internal examiner, D.H. (David) MacGregor, who co-edited the *Economic Journal* with Maynard Keynes from 1925 to 1934. However, Brown suspects he had few conversations with Keynes about the embryonic macroeconomics, although in 1932 he had co-signed a letter to *The Times* (with Arthur Pigou, Josiah Stamp, Walter Layton, and Arthur Salter) advocating more public and private spending.

There were various paths through the PPE course, and Brown steered one that offered the most economics: *de facto* two special subjects in economics.[12] Within this, we know a remarkably large amount about what Brown was taught, the environment in which it was taught, the ways in which it was taught, and how he approached his university period. His papers from his Oxford days are remarkably complete, and indeed form part of the foundations upon which Young and Lee (1993) base their book *Oxford Economics and Oxford Economists*.

Brown's lectures, which also provide useful general insights into the flavor of economics courses at the time, were often given by those who were to become some of the leading academics and economic policy advisers of the post-war period. R.L. Hall, for example, who later became chief economic advisor to the British government from 1947 to 1961, lectured on "Questions in advanced economic theory"; Roy Harrod on "The Federal Reserve system"; Lindsay Fraser on "The value of money"; Eric Hargreaves on "Public finance"; David MacGregor (later Drummond Professor of Political Economy) on "The national income and its distribution"; and Redvers Opie, later one of the five members of the UK delegation to the 1944 Bretton Woods Conference, on "The theory of international trade."

Brown carefully recorded in neat notebooks the lectures he attended. As an aside, and as one of his ex-students, I can also attest to Brown's frugality in the use of paper, clearly a habit he acquired as an undergraduate (if not earlier). In later life Brown made use of notes on the back of used envelopes (some in my classes on Welfare Economics in 1970 with stamps bearing the face of King George VI, who died in 1952). In the same vein, at Queen's he used hardback notebooks, taking lecture notes from one end and then turning the book over before taking notes for another course from the other end.

Brown took the more advanced seminars, such as MacGregor's, whom he considered "good value"—although by that time, and after war injuries in 1918, Brown thought him prone to be forgetful.[13] This teaching involved groups of six to ten students. He also benefitted from his tutors: first Lindsay Fraser, a converted philosopher who taught Brown for over two years; then Charles Hitch, whom Brown considered a great influence, and who pushed him towards his doctorial subject, liquidity preference. Oliver Franks (later Lord Franks) who, among many things, became vice-chancellor of the University of East Anglia and Provost of both Queen's and Worcester Colleges (turning down the Governorship of the Bank of England for the latter), was Brown's moral tutor and tutor in philosophy.

It was suggested to Brown that for his Pass Moderations (his first examinations), because he was a natural science scholar who had switched to PPE he should spend two terms on economics. This involved reading Henderson's (1932) *Supply and Demand*, Robert Lehfeldt's (1926) *Money*, and Hugh Dalton's (1923) *Public Finance*. Basically, he got a diet of Marshallian economics. In tutorials for the Trinity term 1934, his reading was more diverse in its orientation, but also more structured. For example, Fraser directed him more to Cassel, Cannon, and Wicksteed rather than Marshall, and advice to read some Marshall came at the end of the second term, along with direction to Wicksell's *Lectures* (1901, 1906) that had just appeared in translation. Among the more contemporary reading material was Lionel Robbins' (1932) *Nature and Significance of Economic Science*, Hicks's (1932) *Theory of Wages*, and an *Economica* paper by Hicks and Allen (1934) on value theory. Before his final year, Brown also read Arthur Pigou's (1920) *Economics of Welfare*, Robinson's (1933a) *Economics of Imperfect Competition*, and Taussig's (1927) *International Trade*.[14]

The reading he embarked upon to prepare for one of his special subjects (Currency and Credit, 1935) pushed Brown more firmly in a Keynesian direction. He was not, however, directed to Keynes's (1930) *Treatise*, rather Pigou's (1927) *Industrial Fluctuations*, MacFie's (1934) *Theories of the Trade Cycle*, and the *Macmillan Report* (Committee on Finance and Industry, 1931) were his texts; but the last of these, with Keynes as a member and the likes of Pigou, Dennis Robertson, and Robbins giving evidence on unemployment, did provide insights into the ongoing movement of economic theory.

For the other special subject (Public Finance) Brown's vacation reading had been the rather traditional *Public Finance* (Robinson, 1922), Pigou's "meaty," to quote Brown (1988a: 23), *Study in Public Finance* (1928), and Josiah Stamp's (1922) *Wealth and Taxable Capacity*. He also obviously read Keynes's (1931) reply to Dr. Hayek because he uses it in an essay about budgetary measures, and the *General Theory* that he had bought on the day of its publication. He also recalls reading Irving Fisher's (1930) *Theory of Interest* before his finals (Brown, 1988a: 23). He did bring ideas of the *General Theory* into his examination responses. As with virtually all students, however, he seems to have little idea of how well he used the material or of its impact on his results.

THE TRANSITION PHASE

Brown did rather well in his finals in 1936, being awarded the best first class honors in PPE for a decade.[15] This was at a time when PPE had a rich field of students, and between 1929 and 1939 these included two subsequent Nobel Laureates in economics and two British Prime Ministers, as well as a battery of future academics, some later becoming heads of Oxford colleges, and public servants. His achievements were no small thing but, perhaps as important, if not more so, he enjoyed Oxford: "My undergraduate years were intensely happy ones."[16] University education was not for Brown a mechanical process to get a "piece of paper."

Having done with the practicalities of graduating, Brown spent a little more time on assessing the *General Theory* and related material. One reason was the need to think of a thesis topic for his D.Phil. UK research degrees at that time meant just that—they were based and assessed purely on an individual's ability to do original research. Keynes had produced a new interesting and provocative way of looking at the economy, and Brown was interested in this not only for its own sake but also because it left open a lot of questions. Not least of these was the need for more empirical verification of many of the novel concepts thrown up by Keynes. But it was important to understand exactly what Keynes was trying to say, and what critics were offering by way of counter-arguments.

It was not easy to follow the *General Theory* when it appeared, and is probably only slightly easier now despite the various translations that have been produced. Brown (1988a: 27) sums up his problems at the time rather decisively:

> After fifty years during which, I imagine, the majority of readers of the book have been told in advance something of what they are expected to find in it, the impact on the first generation of readers who lacked this (true or false) guidance is not easy to recapture. The *General Theory* is the work of an author who has a number of new things to say, several of them of major importance to his theme, one or two much less so, and who has not had time to stand back and sort out his priorities for optimal exposition. It tends to start with the difficulties. By the time I had got to the Appendix on User Cost . . . I was in need of comfort and reassurance, which my mentors were not yet wholly able to supply.

> I cannot remember how far I got—certainly not to the end of the book—before word came to us, I think in a revision seminar which Charles Hitch was running, that Harrod had spoken. What he was reported to have said was an augmented version of the now famous passage of correspondence with Keynes in the previous summer, by which he had established his claim to have understood what Keynes was trying to say . . . The augmentation consisted of a similar account of the "classical" system of which Keynes might not have approved but which appeared later in Harrod's "Keynes and Traditional Theory."

When prompted to provide more details of Harrod's approach, Brown replied:

> I'm sure that an equation system purporting to represent the skeleton of the *General Theory* attributed to Harrod, was being passed around Oxford within the month after the *General Theory*. What I took to be the nature of the *General Theory* became clear when I first learnt of the Harrod equations, the four equations which I took to be its underlying structure.

Luckily for Brown, rescue also came in another, even more digestible visual form soon after this.

In September 1936, New College, Oxford hosted the annual meeting of the Econometric Society. At this meeting, Harrod spoke on "Keynes and the traditional theory," Meade on "A simplified Model of Mr. Keynes's System," and John Hicks on "Keynes and the 'Classics.'" The key thing to emerge from this was the public appearance of the IS/LM system.[17] There were articles by David Champernowne (1936) and Brian Reddaway (1936) that sought to make Keynes's words more exact as systems of equations, but these were not much easier to follow than the original. The reduction of macroeconomics to two lines in a single diagram was a major pedagogic advance, even if not altogether intellectually satisfactory.

Brown attended the meeting and took careful notes. He recorded the diagrams drawn by Hicks.[18] These are the oldest known surviving depictions of the IS/LM system. Brown, in a later interview by Young (1987:

43), when asked if Hicks drew the diagrams and equations he recorded on a blackboard, his recollection was: "My impression was yes, but it's possible that they were in his paper . . . we may just have followed what he was saying from the paper, that's possible. But the IS and LM curves were physically present in some form."[19]

The other analyses present by Roy Harrod and James Meade were in equation form and, according to Brown, did not strike the "fancy" of the other participants. But Brown also says, regarding Hicks and Harrod's equations:

> We knew they were the same equations . . . It was clear to those who had a preview of Harrod that the equations Hicks used as a starting point were old friends. They were the Harrod equations and what he was just doing was playing with them a bit, and the playing with them was the new thing that was exciting and helpful . . . My assessment of Harrod rises in the course of thinking back. Hicks was a mathematician and this is what made the difference really . . . I think that Harrod is not the mathematician of the party, but his great contributions have all been of mathematical kind in an odd sort of way . . . There are things that are mathematically very simple but profound, like growth equations. I think that the further step that Hicks took of condensing the thing into two functions was important. He has the IS curve and the LM curve, and the solution of the system. But Harrod did it in words. (Young, 1987: 88–9)

Harrod must also have been disappointed at the lack of interest in his recently published book, *The Trade Cycle* (1936). Brown, however, saw some important insights in Harrod's comments on Hicks's presentation (Young, 1987: 43). As Brown wrote in his notes: "Harrod thinks that not 1 but dI/dt should be in 2 [Hicks's investment equation]." In other words, Harrod was thinking in terms of a dynamic rather than a comparative static framework, but this approach did not seem, however, to resonate with other attendees. Nevertheless, the importance of what went down that September was clear to Brown, as he pointed out in a subsequent interview with Warren Young (1989: 135) regarding whether Harrod was disappointed:

> I'm sure . . . I'm sure he was. I mean the word went round . . . Charley Hitch remarked that Harrod was peeved that nobody in Oxford appeared to the reading of his great book on trade . . . I wasn't aware of a great splash made by *The Trade Cycle* in Oxford, whereas the Hicksian IS–LM thing had made a considerable splash . . . But we knew where Harrod was going and he got there in 1939 in "Essay in Dynamic Theory."

NOTES

1. For biographical details this chapter draws on Brown (1988a), William Brown (2011), Thirlwall (2003), Bowers (2003), *The Times* (2003), and Waller (2013), together with the extended notes of an interview with Brown by Keith Tribe, *Interview with A.J. Brown, 25 May 1994, Headingley, Leeds* (no date, AJB C&P), part of which became Brown (1997a).
2. *A.J. Brown: Note on Family and Early Life* (1991, AJB C&P).
3. George Orwell's *The Road to Wigan Pier* (1937), while fictional rather than academic, and centered on the west side of the Pennines, provides a good picture of life in Northern England at the time.
4. Arthur Mee founded the *Children's Newspaper* in 1919 as a title aimed at pre-teenage children; it ran for 2,397 weekly issues.
5. Hastings closed scholarships to Queen's were highly competitive and financed through a fund established in the 1740s to assist outstanding pupils in Northern England attend university. He also took, and failed, the Ackroyd Scholarship examinations limited to certain Yorkshire schools.
6. In political economy, the "Prescribed Books" examination required students to have read Adam Smith, *Wealth of Nations*; the works of David Ricardo (McCulloch's edition); Marx, *Capital, Vol. I*; Jevons, *The Theory of Political Economy*; and Friedrich List, *The National System of Political Economy*. For the specialized paper in political economy, (1) currency and banking; (2) capital and labor; (3) labor movements from 1815 to 1875, were covered.
7. The Economic Curricula at Oxford and Cambridge, *Economic Journal*, **31**, 400–406, p. 400 (italics in the original).
8. Eric Hargreaves compiled the economics list in 1935 and Meade in 1937. Brown (1988a: 29) observes that anyone expecting "some sign of the *General Theory*'s impact" in the later version "would perhaps be disappointed." In fact, six new publications were added to the original 69, including *General Theory*, but none removed. Consequently, the simple expansion of the list must have gradually dulled the guidance intended.
9. Not all of Brown's subjects were this broad: the political economy course for Pass Moderations, for example, had explicit reading matter set out. Brown essentially taught the course later when at Hertford College, Oxford, and found that the problem with such a structured approach was that it was difficult to bring in more recent material.
10. He provides details in Brown (1988a).
11. Keynes (1931: 394) later said in a similar, but perhaps more aggressive vein, regarding Friedrich Hayek's *Prices and Production*: "The book, as it stands, seems to me to be one of the most frightful muddles . . . It is an extraordinary example of how, starting with a mistake, a remorseless logician can end up in bedlam."
12. *Interview with A.J. Brown, 25 May 1994, Headingley, Leeds.*
13. As mentioned earlier, he was Brown's D.Phil. internal examiner and, as Brown put it, "was all there" when he pointed out that the explanatory power of one of Brown's regressions would fall from 90 percent to 60 percent if Brown had omitted two dates (Brown, 1997a: 141).
14. He seems to have mastered the basic of economics quite quickly and won the Cobden Club's Ogden Prize in 1934 for an essay entitled "Economic Nationalism, and the Peace of the World."
15. The economic examiners for 1935 were Harrod and Fay (Young and Lee, 1993). First class honors (firsts) were not common in those days, with only 8.5 percent of PPE candidates obtaining them between 1930 and 1939. The percentage was particularly brought down by the low marking of Redvers Opie between 1937 and 1939, who felt that previous examiners had been over-generous. This caused some friction with the college fellows who, at the time, were primarily judged (for example when it came to tenure decisions) on the exam results of their students.

16. *A.J. Brown: Note on Family and Early Life*, p. 8.
17. They were all subsequently published, in revised form, as Harrod (1937a), Meade (1937), and Hicks (1937). Young (1987) gives accounts of the events.
18. These photos are reproduced in Young (1987: 44–5).
19. The figures are reproduced, along with Brown's notes, by Warren Young. These are not, however, the diagrams from Hicks's subsequent (1937) *Econometrica* paper but rather a conflation of Figures 2 and 3 from the latter.

3. Early career and Keynesianism

GETTING ACQUAINTED WITH *THE GENERAL THEORY*

A.J. Brown was essentially a Keynesian economist, although not as diehard as others like John Brothwell, with whom he later worked at Leeds.[1] He was rather more pragmatic than that and, although very willing to place values on parameters of key variables where possible, these were always treated with care and invariably accompanied by the caveat that they were approximations. His main concern was not with Keynesianism *per se* but rather whether it was a useful way of understanding the main macro-economic forces in play in the 1930s, and with trying to evaluate the key parameters in the eight equations that essentially make up the Keynesian system.

Brown (1988a) provides a pretty full explanation of how he came into Keynesian economics, and it very conveniently came four months before he took his finals at Oxford. In a way, it was then when he transitioned from being a student to becoming a scholar. The segue was, as mentioned, the appearance of a note on 4 February, 1936 in the *Manchester Guardian* announcing the publication of Keynes's *General Theory of Employment, Interest and Money*. Brown invested five shillings (25 pence in decimalized prices, with no allowance for inflation) in buying it. He then tried to read it rather than study for his examinations.

The opportunities for graduate work and the nature of the institutions and the individuals to study under varied in the 1930s. Brown was famil-iar with Oxford, knew many of the faculty and researchers, and it was an obvious place to remain. Added to this, just as Oxford was somewhat adventurous in the early 1930s as it developed the PPE degree, so in the mid-1930s it began to develop new structures for conducting economic research and for collecting economic data. These must have appealed to Brown, both because of the academic issues being debated and, perhaps more so, in the applied nature of the methodologies that were to be applied.

There was, however, initially a practical problem to overcome: Brown did not come from a moneyed background, and needed funding to stay at Oxford after graduation. His undergraduate results helped him in this, and he obtained a Webb Medley Senior Scholarship. There was a junior version of this that Brown competed for and won at the end of his second undergraduate year, and a senior version that he was awarded on after finals. "The Junior Scholarship was small; it didn't revolutionise my life! But the Senior Scholarship was such that I didn't have to bother about being financed" (Brown 1997a: 143).

He also took up a temporary lectureship at Hertford College in 1937, which he held until 1941, whilst James Meade was away at the League of Nations taking responsibility for the World Economic Survey.[2] At Hertford, Brown lectured on economic principles and economic theory, although, as we see later, this was not altogether something he was happy about.

Moving from the undergraduate to the graduate student was perhaps easier in the 1930s than today. The number of students involved, especially in the UK compared to the United States, was small and the methods of undergraduate teaching (and notably the tutorial system at Oxford and Cambridge) meant that students and academics became to know each other well. Living and eating in college, which many of the undergraduates did for at least part of their time, also produced a degree of familiarity not perhaps so common today. The relative youth of the faculty at Oxford also meant that some of the problems often associated with generation gaps were smaller. Brown, by the time he graduated, would have known virtually all the economists at Oxford and those in related academic areas, pretty well.

OXFORD AND KEYNESIAN ECONOMICS

The 1930s, while bringing in the Keynesian revolution in macroeconomics, was also important in refining microeconomic theory. In both senses the period saw a questioning of the neo-classical economics of Alfred Marshall, both intellectually and in terms of making greater use of empirical analysis. It was also, what many may consider, a golden age of British economics—or, as George Shackle (1967) later called it, *The Years of High Theory*.

The supply-side of economists at Oxford, Cambridge, and the London School of Economics (LSE)—which had the major economics departments in England at the time—differed considerably. Despite this, there was considerable interchange between them; after all, they formed an almost equilateral triangle with sides of 58, 62 and 97 miles, although the peculiarities of the rail network (with inadequacies in its east–west links) suggested London as a natural hub.[3]

Not only were there common seminars but also several of the key figures, particularly the younger ones, spent time other than at their non-domicile institutions. James Meade, for example, spent 1930–31 at Cambridge, and several moved between the three universities as career progressions in the 1930s, Hicks, for example, moved from LSE to Gonville and Caius, Cambridge in 1935, while Dennis Robertson made the reverse trip in 1938. In addition were those such as Roy Harrod (who graduated from New College, Oxford but soon moved to Cambridge) and David Champernowne (a King's College, Cambridge graduate who took a lectureship at LSE in 1936 before returning to King's two years later), who, while being students at one institution, moved, at least for a period, from their *alma mater*.

In terms of what would probably be called "teams" in the modern world of competitive academia, many of the players were by any standard exceptional.

The University of Cambridge was by far the most visible and, although LSE had a larger faculty overall, probably had the largest group of what today would be considered economists. It also had many of the towering economists of the day, including John Maynard Keynes, Arthur Pigou, Richard Kahn (later a Professor of Economics at Cambridge and Bursar of King's College), Maurice Dobb (a pre-eminent Marxist economist), Dennis Robertson (subsequently Sir Ernest Cassel Professor of Economics at the University of London and of Political Economy at Cambridge), Piero Straffa, Alex Cairncross (subsequently Head of the Government Economic Service, Master of St Peter's College, Oxford, and Chancellor of the University of Glasgow), Gerald Shove, Colin Clarke, and Joan and Austin Robinson. Alfred Marshall had established the Economics Tripos, which provided an incubator for subsequent generations of economists in 1903, and not only at Cambridge.

Alfred Marshall and neo-classical marginalism from the late 1800s had dominated economics at the University of Cambridge, but the powerful intellectual influence of Keynes had begun to influence thinking there from the onset of the Great Depression.[4] But by the end of the decade major schisms had emerged between those refining Marshall and the "Cambridge Circus" of Keynes. Maynard Keynes's outside activities in business and government, and his frequent interaction with the press and appearances on the radio, were a large part of the high public profile of economics at Cambridge in the 1930s (Donald Moggridge, 2010).

Turning to London, the leading figures at the LSE during the 1930s included Lionel Robbins; the subsequent Nobel Laureates Friedrich Hayek (who had joined the school at Robbins' behest in 1931) and John Hicks (who subsequently became Drummond Professor of Political Economy at Oxford); Hugh Dalton (later Chancellor of the Exchequer); Edwin Cannon;

Nicholas Kaldor (subsequently Professor of Economics at Cambridge); Theodore Gregory (who served on the Macmillan Committee); and Paul Rosenstein-Rodan. The student body in 1930s was also particularly rich, and included later Nobel Laureates Arthur Lewis and Ronald Coase, John Kenneth Galbraith, Abba Lerner, George Shackle (who A.J. Brown later appointed to a post at Leeds University), Arnold Plant, Thomas Balogh, Vera Smith, L.K. Jha (a future Governor of the Reserve Bank of India), Arthur Bowley, Arthur Seldon (joint founder President of the Institute of Economic Affairs), David Champernowne (subsequently Professor of Economics and Statistics at Cambridge), and Oskar Lange.

Although Lionel Robbins was the main driving force in economics at LSE during this time, economics was very receptive to new ideas which Coase (1982) largely credits to Hayek. This was before Hayek's main volumes had appeared, but he had brought to the school an in-depth knowledge of economic theory and powerful tools to develop economic arguments. Despite serious limitations as an undergraduate teacher, John Hicks also exerted a strong influence through his use of mathematics and advanced theory. Robbins argued that while Hayek brought Austrian and Wicksellian ideas to LSE, Hicks introduced Léon Walras and Vilfredo Pareto. Many of these new ideas came from Continental Europe and America, and LSE perhaps took a wider look at what was happening else-where than Oxford and Cambridge. Indeed, it enjoyed a high proportion of foreign students, which rose from 291 in 1919–20 to 717 by 1936–37, although not all were economists and some were part-time mature students (Alfred Coats, 1982). But above all, unlike Cambridge, it was not overly-doctrinal in the 1930s.

Oxford, by contrast had, as we have seen earlier, been much slower to see economics as a distinct discipline, and the internal academic machinations over its place during the first 30 years of the twentieth century would supply enough material to fill several C.P. Snow novels (Young and Lee, 1993). The emergence of Keynes's macroeconomic analysis, together with its underlying microeconomic implications—plus the practical matter of expansion of economic in general at Oxford—led to a broadening of economic interests at the university, and particularly so in research rather than teaching. But Brown, after getting a lectureship at Hertford College, had to consider teaching as well as working at his research interests.

This was at a time when there were institutional changes at Oxford (both formal and informal)—with, for example, the establishment of the Institute of Statistics—and changes in faculty, with Fraser, Wilson, and Meade leaving and Hitch, Richard Sayers, and Brown taking their places. Brown was, however, little engaged in the institutional changes, other than essentially going with the flow as a participant, as Young and Lee (1993:

22) put it in their comprehensive account of economics at Oxford at this time: "Sayers and Brown were too involved with teaching commitments and writing doctoral dissertations ... However, Brown and Burchardt did contribute something to the research side of Oxford economics." Indeed, Frank Burchardt, who had held a position at Oxford from January 1936, later became much more involved in institutional change, and was subsequently made director of the Institute of Statistics in 1948.

Brown lectured on several courses, largely involving economic theory. But he did not seem to relish all of this. Much of what was required was circumscribed. The main book used when he started lecturing in 1938 was Frank Taussig's (1915) *Principles of Economics*. This was a massive two-volume work that Brown later described as "Not an inspiring work. Well the question is, what sort of alternative was there? Taussig is a bit like Marshall, but not quite" (Brown, 1997a: 142). It was dated (the 1921 edition was still used), American in its orientation, and did not go beyond *Indian Currency* (Keynes, 1913) in recognizing the existence of Maynard Keynes. From 1940, the economics sub-faculty recommended Frederic Benham's (1938) *Economics*, which Brown (1988a: 30) critiqued as "excellent and deservedly popular though the book was, it was no Keynesian work. 'Considerable concessions', says the author in his Preface, have been made to the views of Mr. Keynes, but I can hardly be regarded as one of his followers."[5]

One of the problems, and Brown mulls over this, was the lack of an alternative. He feels Meade's (1936) *Introduction to Economic Analysis and Policy* was a possibility, but never seemed to be suggested, possibly because there was a feeling amongst the faculty that there was a need to provide students with more traditional theory prior to moving forward. Brown (1988a: 30) also considered it prudent to stay with the standard books for his introductory lectures.

A little later, with the arrival of Paul Samuelson's (1948) *Economics*, Brown did find an alternative much more in line with the way he thought about the subject. In a review of the book for *Nature*, Brown (1949c: 464) explained the difference between the old textbooks and Samuelson:

> Prof. Samuelson who, like Mr. Hicks, is one of the most brilliant mathematical economic theorists of his generation, adopts for his students an approach which is far more empirical and far less deductive than the older one. The latter approach, with the emphasis on the theory of value and on the presumed behavior of business men, assumed that the main task of economics was to explain and interrelate the almost universally known facts of economic life, which meant, largely, the facts relating to private business and private consumption. The newer approach puts far more emphasis on the discovery and exposition (mainly statistical) of the economic facts about society as a whole,

and approached the task of explaining or interrelating them with something more than scientific humility. It constitutes, in fact, a step towards presenting economics as an empirical science.

THE OXFORD INSTITUTE OF STATISTICS

New research-based institutes were also being established in the mid-1930s. This was at the time Brown was moving through his undergraduate education, his Hertford College lectureship, and to his All Souls Examination Fellowship in 1937, which he was awarded along with the historian David Cox.[6] Of importance was the creation of the Institute of Statistics in 1935, which provided an institutional base for empirical work, and of the Oxford Economist's Research Group (OERG) a year later. The Institute was, although not entirely, designed to meet the increasing interest of economists to build economic theory on a foundation of sound data analysis. Its initial director, Jacob Marschak, the Ukrainian-born economist, went on to have a distinguished academic career in the United States, including heading up the Cowles Foundation. The Institute was Brown's base for his graduate work. The OERG provided a peer group that offered a sounding board for his work, as well as a forum where outside speakers offered their ideas.

Stepping back a little chronologically to provide more institutional background, the notion of making economics teaching and research at Oxford more structured was first broached by the Hebdomadal Council in 1931 when it was reviewing the finances of the university (Young and Lee, 1993).[7] In the process of consultation, the Social Studies Board surveyed the needs of the Honour School of PPE. Besides highlighting the need for several specific faculties, it was recommended that the successful development at Oxford required an Institute or Department of Economics. The outcome was an expansion of faculty, for example a Chair in Finance and Currency, together with more space for economics research.

The visit of Wesley Mitchell, one of the founders and first director of the National Bureau of Economic Research (NBER) in the US at this time, also stimulated some of the younger academics to think in terms of a department and of developing postgraduate research in economics, and thus injecting a longer-term vision into the debates. Mitchell's arguments rested largely on the need for more joint and collaborative activities.[8] The younger faculty—such as Harrod, Opie, Meade, Allen, and Phelps Brown—responded by drawing up plans for a statistical laboratory housing the computers of the day, essentially hand calculators, a secretary qualified as a statistician, and an economic statistics library. The aim, at least initially, was a self-contained unit designed to conduct its own work rather than as an aid to fellows and students to do their work.

It was All Souls that pushed things forward in 1934 by agreeing to support a Readership in Statistics as part of an Institute of Economic Statistics.[9] They used this as leverage in seeking funds from the Rockefeller Foundation to support social science at the university, which the Council believed would be a more attractive proposition for the Foundation than a more specialized unit. In the 1920s, under Beardsley Ruml, the Foundation was giving grants mainly to support interdisciplinary plans for empirical work in the social sciences. By the mid-1930s, under Edmund Day, however, the focus had moved more to providing finance to specific projects, including institutes that were specializing in empirical work of the business cycle (Craver, 1986).

A committee that included Roy Harrod and Alexander Lindsay, the Master of Balliol College, was set up, and advice sought from faculty boards. James Meade drew up plans to go forward as the economics element of the proposal, and consulted Jacob Marschak, the newly appointed Chichele Lecturer at All Souls College, for comments on the vital need for an institute to conduct empirical work on a diversity of "fundamental elasticities" to support his mathematical analysis of labor markets. The data requirements covered banking, industry, national income, consumption goods, fixed capital goods, capital depreciation, price indices, and taxes. Marschak was highly attracted to this because it coincided with what he would require for his own work on capital and money markets. The outcome of this was a memo drafted by Harrod that argued an economic institute encompassing both statistics and theoretical research was essential for the future of economics at Oxford. In doing this the various function and activities of such a unit, as well as suitable subjects for research, were outlined in some detail.

It transpired that, given the shift in focus of the Foundation, the subsequent revised request for £5,000 per annum for five years (including £750 for capital expenditure on a statistical institute) was approved in January, with funding beginning in July 1935. It was housed in an old house in Broad Street with a medieval Dance of Death painted on the wall of its rear door passage.

The actual work to be done at the Institute was initially somewhat contentious, and while Harrod's memo had focused on applied economics, there were others who felt that it should embrace mathematical statistics and economic theory. Lindsay felt it should be multidisciplinary and embrace politics, anthropology, and psychology as well as economics, and focus on more general topics (Chester, 1986).

The outcome was the Council expressing its view that the Institute would extend its work beyond economics and consider issues confronting modern society. But the actualities of the matter were left vague. In June, a standing committee consisting of Macgregor, Cole, Harrod, Phelps Brown, and Marschak was appointed to manage the Institute, with the latter as the director.

Marschak saw as part of his remit not only to look at the diverse implications of business cycles but also to improve the organization of D.Phil. and undergraduate work not only in line with Harrod's memo but also as a wider obligation to the university. He also had to provide additional research funds and physically accommodate the needs of economics fellows. Added to this was the need for an outlet for the findings of the Institute, and for this the *Bulletin of the Oxford University Institute of Economics and Statistics* was established in 1939.[10]

It was just after its outset, in 1936, that Brown joined the Institute to work on his thesis. The number of doctoral students studying economics in the UK was, at that time however, small, perhaps 12 at Oxford, and only a few had links with the Institute. They were an eclectic group. Brown in his interview with Keith Tribe remembers Teddy Jackson, who later became director of the Institute and steered it towards development economics in the post-war period; George Shackle, who was Phelps Brown's part-time research assistant; Betty Ackroyd, later chair of the Consumers Council, who was involved in an Oxford Social Survey; Helen Makeover, who worked with Marschak on labor and mobility; and Goronway Daniel, who became principal of Aberystwyth University.[11] Added to this, Harold Wilson, the future Prime Minister, began working with William Beveridge a year after Brown joined the Institute.

THE OXFORD ECONOMISTS' RESEARCH GROUP

From a more directed research focus, the late 1930s saw the initial challenge to the Marshallian supply and demand framework that was subsequently reawakened in the Cambridge capital controversy. This primary challenge came when a group of Oxford economists, led initially by Hubert Henderson, who was a Fellow of All Souls after being Joint Secretary to the Economic Advisory Council (Robinson, 1985), and subsequently by Roy Harrod formed the Oxford Economists' Research Group (OERG). After some preparatory work from 1934 deciding on methodology and subject matter, it emerged in 1936.[12] The major focus of the group was to be the investigation of trends in economic activity in the United Kingdom since 1924, with an emphasis on the reaction of businessmen to the trade cycle. In a way, the OERG was a somewhat belated response to the creation of Keynes's informal "Cambridge Circus" that had started in 1930, but was more concerned with quantification than theorizing. The aim was basically to test the empirical question of whether the Great Depression was, as conventional Marshallian arguments went, largely due to structural problems in the economy or to demand factors (Lee, 1981, 1991). Arthur Brown, who prior to taking up his All Souls Fellowship in 1937 was a lecturer at Hertford College, not surprisingly given his dissertation subject, very quickly became involved.

The OERG was comprised of economists who were fellows at the Oxford colleges. The Group included, besides Brown, Roy Harrod, James Meade, Robert Hall, Charles Hitch, Eric Hargreaves, Henry Phelps Brown, Redvers Opie, Frank Burchardt, E.M. Hugh-Jones, W.M. Allen, Russell Bretherton, and R.S.G. Rutherford. Henderson was chairman. There were two research students, P.W.S. Andrews and George Shackle, because their work was connected to that of Phelps Brown. Many of these characters make appearances throughout Brown's later career, both in terms of his academic work and his public service (Lee, 1981). Others at Oxford who also were important in Brown's career, including Richard Sayers who was at the Institute of Statistics for four years before the war, were not engaged in the OERG, mainly because of a lack of commonality in their research interests. However, the academic community of the time was small—with, for example, only 9,311 students in the UK obtaining undergraduate degrees in 1938—and collegiality more pronounced than now.[13] This was not an age of mass higher education.

Since economics had only explicitly being introduced at Oxford in the 1921 as a subject for undergraduate study, all the fellows were relatively young and keen to test traditional doctrines and to look at the practical implications of economics for policy. There was a bent for grounded empiricism stimulated by the work of Arthur Bowley and Josiah Stamp, the Balfour Committee on Industry and Trade, the Macmillan Committee on Finance and Industry, the creation of the Institute of Statistics at Oxford in 1935 (where Brown first went for his graduate work in 1936), and by Wesley Clair Mitchell spending 1930–31 in Oxford (Harrod, 1949).[14]

The newness of the subject at Oxford, at least in any depth of academic numbers, the fact that a number of faculty were not Oxford graduates (and indeed not economics graduates), and the lack of any historical "school of thought" also meant those in the group were initially quite eclectic in their interests. As Brown (1997a: 142) put it later: "There wasn't anything corresponding to the founding fathers who though it was all in Marshall. They were all bright young things and they were all a bit different from each other. . . . I think the main difference is that we didn't have a bible called the *Principles of Economics*." In general terms, however, by 1933 the ethos at Oxford was moving away from the political economy bent of the early years of PPE, and "the theoretical orientation of Oxford economics was clearly becoming neoclassical, mathematical, and non-historical" (Young and Lee, 1993: 21).[15] It had traveled away from the traditional Oxford political economy to combine neo-classical economics with an interest in applied statistical methods as an instrument of verification (Chester, 1986).

The vehicle for disseminating the OERG's ideas and for stimulating external debate was the *Oxford Economic Papers* (*OEP*). This was at a time when many economics journals in the United Kingdom were largely institution based. *Economica*, for example, had been founded in 1921 and revamped as a New Series in 1935, and was largely, although not exclusively, an LSE vehicle. *The Economic Journal* had begun in 1891 as an initiative of Herbert Foxwell, who was at University College London, and its first editor was Francis Edgeworth, who had just moved to Oxford. While a broad journal produced by the Royal Economics Society, its contents were heavily influenced by Cambridge. Maynard Keynes was editor from 1912 to 1945, although balanced to some extent by Edgeworth, who returned as joint editor between 1918 and 1925, and by D.H. Macgregor between 1925 and 1933. One of Keynes's former students, Austin Robinson, was, however, assistant editor between 1934 and 1940 (Coats, 1968). In addition, but less influential in the 1930s, there was the *Manchester School*, edited since 1932 by the School of Social Science at the University of Manchester. *The Bulletin of the Oxford University Institute of Economics and Statistics*, which has a more mathematical leaning, was established a little later in 1939.

Founded in 1938, the initial three issues of *OEP* contained an array of papers that, in combination, led to two highly upsetting conclusions (Robinson, 1939). The first conclusion, which led to a plethora of subsequent studies in industrial economic and management science, was that businessmen did not set prices in accordance with marginalist principles. The second conclusion was that investment decisions were not responsive to changes in interest rates, of which Brown's work on liquidity preference was a key element.

Regarding the work of Hall and Hitch (1939), evidence from businessmen showed that they did not use marginalism to set prices, but rather set prices on a cost-plus formula largely stable in the face of changes in demand: the idea of full cost pricing. To allow for firms facing downward-sloping demand curves, Hall and Hitch developed the notion of a kinked demand curve. From the group's pricing data and a business survey of 39 large manufacturing firms, they found that businessmen tend to follow price cuts and ignore price increases.[16] While this issue of hysteresis is inconsistent with marginalism, the various concepts explaining the behavior of individual firms were derived from the Marshallian supply and demand framework.[17]

In many ways, this work on business behavior has been the enduring legacy of the OERG, at least as found in textbooks. As Brown later put it in a personal letter to Frederic Lee of October 22, 1979:

> My own recollection is that the Hall/Hitch article made a considerable impact on Oxford economics. It was considered a reconciliation of the logic of marginalism with the empirically established practice of full cost pricing-or, at any rate, of pricing in some relation to either average total or average variable cost at some conventional level of capacity utilization. (Lee, 1981: 346)[18]

GETTING A D.PHIL.

A.J. Brown stayed at Oxford to pursue a D.Phil. degree under the supervision of Jacob Marschak at the Institute.[19] Until the mid-1980s or so a research degree in the United Kingdom was just that. It was entirely based upon writing a thesis of publishable standard that was evaluated by at least one internal and one external examiner appointed by the examining institution. The examination involved assessment of both the thesis and an extensive *viva voce* held in private, unlike the US or Continental public defense. There were no formal courses involved, although candidates did of their own volition often attended seminars and public lectures, and conducted joint work with established academics.

The interest in the late 1930s in getting more closely to grips with the magnitude of some of the parameters in the Keynesian system provided an array of empirical questions to be answered. Brown started work on what was to become his thesis on "Liquidity Preference: A Study of Investment"; the broad topic was suggested to him by Charles Hitch and the sub-title by Marschak, whom Hitch had drawn in as Brown's supervisor (Brown, 1988a: 34).[20] This had an advantage for Brown in that the OERG had several people who were also working on the role of interest rates, and who could act as useful sounding boards for his ideas as his thesis developed and as academic papers where drafted.

The upsurge of interest in Keynesian ideas of liquidity preferences, and with the possibility of a liquidity trap, meant there were new lines of enquiry regarding the role of interest rates in need of analysis. Keynes's (1936: Chap. 15) thinking was that interest rates are payments for giving up liquidity, of which money is the most liquid asset, and not, as neoclassical economics held, a reward for saving:

> [T]he rate of interest at any time, being the reward for parting with liquidity, is a measure of the unwillingness of those who possess money to part with their

liquid control over it . . . It is the "price" which equilibrates the desire to hold wealth in the form of cash with the available quantity of cash.

A liquidity trap, in this context, is a situation in which injections of cash into the private banking system by a central bank fail to decrease interest rates, and hence make monetary policy ineffective—a problem that, Keynes argued, occurred in the 1930s. Such a trap exists when people hoard cash because they expect an adverse event such as deflation, insufficient aggregate demand, or war. Common characteristics of a liquidity trap are interest rates falling close to zero and when fluctuations in the money supply fail to translate into fluctuations in price levels. The main thing that beggared the policy makers in the 1930s was, did such a trap exist and, if so, when did investment became insensitive to the interest rate, and to what extent did liquidity preference vary at higher levels of interest?

The path to his thesis topic, as is often the case with these things, was slightly circuitous. Initially, on the advice of Marschak, Brown (along with an undergraduate student, William Blair) had been directed to the idea of looking at security prices. This provided Blair with a useful B.Litt thesis on *Risk, Interest Rates and Security Prices*. Brown's initial idea was to analyze the stock prices of British railways, which were privately owned at the time, in relation to the weekly statistics of railway returns and in connection with more general developments in the capital market. As so often happens with these things, this did not work out very well. Brown could find no security valuation attributable to liquidity, and so he "wandered into a different part of the forest" (Brown, 1988a: 34).

Turning to the balance sheets of the London Clearing Banks, Brown sought:

> to see if the "liquidity-preference schedule" which Mr. Keynes has introduced into the theoretical discussion, can be used in this field as an instrument of statistical analysis with the same limited, but important measure of success that Mr. Schultz, for instance, has attained with the Marshallian demand-curve in another one. (Brown, 1938: 49)

The problem was that the balance sheets of the banks contained five main types of assets. Nevertheless, he thought there may be interesting relations between the ratios.

By employing confluence analysis, Brown did find some links, and well before completing his thesis. He published his work as "The liquidity-preference schedule of banks," after making revisions following discussion within the OERG, in the first issue of the new *Oxford Economics Papers*. This paper contains what was probably the first application of the technique in the UK. Confluence analysis, as developed by Ragnar Frisch

(1934), helped Brown deal with two statistical problems. First, it was a way of meeting the challenge of separating out different linear relationships which might hold between any set of observable variables. Second, it overcame the difficulties caused by estimation when all variables are measured with error. More recently, however, David Hendry and Mary Morgan (1989: 51) have shown that the use of bunch maps, as used by Brown "to uncover confluent relations, have faded out. There were good historical reasons for their demise and, as our analysis shows, there are good intellectual reasons why they should not be resurrected."

Empirically Brown finds or, as he says, "persuaded" himself, that:

> It is very clearly seen that the 'total liquidity-position' of the banks was low in early 1921, very high in 1922–23, and had a downward trend from then till 1929. It then fell to a very low minimum in 1931, and recovered rapidly (with a small setback in 1933) to a very high point in 1934, from which it fell away. This means the banks are most illiquid in the slump, gain liquidity in the depression, to attain their most liquid position in the early or middle years of recovery, and gradually become less liquid through later recovery and boom. (Brown, 1938: 80)

In fact, the results were not that satisfactory, and Brown surrounds his conclusions with copious caveats: "The chief conclusion from the foregoing analysis seems to be that the liquidity-preference schedule defined in some such way as that used here is, in favorable circumstances, quite a useful instrument for quantitative analysis" (Brown, 1938: 80).[21] The generality of his findings are also limited to only London clearing banks. His companion on the securities work, William Blair, was also "not equally persuaded" by the results (Brown, 1988a: 34). The paper had only limited impact.

Brown then, getting the idea shortly after moving to All Souls in November 1937, shifted his energies to estimating a broader demand schedule for money, with what can be called side excursions into Wicksellian theory and Gibson's Paradox.[22] He also attempted to defend and to address and refine some of the findings of a survey by Meade and Andrews (1937) involving 37 businessmen regarding the effectiveness of the interest rate in influencing business decisions. To summarize, the latter's survey found business investment decisions little influenced by short-term interest rate changes, largely because they did not borrow from banks, and any changes were small relative to profit margins. That there may be some effect of a decline in the rate was a signal for easier borrowing in general. Equally, long-term rates also seemed to have limited direct impact because they had no need to borrow or it was a small element in their costs compared to depreciation, market uncertainty, and so on. What was mentioned as important by some was that the willingness to invest was influenced by the availability of liquid assets. Brown (1939a: 66) reads this as saying:

> It would perhaps be presumptuous to assert more than that the entrepreneur's liquidity position is probably of considerably more direct importance to him than is the rate of interest, but so much, at any rate, seems justified by the evidence . . . low interest merely a result of abundance of idle funds, which is the real stimulant.

What Brown (1939a: 45) set out to do was "to show that Mr. Keynes' general liquidity-preference schedule can be made a useful instrument of statistical analysis, and that there is some evidence that it remains fairly stable through time." After presenting his findings, under the title "Money, interest, and prices," to a joint Oxford–London–Cambridge economics seminar in May 1938 at the Institute of Statistics, the paper was published the following year, again in the *OEP* (Brown, 1939a). The multiple regressions in the paper, involving up to four independent variables, must have taken time and effort given the lack of computing power available in the 1930s for inverting matrices.

Brown's analysis essentially entailed estimating the relationship from 1926 to 1931 between British idle balances and interest rate and price changes, and trying to relate total cash holdings to interest rate, price change, financial transactions, and non-financial transactions—but this was not as satisfactory as using idle balances. To gain a handle on the levels of liquidity, active and idle balances are separated by estimating velocity of circulation when there are no idle balances: the so-called maximum velocity. Idle balances are then calculated by taking the difference between total balances and the ratio of transactions to the maximal velocity. Superficially, his approach deviates from the Keynesian framework by including more than one alternative to holding cash, security, or goods. Brown argues that businesses may hold goods when prices are rising and hence are relevant, but with no price changes, in an equilibrium situation the underlying model reduces to the original Keynesian formulation with liquidity preference defined as the relationship between the total of idle money in the hands of the public and the rate of interest.

What the data tells him is that liquidity-preference, in terms of idle money, does influence business decisions provided that the real turnover of commodities varies little with the trade cycle or prices relative to the variation of total money.[23] Regarding Knut Wicksell's work and the Gibson paradox, Brown (1939a: 67–8) finds that:

> the Gibson relation may be accounted for as well on the assumption that the rate of interest is a comparatively unimportant price, relative to the quantity

of idle money and to recent trends in the general price level by the liquidity-preference schedule, as on the Wicksellian supposition that it is the chief regulator of new enterprise.

From a policy perspective, Brown's paper concludes:

the number of causes capable of starting the snowball of recovery is probably large, yet the statistical evidence that recovery is associated with low interest rate (or some condition that generally accompanies it) is very strong. It may well be that abundance of idle money, acting either as a stimulant itself, or as an enabling condition permitting other miscellaneous stimulant to work, is the systematic causal factor lying behind this regularity. (1939a: 69)

The onset of war obviously had a diversionary effect in terms of the impact of Brown's paper; academic energies as well as personnel were being diverted to the war effort, and a new set of economic issues to tackle had come to the fore. His analysis did not go unnoticed, however, although Brown did suggest that James Tobin's (1947) work in the same area in the late 1940s was independent of his, presumably because he was unfamiliar with it.

Nearer home, prior to the publication of Brown's paper, for example, Dennis Robertson was addressing the Oxford Economics Society, and likened liquidity preference unfavorably to loanable funds mechanisms; and, after someone mentioned Brown's work, Brown was drawn into an argument on the topic.

Richard Sayers, a fellow of Pembroke College at the time (and who had just published his book *Modern Banking* in 1938), in the May 1940 issue of the *Oxford Economic Papers* also offered comment on Brown's work as part of a more general critique of the OERG's study of interest rates. His arguments firstly revolve around the low response rate to the OECG's survey and whether responses were, thus, potentially biased towards firms who did feel interest rates are effective in affecting borrowing. The potential of ambiguous interpretation of questions was also seen as an issue. Adjusting for this, Sayers only finds new fixed and net investments in stocks seemed sensitive to interest rates, and maintenance of fixed stock hardly at all; but even in the first two cases, bank charges and the attitude of the bank seemed to dominate. Brown's defense of the OERG findings was somewhat battered by this.

Regarding Brown's work more specifically, Sayers found no evidence to support Brown's finding that the real stimulant to increased trade may not be low interest rates but the availability of idle balances which, in themselves, can result in low interest rates. Sayers argues that unless there is a mechanism to pump the idle funds into the ownership of firms, the only way he sees for entrepreneurs to increase their resources is by reducing maintenance or reserving profits, but this will adversely affect the profits of other firms. He concludes: "the evidence in our possession does not allow us to hope that the banking system can give substantial direct help by varying the amount of 'idle money' in existence" (Sayers, 1940: 31).

A major underlying problem with Brown's approach, and certainly not one unique to his analysis, was that of the inherent "identification problem" involved—basically, whether the rate of interest depends on liquidity or vice versa.[24] The challenge in circumventing these problems was a lack of data to build complete systems of equations that would allow for the clear identity of the demand for liquidity to be isolated from the supply. This was a difficulty that existed for some time, and certainly well into the analysis conducted from the post-war period into the 1960s, and is seen in a slew of American studies—including those by Allan Meltzer (1963), Brunner and Meltzer (1963), James Tobin (1965), and by Khusro (1952) and others in the UK.

Besides keeping in touch with the literature, Brown also participated in the economics and statistical seminars that were regularly held at Oxford and London. This provided meat to his understanding of Keynes, and allowed him to keep abreast of wider developments in economics whilst working on his thesis. Brown recalls (1988a: 35), for example, listening to Roy Harrod explain the concept of the warranted rate of growth at the Oxford Economics Society, and to discussions at the Institutes by Marschak and Opie of Wicksell's recently published *Lectures*, John Hicks's (1939) *Value and Capital*, and, apparently less successfully, Maynard Keynes's *General Theory* when Robert Hall stood in for Marschak.

He had also been an attendee at the London and Cambridge Economic Seminar (Oxford was added to the title later) since his undergraduate days, but not frequently so. He did find, however, that "gatherings involving Nicholas Kaldor could not avoid a certain liveliness."

More locally, at the Institute he was continually engaged, initially partly for the practical reason he needed to enhance his statistical skill base, with its informal discussions, and especially with visitors such as the later Noble Prize winners Trygve Haavelmo and Tjalling Koopmans. He also was involved in a seminar that considered Jan Tinbergen's 1935 *Econometrica* article on business cycles, and found satisfaction in developing a second-order differential equation version of Hawtrey's theory; it also had the useful value that, "Tinbergen's short-term scheme formed the basis of my final answer on the economics paper in my second, and successful assault on All Souls in October, 1937" (Brown, 1988a: 37).

It was these statistical seminars that also brought him into contact with confluence analysis, and he and Edward Radice, who subsequently served

30 years as a British civil servant, mostly working in economic intelligence, were drawn into using it—in Brown's case in both his 1938 and 1939 papers. Just as his 1939 paper was essentially drowned in the need to reorientate for war, so his pioneering use of confluence analysis, for all its warts, was at least partially forgotten. Indeed, so much so that when Richard Stone published some of his work in the *Journal of the Royal Statistical Society* in 1945, his discussant, M.G. Kendall, thought it was the first appearance of the technique: "The third feature of the work is the introduction—I think for the first time in a paper in England—of confluence analysis" (Stone, 1945: 385).

THE WAR AND THE CIVIL SERVICE

Brown, with his All Souls fellowship, stayed at Oxford until 1943 but became increasingly involved with the Royal Institute of International Affairs (more commonly referred to as Chatham House), which had been moved to the city not long after the war began. The foreign press section of the Foreign Office, to which Chatham House was strongly linked, also moved to Balliol. Brown initially got pulled into writing regularly for the *Bulletin of International News*, and subsequently became a member of the economics section under A.G.B. Fisher. When the foreign press section removed back to London in 1943, becoming the Foreign Office Research Department, Brown remained in Oxford with the peacetime Chatham House and, as head of its economics section, he had three assistants!

His time with the Foreign Office produced a steady flow of articles, not only for the *Bulletin of International News* (to which he contributed 50 or so papers) but also more theoretically oriented academic pieces, for example for the *Oxford Economic Papers* (Brown, 1942a), and reviews of the work of others.[25] He also wrote what was really an explanatory pamphlet early in the war on *The Arsenal of Democracy* (Brown, 1941a), looking at the role of the US in a global geo-political context, another pamphlet on *Industrialization and Trade* for the Royal Institute (Brown, 1943a) that looked at the changing economic position of Britain in the world economy, and contributed to a number of edited volumes. Later, with peace, he brought together some of what he had learned from writing for the *Bulletin*, with some additional material that was published, for example, as a pamphlet on *The America Economy and World Economy* for the Institute of Bankers (Brown, 1949b), and his book *Applied Economics: Aspects of the World Economy in War and Peace* (Brown, 1948; reviewed by Clough, 1949).

The articles in the *Bulletin of International News* were exactly what the journal title suggests; they covered a whole range of subject matter germane to the war. The journal was topical in the sense that its articles were on subjects, if not quite of the day, of at least relevance in the short period. They generally contained large amounts of information and data, and put this into context. Since many of them involved the economies of the Axis Powers, or countries that had been overrun by these powers, the information was often somewhat dated and probably not entirely accurate.[26] It was also inevitably incomplete for security reasons. But the intention was that this was made up for by clear exposition of the situation. They moved, and particularly so towards the end of the war, more into matters of post-war UK economic challenges and policy options.

As common to all the *Bulletins*, the relevant articles were drafted for the interested non-specialist and reflect Brown's own thinking based on the theories of the day and the data then available.[27] To overview these papers, and his Oxford pamphlet on America's entry to the war (Brown, 1941a), is not the aim here. Besides much of it being heavily descriptive, conditions at the time often prescribed the subject and subject matter of what was written. There were some papers, or groups of papers, however, that indicate his thoughts at the time on topics he returned to later in his life. Added to this, the period stimulated his much broader interest in international economics, a point he made in his later application to the University of Leeds: "My wartime work, however, has turned my interests more in the direction of international economics and especially towards (a) the pure theory and statistical analysis of elasticities and stability-conditions of international trade, and (b) the statistical analysis of social patterns of international trade."[28]

One topic that he addressed in some detail, and that offers a few thoughts about his later major analysis of the subject, was inflation. The situation as he saw it as the war moved towards its close was that:

> "Inflation" has been held up as a danger before all the belligerents in this war; it is not clear, however, that the understanding of what it is (still less of how it is caused and how it can be avoided or remedied) has become a widespread as the fear of it. (Brown, 1945a: 11)

Having said that, most of Europe still had recollections of the hyperinflation in Austria in 1922, and Germany and Hungary in 1923; but memories of extreme events and an understanding of the forces that cause them are not the same thing. Brown gave some thought to both the causes of inflation in general but obviously, given the context, focused on those peculiar to wartime conditions, and policy options for limiting them and handling the consequences.

Of importance in his later career, and in particular in his thinking when conducting his Royal Institute of International Affairs study of post-World War II inflation in the early 1950s, Brown provides an explanation of what inflation is and what may cause it as a sort of warning of what might be expected as hostilities decline, but with an array of possible policy options.[29] His focus in several articles in the *Bulletin* was on "ordinary inflation" and not hyperinflation, and focuses on the causes of excessive money supply, and in particular the challenges of coping with large-scale government borrowing to finance the war. His diagnosis of the situation to the end of 1944 was relatively optimistic: "It is note-worthy that strong and determined governments have had little difficulty in preventing serious inflation in this war so far, only in countries with weak executives or countries under enemy occupation has it assumed alarming proportions" (Brown, 1945a: 15).

As for policy, price controls and rationing were generally viewed favorably, with very strong caveats regarding the method of application, a position that he retained in his later, more substantive work on *The Great Inflation* (Brown, 1955). In this he was in line with Galbraith, (1952). As he put it:

> The far greater success attained by the belligerents in this war, as compared with the last, has been largely due, not to any improvement in fiscal or monetary policy in the narrow sense—governments have again had to borrow extensively from banks and cannot possibly be sure that their patriotic appeals will increase savings sufficiently to neutralize the extra purchasing power so created—but to improvement in price-control and rationing. (Brown, 1945a: 15)

The caveats about price controls revolve around the need for complementary rationing strategies that ensure the individual can "meet his essential needs—or secure his fair share of the available supplies." Which countries were successful in achieving this up to this point are investigated in some detail in his subsequent contribution (Brown, 1945b).[30]

Brown's focus on the effectiveness of price control strategies had begun earlier, and inevitably was highly speculative given the data shortages on inflation when looking at the occupied countries of Europe. Here the rationale for price controls as an inflation control was somewhat different to that of the UK. Germany had fixed the exchange rate between itself and the territories occupied at an artificially low rate to encourage Germans to buy from the occupied countries, but the latter not to buy from Germany (Brown, 1941e). In normal circumstances this is because the rise in demand for production in the occupied territories would be inflationary unless production rises considerably, which it did not. To combat this, price controls were imposed and enforced externally by the Germans.

Brown took away several messages from what he observed in the three occupied countries he looked at, Norway, Denmark, and France. One was the differential reaction of the wealthy to price control with this, who "seemed to have a lot of confidence in the currency . . . and to have escaped from bank-deposits and bonds into shares and real property," whereas "it seems that the general public's confidence in their value [that is, of notes] is not seriously shaken" (Brown, 1941e: 1872). He foresaw a longer-term issue:

> There is preparing in the three countries a very dangerous inflationary situation at some time in the future when the price control (the poor man's barrier against 'escaping from money into real values') breaks down, and when, at the same time, the rise in prices increases his desire to escape. (Brown, 1941e: 1872)

At about this time, Brown also reviewed, for the *Economic Journal*, the *League of Nations' World Economic Survey, 1939–41*. While much of his space is devoted to production levels and trade as economies transitioned from a peace-time to a wartime footing, he does devote some time in his review to inflation policies. Looking at the data presented, he, as he did earlier in the *Bulletin of International News*, concludes:

> More generally, perhaps the most striking financial difference between this war and the last which emerges here is the efficiency of the various means now employed to limit private spending, one result of which has been that, in practically all belligerent and occupied countries, unspendable money has accumulated, an unprecedented degree of liquidity has been attained, and interest rates have nearly everywhere fallen. The undesirable aspect of this development may become apparent when the power of the administration in any of the countries concerned is threatened: the difficulty of preventing drastic price-inflation will presumably be greater when the sole barrier against it is direct control of process and of amounts of goods which can be bought than it would be if the supply of currency were also kept on a tight rein. (Brown, 1942d: 237)

In 1945, Brown joined the Economic Section of the Cabinet Office, where, under the invitation of James Meade (who had just taken over as head from Lionel Robbins), he worked on the German re-armament and on the creation of the Government Statistical Service. The team was small—two advisors plus secretarial staff—and over his time there included people from the now defunct Prime Minister's Statistical Branch, including George Shackle (whom Brown had known at Oxford and would be subsequently recruited to Leeds) and Jack Parkinson, a Leeds graduate who would later be a lecturer there when Brown arrived. Again, important for his future, it was at the Economics Section that Brown met Ronald Tress, with whom he later worked on the Tress-Brown Index of university costs and on African economic issues. Tress was also later Secretary General of the Royal Economic Society when Brown was President.

Brown's main function during this period of government service was to provide day-to-day briefings and the writing of material for internal government circulation of a semi-annual world economic survey highlighting things that may in future be of interest to the government.[31] The latter was a stopgap measure necessitated by the ending of the League of Nations' survey at a time that new bodies such as the secretariats of the United Nations and the Organisation for European Co-operation (later the Organisation for Economic Co-operation and Development/OECD) had not become fully operational. His stay there, however, was limited and he wished to move back into academia; indeed, whilst at the Cabinet Office, he spent a year as a special lecturer at University College London (UCL) in 1946.

TRADE ISSUES

As we see later, in 1947 Brown moved to the University of Leeds where he became immersed in the challenges and excitement of developing a major academic unit, and the time-consuming administrative burden that goes with this. (His later memos suggest he found the issue of dealing with noise from a garage adjacent to the Economics Department particularly wearisome.) What did inevitably carry over, however, were his research interests. While he initially had little time to develop a new research agenda there were things he had become interested in whilst at Oxford and in the civil service that had grown in national importance after the war. He also had intellectual capital invested in them. Therefore, if for no other practical reason than that running a department of a somewhat different educational structure to that of Oxford, and getting familiar with the politics of Leeds University required moving up a steep learning curve, his research in the late 1940s and early 1950s tended to involve more consolidation that novelty. Equally, inevitably these research interests he carried over were initially linked to his work in government and in international trade; they were a continuation of matters he had been involved with at the Foreign Office, for example regarding commodity prices (Brown, 1954).

But we move a little ahead of ourselves. Brown's articles in the *Bulletin of International News*, together with *Industrialization and Trade*, besides providing insights into the economic conditions in the various belligerents and comments on some of the implications for the future, touched upon several more explicit international finance and trade topics. In particular, part of the analysis had looked at some of the global challenges of developing a sustainable international exchange system. Much of what he wrote, however, was a retrospective assessment on the failures of previous systems, most notably those of the gold and gold bullion standards; and, in a sense harking back to his D.Phil thesis, the problems of ensuring adequate future global liquidity. The events at Bretton Woods had, however, made this rather *passé*, but they had also established a major agenda for a fresh look at the implications of the gold exchange standard that had emerged.[32]

Regarding international trade, Brown's interests run somewhat differently and was more focused, but not unrelated. Even while doing government work during the war he began to be engaged in thinking about exchange stability in circumstance when currency depreciation leads to an increase in the value of imports rather than their reduction. To that end, his largely theoretical paper in the *Oxford Economic Papers*, published while working for the Foreign Office, sought to both exact conditions that lead to this unsustainable situation and "to assign reasonable values to the relevant elasticities" (Brown, 1942a: 57) that would allow estimation in the UK's case of the effects of a sterling depreciation from its equilibrium level against all other currencies, and the subsequent impacts on the trade balance. This differed from conditions where currency depreciation can lead to an increase in the value of exports, a subject covered earlier by Keynes (1929).

The modeling breaks away from the conventional Marshallian approach that takes it as axiomatic that in the presence of Say's Law all income is spent in all countries, and instead follows one that, at least in the short term, can deviate from this.[33] Following a Keynesian approach, labor supply is assumed infinitely elastic in both countries at the going real wage rate, reflecting short-term unemployment, with goods being produced under competitive conditions in the absence of any scale effects. This effectively means that the price of each national good is the unit of currency of that country and assumed to be stable.

Under these conditions, production in each country is determined by the equilibrium of total demand for its national good with its infinite elastic supply of labor and, given the exchange rate, the total demand for each good would be determined by the levels of production in both countries. This leads, unlike the classic Marshallian framework, to a Keynesian situation whereby there is the possibility of underemployment and continued disequilibrium in the balance of trade even if a currency is depreciated. The Robinson–Brown outcome is that with variable production there is no change in the critical value of the sum of the elasticities of demand for imports, but that it acts only to lower the absolute effect of depreciation on the balance of trade.[34]

Applying this framework to the UK requires some assumptions, including many which cover: whether economic activities in the UK and the rest of the world remain constant; whether elasticities of supply are infinite if there are variations in economic activity due to the trade balance; and whether, if the elasticity of supply of UK exports is finite, other elasticities of supply are infinite. Funneling these assumptions through several options, Brown (1942a: 75) concludes:

> The impression left is that the British exchange equilibrium is likely to be stable in practically any imaginable circumstances, but that the extent of depreciation of sterling necessary to make up for any given loss of (say) foreign investment income, or to make possible the transfer of any given loan is highly problematic.

In the post-war world, the new global institutional structure posed many challenges for the United Kingdom. The matter of currency valuation under the Bretton Woods gold-exchange system, and the very rapid return to convertibility for sterling after the war, found the pound seriously overvalued and the UK short of sufficient reserves to tide over the run on its currency. The UK thus devalued the pound from the rate set on 27 December 1945 of £0.2481: $1 to £0.3571: $1 on 18 September 1949. Setting aside any commentary on the Bretton Woods system *per se*, one of the major problems with any fixed, or in this case quasi-fixed, exchange system is to determine what the initial exchange rate would be and the implications subsequently of the various pressures that may be imposed upon it. A key parameter in assessing both these questions is having good estimates of the price responsiveness of imports and exports, a topic Brown turned to both specifically in the United Kingdom's context (Brown, 1951b) and, more generally (Brown, 1951a), in his early years at Leeds.

The importance of knowing the relevant elasticities is that they provide insight into whether a depreciation of its currency will improve the trade balance of a country or not. The assessment of whether the outcome of a currency depreciation would be favorable still in the 1940s relied largely on thinking in terms of the Marshall–Lerner condition; namely that a depreciation will only lead to an improvement in the balance of payments for a country if the sum of its demand elasticity for imports and exports is greater than one. It was only in the 1950s that the "absorption approach"—which, in addition to the Marshall–Lerner condition, considers flows of expenditure and income—was adopted, and the 1960s, when a synthesis of the two was developed.[35] A major practical problem when Brown was working on the effects of currency depreciation was the lack of quantitative information of the relevant elasticities to feed into the Marshall–Lerner arithmetic.

The challenge, therefore, was getting an empirical handle on these parameters, and especially the elasticity of substitution. The practical problems in the 1940s of doing this were numerous, and many remain today despite the long-term interest in improving national economic statistics that has taken place.

> The actual measurement of the price-elasticity of demand for a country's exports presents enormous difficulties. In the first place, the measurement of their price is difficult; second, the prices of competing foreign goods should be considered; thirdly, effects of price-changes should be sorted out from those of income changes; fourthly, trade barriers of all kinds, and, still more, changes in them, introduce innumerable disturbances; and fifthly, full adjustment to price-changes takes place only after a time-lag which it is difficult to allow for in empirical investigations. (Brown, 1951a: 91)

The data that was available also tended to bias the work that was done towards a focus on demand elasticities with much less focus on the supply side, even though that on demand was itself inconclusive. Even when there is data, there are econometric problems to overcome, not least of which is sorting out issues of multicollinearity: the prices of both exports and imports that had historically tended to follow much the same cyclical pattern as world income, or as almost any importing country. Brown's (1951a) survey of material up to 1950 suggests that most empirical work until then had failed to deal with this, demonstrating "the inherent unreliability of the result" (Brown, 1951a: 91). As Brown also points out, however, this problem was, at the time he was writing, likely to be soon resolved because there was occurring "a set of adjustments in currency-values and relative prices, delightfully uncorrelated with changes in income" (p. 106).

The theory, or perhaps implicit assumption, when Brown was working on his own estimations in the early 1940s was that countries tended to have a fairly general pattern of consumption (including their imports) but a much more specialized pattern of production (including their exports), leading to a low elasticity of demand for imports because of limited competition between specialized domestic production and more general imports, but a high elasticity of demand for exports because of global competition for markets. (As he writes later, in the British context (Brown, 1951a: 94), "one would expect only a very low elasticity of substitution between (say) British exports, three-quarters of which were finished manufactures, and all other countries' exports, two-thirds of which were goods of other classes.") This model was often refined a little to include the effects of the existence of some domestic consumption of potentially exportable goods possibly increasing the elasticity of supply and demand for exportable goods, and that some production of some importable-type goods could raise the elasticity of demand for imports. Overall, despite these refinements, the theory still suggested export elasticities would be high and import elasticities would be low.

From the policy makers' point of view, a major problem was that early empirical studies, notably those by Hans Adler (1945) and Tse Chun Chang (1948), produced results that contradicted the relationship or often showed no statistical relationship of the anticipated kind. Brown's work on the UK based upon elasticities of substitution rather than quantity elasticities, however, produced a statistically significant elasticity of –1.96 exports for 1929 to 1938. Extending the analysis to a range of countries, using changes in export volumes to changes in export price, Brown (1951b) found an elasticity of substitution of –1.27 for Germany, Switzerland, France, the UK, the US, Italy, and Japan for 1929 to 1936/38; –2.87 for the US, UK, Switzerland, Sweden, Czechoslovakia, and France for 1937 to 1946; –2.53 for the same countries for 1937 to 1947; –1.56 for the same countries plus Belgium for 1937 to 1948; and –1.89 for the period 1946 to 1948.[36]

In general, these results yield elasticities of substitution higher than the broad figure of unity that Brown obtained looking at the impact after one year of the UK depreciation of sterling in 1949. This implies that the full positive effects of depreciation of its currency on a country's exports, or at least in the UK's case, may take longer than a year, which is in line with subsequent thinking regarding the "J-curve" effect.

Much of the subsequent analyses of currency depreciation has tended to support Brown's findings regarding higher elasticities of demand for exports over the longer period, this being a simple reflection of the greater flexibility in market responses over time after any shock; but even allowing for this the data used by Brown may well have underestimated the sensitivity of exports to prices because of the trade interventions during the 1930s. Added to this, Brown's work was at the aggregate and, as intuitively accepted by those such as Jan Tinbergen (1946) and the subsequent systematic testing of Junz and Rhomberg (1965) and others confirmed, this can produce aggregation bias, and in particular the underestimate of the export elasticity. This was, however, a problem Brown was clearly aware of given comments in his previous writing (Brown, 1942a: 61), and in his 1951b survey paper he specifically cites Kubinski (1950), who was working at the time at Leeds, and his analysis of individual elasticities of substitution for 286 commodities imported into the UK between 1921 and 1938 that produced elasticities ranging from +6 to under –18.[37]

While a little later in his career, it is also perhaps appropriate here to bring in a Special University Lecture delivered at LSE in February 1957, subsequently published in the *Yorkshire Bulletin* (Brown, 1957), that stems from the wartime *Industrialization and Trade* pamphlet he produced for the Royal Institute in 1943. In the pamphlet, Brown spends time looking

at ways that natural endowments, including those that may affect migration, influence the long-term "territorial distribution of economic activity"
(Brown 1943a: 16): this distribution being a major factor in determining
the comparative advantage of countries when it comes to international
trade. While, not unsurprisingly given the intended readership, the pamphlet does not go into the Ohlin–Heckscher theorem, this is essentially an
examination of the sorts of endowment patterns that produce trade—the
latter espousing the principle that a country tends to specialize in those
commodities which depend most heavily on the factors of production with
which it is relatively best endowed.[38]

This issue resurfaced, and got a much fuller treatment at the LSE lecture
because of the publication of a speech given by Wassily Leontief (1953)
to the American Philosophical Society.[39] This looked specifically at the
role of capital in facilitating American trade. Brown's concern was that the
essential simplicity of Leontief's underlying model framework was likely
distorting his conclusions.[40] The trouble with Leontief's paper was that,
in Brown's view (1957: p. 64), "Professor Leontief has thrown a singularly
destructive bombshell. Not that his intentions were, in all probability,
hostile—he simply set out to provide the Ohlin–Heckscher principle with
the direct verification which it had hitherto lacked"; but "The conclusion
which emerges from the examination of Professor Leontief's findings is
that the Ohlin-Heckscher principle, while logically unassailable on its own
assumptions, is of only moderate usefulness in the practical interpretation
of the pattern of world trade" (p. 73).

The difficulty, as he saw it, and harking back to his 1943 pamphlet, was
essentially that of production being more complex than the basic Ohlin–
Heckscher framework suggests and Leontief's calculations capture. In the
pamphlet Brown, after considering the available data, had divided countries into four groups; (i) countries with plenty of all kinds of resources
in relation to population; (ii) countries with fair or good endowments of
power and minerals but little agricultural land in relation to population;
(iii) countries with much land per head but few power resources; and (iv)
countries with few resources of any kind per head of population. The
application of the Ohlin–Heckscher model would place the United States
in the first group, which involves specializing in producing less labor-
intensive agriculture and capital-intensive manufactures. But Leontief
finds that the country specializes on the labor-intensive side in a range
of manufactures, and on the capital-intensive side basically on primary
products.

Leontief's explanations for this are, first, that the US is capital-poor
and labor-rich rather than the reverse. But, as Brown points out, making
several comparisons with Europe, this just does not stand up to statistical

examination. The second line of explanation, posited by P.T. Ellsworth (1954) in critiquing Leontief, is that there are missing factors of production, and especially raw materials that are geographically unevenly spread across countries. This results in the various US industrial production functions being poorly specified. Boris Swerling (1954), again critiquing Leontief, takes this even further by suggesting that trade depends more on the distribution of raw materials than of labor and capital. Brown is not convinced by Swerling's argument which, "may well go too far"; and, regarding Ellsworth's, he feels that, while it has some relevance, it is limited because even if raw material endowments are location-specific, they can be transported and transportation costs generally only form a small element of manufacturing costs. Another way of looking at this is the survey evidence showing that distances from raw material are seldom a large factor when businessmen locate their activities.[41]

Thirdly, it was argued that even if the production functions regarding the factors measured are the same in two countries, the production may be more capital-intensive in one because of differences in relative factor prices. This could occur if the production functions are of varying flexibility once outside of the narrow range examined. Empirically, this can be explored by looking at, say, the range of possible capital intensities for each industry. Brown accepts this may be valid but that capital intensity between industries may reflect other factors, and he examples water availability for agriculture. This swings the argument back to omitted variable problems when estimating the production functions.

Finally, Leontief's apparently paradoxical results may be explained by a misunderstanding of what capital- and labor-intensity mean. In the Ohlin–Heckscher approach these are seen as economic abundance of factor of production, and not physical abundance. Thus, the United States may have a physical abundance of capital but, because of the high demand for its use, there may be a relative capital scarcity; this would be broadly in line with Leontief's finding that final demand in the US is largely for services and highly finished goods. Despite this, Brown, following Stefan Valavanis-Vail (1954), argues this situation is, given the physical abundance of capital in America, likely to lead to situations where labor is plentiful and capital scarce in the context of the capital situation elsewhere. Another way to look at this is in terms of the cost of capital, which is the interest rate paid to acquire its services. Brown finds that historically over half a century or so this cost of capital was as low as anywhere, and that the US over this period was a major exporter of machinery, indicating it was, in global terms, not expensive. In contrast, labor costs, in terms of wages, were relatively higher than in other countries.

Brown thus accepts some element of the omitted variable problem and of different relative factor prices in accounting for the Leontief paradox, but focuses more on what is essentially an aggregation problem. His general conclusion is that:

> So far as specialization within the field of manufactures is concerned, is seems that the Ohlin–Heckscher principle, in the broad form in which it is usually stated, is altogether less useful, because the single factor labour is for most products so predominant over others that international and interproduct variations in its "quality" or "efficiency" tend to swamp the cost-differences due to diversities of factor-proportion and relative factor price. There are, of course, exceptions—those products (largely intermediate goods rather than finished manufactures in the strict sense) which require exceptionally large quantities of capital or of raw material transport in relation to their value. For very many manufactures, however, the predominant factors conferring comparative advantage on one country or another are matters more of human than of physical geography; forwardness in research and design, speed and efficiency in translating new ideas into production, skill and adaptability of labour, good day-to-day industrial relations, and, one must add, good selling methods. . . .
>
> This is, of course, nothing but a re-assertion of the Ohlin–Heckscher principle, though not in terms of the traditional factors of production. (Brown, 1957: 74)

Brown returned to trade matters, and especially those involving developing countries, later in his career. But from the early 1950s, when not running the Department of Economics and Commerce at Leeds, his immediate research attention switched to the causes of, and policy responses to, excessive inflation.

NOTES

1. In a much later review of Brown's joint book with Jane Darby, *World Inflation Since 1950*, Anna Schwartz (1986: 671) was somewhat off the mark when she says: "Brown is caught in a time warp of Keynesian views that no longer command the assent of economists." Certainly his works are Keynesian in their orientation, but her comment may be more reflective of Schwartz's position, which itself was not neutral, and in inherent disagreement with the empirical findings.
2. Brown's only prior teaching experience had been as tutor to the Prince von Hohenlohe who, apparently, was the "least academic" pupil of Brown's career.
3. The literature on economics in the UK in the 1930s is extensive, and especially so for Cambridge. The links and ties between these institutions at this time, and some of the intellectual waves associated with them, are well covered, albeit with an inevitable Cambridge focus, by Robert Skidelsky (1992) in the second volumes of his biography of Keynes.
4. Keynes's presence at Cambridge was almost entirely intellectual rather than physical in the 1930s given his life-style pattern (Kahn, 1984: 171–3).
5. Brown did admit to finding nothing of liquidity preference in Benham, but not in the determination of interest rates; and the notion of unemployment equilibrium was found to be absent, and that of the multiplier obliquely mentioned in terms of a snowball effect.

6. He had attempted to gain a fellowship in the previous year but had failed, whereas the philosopher Stuart Hampshire and Dennis Routh, who subsequently had a career as a civil servant, had succeeded.
7. The Council was the chief executive body for the University of Oxford from its establishment by the Oxford University Act 1854 until its replacement, in 2000, by the University Council.
8. In Mitchell's papers, *Talk to Economics Tutors*, 5 November 1931 and *Organisation of Economics Teaching*, 23 February 1932.
9. The funding of this was fortuitous, as Brown (1988a: 32) later explains: "Part of this development—certainly the financing of the Readership which went with it—was due to decisions at All Souls, which had for most of its history been a poor College, but which struck oil (or the equivalent) in the late 1920s when one of its agricultural estates was overwhelmed by the sprawl of the north-west London suburbs."
10. Although Brown's time in the Institute overlapped slightly with the birth of the *Bulletin* and his D.Phil. would have fitted with its ethos, he published his 1939 paper on liquidity preference in the *Oxford Economic Papers*. This may have been because, in a way, it was a reaction to a previous article in the *Papers*.
11. *Interview with A.J. Brown, 25 May 1994, Headingley, Leeds.*
12. Harrod, possibly partly because of his own work at the time, tended to call the OERG "the trade cycle group," but its interest extended beyond this. Indeed, none of the published output of the group prior to the war was on economic fluctuations (Daniele Besomi, 1998: 536).
13. Data from *Education: Historic Statistics*, Standard Note SN/SG/4252, House of Commons Library.
14. Although, as Harrod (1949: 459) put it, "Professor Wesley Mitchell had been with us for a year a short time before and, although he failed in 'selling' his specially favored methods of time-series analysis, he sowed seeds of the desire for and empirical approach." See also Harrod (1937a).
15. This was also the time when, as Coase (1982: 31) put it, "The 1930's [*sic*] brought about a great improvement in the analytical tools available to economists."
16. Getting primary information from business followed the general sort of quasi-stated preference-cum-Delphi approach of the group at the time. This involved conducting interviews with businessmen and "confronting certain points of theory and the ascertainment of how their own experience tended to confirm or conflict with the theory" (Harrod, 1953: 60). Lee (1991: 491–2) explains, having interviewed members of the OERG, how senior businessmen were approached personally by Henderson using his wide range of contacts, and through letters asked a series of questions. These questions were continually updated to ensure that the respondents were clear about the issues being addressed. The businessmen then came to Oxford, usually to dine with Henderson at All Souls, and then, broadly in line with a Delphi methodology, to meet with other members of the group to discuss the question. A second approach involved field interviews, with members of the OERG visiting businessmen to write up the responses and to send these to other members of the OERG and the business for comment.
17. For an account of the development of the kinked demand curve, see Gavin Reid (1981).
18. Given the array of talent that was attracted to the Group, together with its obvious relevance for tackling the economic questions of the day, Ray Petridis (1994: 146), in reviewing Young and Lee's history of the unit, raises the interesting question of why "historians of economic thought are yet to explain why the empirical work of the OERG with its profound implications for theory did not have an even greater effect on the economics profession, and why more technical but related versions of non-market clearly apparently had to wait for rediscovery in the 1960s."
19. D.Phil. (*Doctor Philosophiae*) is the Oxford term for a Doctor of Philosophy, more generally called a PhD (*Philosophiae Doctor*).
20. Marschak transpired to be a useful supervisor for Brown: "Marschak was an ideal supervisor; he always had suggestions on where I should go next, but pretended to have

forgotten them if I, in fact, went somewhere else—provided that it was interesting"
(Brown, 1988a: 34).

21.   Basically, he found the elasticity of substitution between cash and short-term claims and
      bills to be –0.2, and between investment and advances to be –0.66; both very low figures.

22.   The Wicksellian view was essentially that the natural rate of interest was that which
      produced stable prices and any effort to keep interest rates below this causes economic
      expansion and prices rise. Gibson's Paradox was the empirical observation that the
      rate of interest and the general level of prices are positively correlated. For example,
      in the 1873–96 depression, prices fell considerably while interest rates remained low.
      Conventional theory argued at the time that higher interest rates would encourage
      savings and thus pull down prices.

23.   Empirical study by Phelps Brown and George Shackle (1938) had by 1939 found that
      real turnover varied little from the trend.

24.   The underlying problem in identifying appropriate equations for estimation goes back
      (Wright, 1915). The solution is either to specify a full set of equations and estimate them
      simultaneously or to use instrumental variables; basically these induce changes in the
      explanatory variable with no independent effect on the dependent variable allowing the
      causal effect of the former on the dependent variable to be seen. Both techniques were
      known in the 1930s.

25.   These are listed in the bibliography prepared by Maurice Beresford (in Bowers, 1979:
      295–304).

26.   Just as examples of what were essentially statistical assessments, Brown looked at
      German mineral supplies (1939b, c), global supplies of petroleum (1940b), synthetic
      rubber suppliers 1943b), and coal and cotton (1945c). In addition, he assessed the eco-
      nomic impacts of the war on the USA (1942b, c) and Latin America (1940c, d). He also
      assessed the economic positions more generally of Italy (1941d), Canada (1941c), and
      Japan (1941b) to wage war.

27.   This may well have been the time when Brown learned the importance of clarity in
      writing economics. Later, Anthony Thirlwall (2003) recalls the first advice Brown gave
      him was to read and digest Ernest Gowers's *Plain Words*, and to remember that the art
      of writing is "the application of the seat of the pants to the seat of the chair."

28.   In Brown's application to Leeds University dated 21 October 1946 (AJB C&P).

29.   Some of the relevant papers were also incorporated, almost unaltered, as Section 3 in his
      later book on *Applied Economics* (Brown, 1947). For a review see, Clough (1947).

30.   Brown also addressed this from a slightly different angle in earlier papers concerned
      with the exploitation of captured territories by Germany (Brown, 1940e, f).

31.   Edward Boyle (1979)—a former Financial Secretary to the Treasury, Minister of
      Education, and Minister of State for Education and Science, and vice-chancellor of the
      university—offers some insights into the role of economists in government. This is a
      subject returned to later.

32.   Ben Steil (2013) lays out some of the debates and the rationale behind the international
      financial system that emerged from Bretton Woods together with an account of some of
      the shenanigans that occurred there.

33.   His assumption very much follows that found in Joan Robinson (1933b), a fact he
      acknowledges in a footnote when he clarifies that he had not read this when writing his
      own paper, and that his approach is more general than hers.

34.   Harberger (1950: 51) critiques the Robinson-Brown model, arguing that it is only appli-
      cable in very particular cases and that it "would require a very special constellation of
      values of the marginal propensities to hoard and to import to invalidate the common-
      place dictum that 'unemployment can be exported by depreciations'."

35.   There is the synthesis work of Sho-Chieh Tsiang (1961) that embraces the elasticities'
      approach into a large framework including that of domestic monetary policy.

36.   These findings run somewhat counter to an earlier paper by Jan Tinbergen (1946)
      that also reported substitution elasticities for a similar period and covering Argentina,
      Australia, Germany, Hungary, Japan, South Africa, the UK, and the United States.

37. Brown also provides updated information in his 1951a paper not contained in the Kubinski reference.
38. This is Brown's originator's attribution for the model; the more normal ordering of names is Heckscher–Ohlin. Brown's attribution is used here.
39. Brown got to know Leontief quite well a few years later when they both served on a UN Group concerned with disarmament (see Chapter 5).
40. Brown also references the reproduction of the piece in the February 1954 issue of the Italian journal, *Economica Internazionale*, where he probably first came across it. Leontief (1956) provides a sort of Part 2 to his paper that is more theoretical and offers support for his initial conclusions and comments on the Ellsworth, Valavanis-Vail, and Swerling articles that Brown also touches upon. Brown does not directly return to the subject, although he does touch upon it in his *Introduction to the World Economy* in a general way (1959a: 104–5).
41. The validity of this falls somewhat if, as modern supply chain management and logistics suggest, inventory costs become important rather than transportation costs *per se*; but even then, since most raw materials are not perishable, this is a one-off, fixed cost.

4.   Building an economics department

LEAVING OXFORD

The period after World War II was one of considerable shortage of economists in Britain, with universities competing with government services, and to some extent industry, for them. This took place at a time when, due to the effects of war, there was physical relocation of faculty, the reconstruction and maintenance of buildings, the demobilization of men and women and making up for lost time in their education, and deciding on the best way to structure higher education in a changed world. There was not just a need for replacing what had been lost in the war but also to expand education to meet the new economic environment. At the same time the return of a Labour government, with its greater interests in nationalization and economic regulation, led to new ideas for implementation of higher education policies and for how to run the system.

In terms of university expansions, new capacity was created in several ways. The University College of North Staffordshire, the last "public university college," was established in Keele in 1949 and was the first university college to receive full degree-awarding powers.[1] In 1962 it was granted a Royal Charter to become the University of Keele. The university college system dated back to Victorian times—for example Nottingham University College was established in 1881 but had to award external degrees ratified by a full university (in Nottingham's case, the University of London)—and provided a framework that could be easily modified. Indeed, between 1948 and 1967 the existing university colleges (except those that had become colleges of the University of London) achieved independent university status. The other expansion after World War II came with existing universities taking more students, and this is where Leeds fits in.

The university system at the time was, however, small. Going back to 1900, only five universities had been established in England and one in Wales. In England were the Universities of Oxford, Cambridge, and London, plus Durham University and Victoria University. The last of these was established in Manchester in 1880 as a federal university in the North of England, instead of the government elevating Owens College to a university and granting it a Royal Charter. Owens College was the sole college of Victoria University from 1880 to 1884. Yorkshire College of Science and later the Yorkshire College, located in Leeds, became part of the federal Victoria University alongside Owens College (later the University of Manchester) and University College Liverpool (subsequently the University of Liverpool).[2]

The Victoria (Leeds) University was short-lived, as the university locations in Manchester and Liverpool were keen to establish themselves as separate, independent universities. In part this had to do with the practical difficulties posed by maintaining a federal arrangement across relatively long distances, but also because of the perceived benefits a university had for the cities of Liverpool and Manchester. The interests of the universities, and their respective cities, in creating independent institutions were spurred by the granting of a Charter to the University of Birmingham in 1900, and in 1904, a Royal Charter was granted to the University of Leeds.

It was these "red-brick universities" that perhaps expanded the most after 1945 given both their locations and their long traditions of applied science and engineering. The latter factors also made them in many ways better bases to conduct applied economics research, and especially that linked to industrial and regional issues. Added to this, for young academics these institutions offered more opportunities for developing their careers than were available at Oxbridge, where expansion was less.

But there was a different feel in the expanding universities system to that before the war. The traditional structure had seen the universities enjoy extraordinary influence on UK public policy. Oxford and Cambridge had enjoyed having their own Members of Parliament, two for each constituency, since 1603. London University had one MP from 1868, as did Glasgow and Aberdeen Universities and Edinburgh and St Andrews Universities from 1868 until merged into one in 1918. The Universities of Wales and Queen's University of Belfast, as well as the National University of Ireland before Ireland's independence, also had representation in the House of Commons at various times. These constituencies were not, as were others, geographical areas, but rather the electorate consisted of the graduates of the universities. These were all abolished in 1950 by the Representation of the People Act 1948. This obviously weakened the political influence of the older universities.

ECONOMICS AT LEEDS IN THE LATE 1940s AND THE 1950s

There were both push and pull factors that influenced Brown's decision to move from the civil service and seek an academic career in Leeds in the late

1940s. The role of economist in the government was nowhere near as influential as it subsequently became. Reflecting on his period as deputy-director of the Economic Section, the Oxford economist Ian Little (1957: 29) felt that the non-economist administrators "abstract too much from the real world" and that he had sometimes been "shocked by the naïve sureness with which very questionable bits of economic analysis were advanced in Whitehall." In a similar vein, another Oxford economist, David Henderson (1961: 11), explains the difficulty of hiring and retaining economists in the civil service at the time:

> It is apparent . . . that when a specific question of economic policy is referred to a committee of officials for their advice, the influence of professional economists is unlikely to be significant, such influence will almost never be decisive; it will usually be slight; and in very many cases it will be non-existent.

The simple fact was that economic expertise was little valued.

The pull side, in addition to the chance to run his own academic unit, was in part composed of Brown's love for the area he grew up in and for the countryside he enjoyed walking through; also his initial efforts to gain a position were not successful.

> Well I wanted to get back into academic life and I had always thought it would be nice to be a Professor at Leeds, because I'm a Bradford lad by upbringing! I applied for one or two posts. I applied for the Chair at Liverpool, which went to Barrett Whales and the next one that came up was Leeds, and I applied for that.[3]

Brown listed three referees for the Chair of Economics on his one-page application, and we have records for two. He seems to have chosen carefully and to have sprinkled the dust around a little. They provided hopeful support from Oxford, London, and the civil service, with some ties to Leeds and some overseas links for good measure.

James Meade, whom Brown had known well at Oxford who had subsequently championed him in the civil service, and was currently holding a senior government post, wrote to Leeds: "Mr. Brown is a first-rate economist. He is a very sound theoretician and analyst; but his main work has been in applied and descriptive economics in the international field."[4] David MacGregor, perhaps chosen slightly for strategic reasons rather than just for being Drummond Professor of Political Economy at All Souls (although that was reason itself), but perhaps more because of his prior contributions at Leeds, stated:"Dr. Brown is highly equipped in the techniques of research, in both its statistical and theoretical sides."[5] We have no record of the letter from the third reference, Paul Rosenstein-Rodan (then at LSE but about to move to the World Bank), and again this was perhaps a strategic choice given that Brown was at that time a special lecturer at London. Other applicants included H.D. Dickinson, who would have been an interesting choice for Leeds!

Brown's credentials, despite his rather poorly typed letter of application, were strong. By 1947 he had extensive research experience and major publications in 1938, 1939, 1942 to accompany his exam performance at Oxford, and his publication of numerous policy papers for Chatham House during the war. He also had diverse experience of high-level government advising. But in addition to this, and relevant for a place such as Leeds at that time, Brown had produced in 1943 a short booklet for Chatham house, *Industrialization and Trade: The Changing World Pattern and the Problem for Britain*, that would resonate well at the university given its history and its perceived role in fostering local manufacturing and commerce largely engaged in international markets. Added to all this, Brown had a textbook, *Applied Economics: Aspects of the World Economy in War and Peace*, in production that, if widely adopted, would heighten awareness of economics across a wider audience. Perhaps the handicap was that Brown was only 33.

Despite its spiritual attraction, Brown did not immediately accept the position at Leeds when it was offered to him; it took him three weeks to decide. The issue was whether it was worth waiting and seeking the Professorship at the Royal Institute of International Affairs that had been vacated by Alan Fisher on his move to the World Bank. This was an area Brown was interested in and it was purely a research post. On hearing that Ralph Hawtrey, who had retired from the UK Treasury in 1945, was likely to get it (which he subsequently did) Brown accepted the Leeds offer.

He arrived at Leeds in July 1947 having secured the post as Professor of Economics and Head of the Department of Economics and Commerce.

The history of economics and commerce, the two subjects were strongly entwined for many years, at the University of Leeds is not only very much shorter than Oxford's but also very different, even for the period they have co-existed. Oxford, and Cambridge for that matter, although gradually moving away from the image conveyed by Noel Annan (1999) in *The Dons*, were still steeped in ancient tradition and were the main route into the high offices of the country. Leeds was much more grounded in manufacturing and in the Industrial Revolution.

In the days of the Yorkshire College, amongst other things, political economy was taught for many years by Cyril Ransome, the Professor of Modern History and English Language and Literature (and, although not germane to our story, father of Arthur Ransome, the writer of children's books). In 1902, the first Professor of Economics, John Cobham an expert on the local textile industry, was appointed when Leeds was still part of

Victoria University. He later returned to Cambridge, and became involved in the post-war expansion of social and economic research in Britain.

MacGregor, whom Brown later came to know well at Oxford, succeeded Cobham in 1908 and established the Bachelor of Commerce degree. After wartime service, he returned in 1918 but left the following year for Manchester before moving on to Oxford, and was succeeded by Harry Jones, whom Brown followed at Leeds but never met there. Brown describes Jones as a "sort of Cambridge Marshallian" who wrote a textbook (Jones, 1926) and worked on the economics of coal mining.[6]

BUILDING AN ECONOMICS DEPARTMENT

The roll call of academics when Brown arrived at Leeds was eight bodies plus himself and a vacancy. The faculty included J. Henry Richardson as one of the first appointed Montague Burton Professors in the late 1920s and was more concerned with the commerce than the economics aspects of the school.[7] At the non-professorial level was H.D. Dickenson, an economist and Marxist who had competed for the Leeds post with Brown, although Brown only overlapped with him at Leeds for a short period before Dickenson went to a readership, and subsequently professorship, at Bristol. Someone Brown was more familiar with was Jack Parkinson, who Brown knew at the Economics Section of the Cabinet Office. He ultimately became a professor at Nottingham University. Richardson had also appointed an industrial relations expert, the economic historian, A.E.C. Hare, who had arrived just prior to Brown, although Brown had been consulted about the appointment. His wife, Nancy, was the sole strict economic historian in the department, having taken over some lectures Dickenson had given, and worked part-time. Added to these for a year was a young academic recently recruited from Birmingham, C.H. Thomson, who later had a career in South Africa, and with the World Bank. There were also individuals involved exclusively in teaching the commerce part of the department's activities, a subject returned to later.

The 1946 Report of the Clapham Committee on Social Sciences resulted in additional resources being made available for economics by 1948, and this gave Brown a budget to refresh the faculty at Leeds. As mentioned earlier, however, in general getting good faculty in the late 1940s was difficult because of the limited supply plus the increased demands within the university sector and from the civil service; and in some areas, such as economics, the needs of a restructuring industrial economy generated particularly strong competition between universities and government. Many of Brown's early appointments, as may be expected, were ex-servicemen.

Despite this, the emphasis was on the quality of the faculty appointed rather than the filling of teaching slots, which seems to be the *sine qua non* of many current departments. That is one reason why four of his very early appointments subsequently became Fellows of the British Academy.

His first appointment was Harold Speight, who produced a well-used introductory textbook, *Economics*. Walter Newlyn, an LSE graduate with specialism in money and development (and who later became central in Brown's involvement with Bill Phillips discussed in Chapter 6), joined in 1948, as did Dennis Sargan, a Cambridge graduate in economic and mathematics (and, when later put up for the British Academy, was described as probably the best theoretical econometrician in the world). George Rainnie was another early member, possibly more relevant for his organizational skills, which should not be denigrated, as for his research output. In 1950 a post was created, with the help of Meade's intervention with the vice-chancellor, for George Shackle, known for his theoretical work on uncertainty, to come to Leeds at the end of his contract with the Treasury.[8] The Marxist Ron Bellamy, an exceptional teacher, was also recruited at an early stage. John Brothwell, a Leeds graduate whom Brown describes as "the best Keynesian I knew," joined in 1953.[9]

Maurice Beresford, an English economic historian and medieval archaeologist, also came in 1948 to fulfill an economic history need. This was partly a tactical move to retain a claim in that field, although apparently the history department did not object, but also was part of Brown's idea for developing an interest in the department in the wool and local textile industry, as well as other aspects of the local economy.[10] Accompanying this, Brown also gained funding from D.H. Dean, a prominent figure in the wool textile industry: £14,000 for a research assistantship and a Dean Fellowship, with Eric Sigsworth, who later moved to the University of York, appointed to the latter. This work subsequently led in the early 1950s to a major study for the Board of Trade on the structure of the wool textile industry headed up by Rainnie.

Despite the efforts required in the initial recruitment of a strong faculty, and the demands of ensuring adequate physical facilities for the department, Brown did take a semester's leave from February to June 1950 to teach at Columbia University in New York—the request that he spend a year he rejected because of the need to attend to Leeds business. He obviously found this time interesting, and discovered the requirements of both students and academics very different to those in the UK.

I had got a picture that it was different from what I was familiar with at home. What teaching I had there was in the graduate school, and it was just like teaching third year students here, just about. I sat in a lot of oral examinations for students at the end of their graduate course work before they start their thesis, and I sat in on some thesis orals too. I got a very clear impression that the American Columbian graduate coursework was very like the final year work here.[11]

Brown's time at Columbia did seem to influence his openness to, or at least gave him experience of, alternative methods of teaching, and particularly teaching to larger groups involving integrated lectures and discussions. This fitted much more with the style that was the norm at a large British civic university rather than the separate lecture–tutorial structure he had experienced and been involved in teaching at Oxford. The stay also gave him direct access to US scholars. At the time, the Englishman Norman Angell, who had won the 1933 Noble Peace Prize, was chairman of the Economics Department; and other faculty included John Maurice Clarke and Charles Kindleberger, who was, as Brown put it, "moonlighting" teaching part-time at his *alma mater* whilst on the faculty at the Massachusetts Institute of Technology (MIT). George Stigler was also there before returning to Chicago University, via Brown University. Stigler had spent much of World War II at Columbia engaged in mathematical and statistical research for the Manhattan Project, and then served on the faculty from 1947 to 1958. Brown also developed links with those at other economics departments on the east coast.

The various experiences he had enjoyed at Oxford and in the civil service, and during the early years at Leeds, interactions with new faculty and local business, coupled with changes in the demands of the student market, led him to restructure degree programs at Leeds. These changes not only resulted in more flexible programs for students, but also in the longer term provided a basis for new initiatives in terms of departmental reforms and the development of research centers.

The degrees inherited on his arrival at Leeds were an honors degree in economics and an ordinary B.Com. degree, and the number of graduates was small—ten or eleven students annually. Brown built this number up to about 20 students in each program by 1956, a number that rose rapidly in the 1960s after the Robbins' expansion of higher education. One change that Brown initiated was to make it easier for those doing the first year of the B.Com. degree to switch to the economics honors program for their second year. This meant a common first year economics course, mainly macro driven, at an honors level for both degrees that then became "with honors." The difference between the BA and B.Com. was that the latter replaced some economics courses with accountancy or a technical subject such as engineering. The BA was also modified to have students specifically opting for it when applying to Leeds rather than taking it as their option after the first year of "General Studies"; in the second-year they could elect either for the BA or B.Com. stream.

In terms of pedagogy, the Leeds system was not dissimilar to the one Brown had experienced when visiting Columbia, with a focus on small group teaching against a syllabus of lectures, with occasion individual tutorials. Third year seminars were a distinguishing feature of Brown's early years at Leeds involving all final year students. Brown also championed a residential course in the early 1950s, initially at the eighteenth-century mansion Grantley Hall. Maurice Beresford had first taken his special subject students there in 1949 when it opened and had recommended it to Brown. Initially involving only finalists and postgraduates, in 1952 it was expanded to include second year students and first years in 1957, when the venue moved to Cober Hill near Scarborough. But as the student population grew, after 1964 only graduate students were involved. Besides student presentations and student-arranged debates, there were guest lectures by the likes of Richard Goodwin (at Cambridge at the time) and the international economist Ragnar Nurkse, and talks by Leeds faculty on their research.[12]

One of the functions of an academic besides research and direct teaching is the production of more general educational material and, what sometimes overlaps with this, publicly accessible articles and pamphlets. Many of Brown's wartime publications fell into this category, but he also found time to continue with this sort of work in his early years at Leeds. He wrote several textbooks, as we have seen, dating back to 1947 when he had effectively brought together some of his wartime writings in *Applied Economics*.

But the work that had the most powerful impact as an educational tool was his *Introduction to the World Economy* (Brown 1959a), which had partly come out of his first-year lecturing. The book is strongly Keynesian in its orientation and reflects the general view of the time—that appropriate fiscal policy could prevent another Great Recession and ensure economic stability. As Brown put it later, the text was "evidence of how completely my generation discounted the possibility of a return to mass unemployment and the rejection of Keynesian policies."[13]

The book was widely adopted, despite competition, and had gone to seven reprints by 1965, including one major revision in 1962. And this was at a time when technology did not allow production of books on demand and the outflow of books was constrained by the necessity, at considerable financial risk, for publishers to hold physical inventory. Textbooks, however, with the occasional exception, get little recognition in the battle for academic acclaim, but are important in attracting students and for educating them.

In his review of the 1965 edition of the book, Edward Horesh (1966: 379) observes:

> Regarding this book, one is struck by the manner in which Professor Brown describes fairly complex theoretical constructs with a virtual absence of technical language. The argument is rigorously phrased and the initiated reader is able to discern the economy that has been used to limit the text to such a short space.

He saw the style as having undoubted merit for undergraduate students. Victor Morgan, in his review for the *Economic Journal*, takes a similar view as to its success:

> As its title implies, this stimulating little book is intended for newcomers to economics; the publishers mention particularly those, "whose interest in economics has been awakened by economic geography, economic history or the survey of current world affairs." It is, however refreshingly different from the general run of first-year texts. (Morgan 1959: 550)

He goes on to say that, "Professor Brown has not tried to write a substitute for the ordinary elementary text. He has, however, written a most valuable complement" (p. 553).

The Leeds faculty grew and changed during the later years of Brown's headship. Sargan left after 17 years to go to LSE and Shackle, Sigsworth, and Jack Parkinson, after shorter periods, to professorships elsewhere. The new faculty included, for econometrics, Kenneth Lomax and for economic history John Killick. In addition, Ken Woolmer, a Leeds graduate who was spending a period at the University of the West Indies, took up economics courses in development, and Victor Allen, industrial relations. Woolmer subsequently became a Labour Party MP, director of MBA programs for Leeds University, and a life peer, while Allen (in 1999) was found to have been an "agent of influence" for the East German Stasi secret police, possessing the code name "Barber." The Montague Burton Professor of Industrial Relations from 1961 to 1963 was Herbert Turner, who left to go to the same position at Cambridge, with Thomas Lupton taking his place in 1964.

THE BUSINESS SCHOOL

During Brown's initial period as head of the Department of Economics and Commerce several strategic initiatives were put in train. When he took over, the second part of the title was not insignificant. The university had strong ties with industry and local business, and the department, as we have seen, offered both B.Com. (from 1946 an ordinary degree, but with honors by the mid-1950s) and BA economics degrees.[14] There was also a growing interest in the UK, following a somewhat longer tradition in the US, in the academic side of management. Leeds had some of this but the demands were changing in terms of the skill sets students and industry required. There were also shifts in the wider economy, and one aspect of this was in the realignment of both the country's industrial structure and its human geography. New questions were arising concerning the nation's requirements regarding mobility and access, and how these were to be provided. Transport had been a major element of immediate national post-war economic policy, with the nationalization of large parts of industry. Brown was engaged in both the growth in managerial studies within the department and, later, that of transport economics.

In terms of management studies, Leeds University was born of the concept that higher education and research should have a large practical use associated with them.[15] The woolen industrial base of West Yorkshire together with the coal mining of adjacent areas underpinned this practical base at Leeds, and its economics department, in its various forms, had always played a key role in this. The inclusion of the word "commerce" in its earliest manifestations was indicative of this.

Accounting was taught in the Department of Economics and Commerce in 1949 by two part-time staff, and after the death of one, Phillip Sheard took over and was joined seven years later by Tony Lowe, subsequently a professor in Sheffield. In 1952, the question of how management might be taught within the department was raised by Thomas Whetton, Professor of Mining Engineering. The economists' reaction at a subsequent faculty meeting was essentially that it could not.[16] The main concern, however, was from the technology and engineering departments, and the wider view in the institution was that the Department of Economics, in part because of the nature of existing teaching activities, was the place to locate it.

In 1953 Gavin Whitaker, who had earlier approached the department about some part-time tuition, began giving some *ad hoc* lectures in management, and subsequently took up a full-time appointment. He had a PPE degree from Balliol and an MBA from MIT. Indeed, in the latter context, Brown had helped Whitaker in 1951 to develop contacts whilst he was in the US. Brown's time at Columbia had allowed him to interact with the international trade economist Gottfried Haberler (whom Brown described as "a great and good man"), and the Keynesians Alvin Hansen (who held the Lucius N. Littauer Chair), Paul Samuelson, and Arthur Smithies (all at MIT).[17]

The Leeds economists were not enthralled with Whitaker's research deploying as it did the American idea of T-groups to explore group dynamics. Brown, however, was somewhat more interested in the general idea that conventional methods of teaching were not very useful for those in business. Managers in decision-making, rather learn about themselves, and about small group processes in general, through their interaction with each other. They use feedback, problem solving, and role-play to gain insights into themselves, others, and groups. Whether Brown felt this sort of things to be genuine research is, however, open to question, as seen later when considering the creation of a specific Industrial Division in the School. He tended to think more of operations research and linear programming as the key areas of research in the field, a reflection perhaps of his own training at Oxford.[18]

Arthur Brown's views may well have been not only influenced by his prior links with Roy Harrod's group at Oxford, but also by a five-month sabbatical he had spent at Columbia University in 1950. Although the first business school in Europe dates from the establishment in 1819 of the ESCP Europe in Paris, the Wharton School of the University of Pennsylvania had been in existence for 70 years when Brown went to the US, and Columbia Business School since 1916.

In 1959, Leeds University provided a full-time post in management accounting, with Tony Lowe moving over to fill it and Alan Witts joining the department as Sheard's "partner." In the same year, an initial grant of £12,100 (rising to £16,000 annually by 1965–67) was made by the Foundation for Management Education for the expansion for the teaching of, and research in, industrial management; and the University Grants Committee (UGC) gave an award that largely went to a one-year graduate diploma course and the introduction of one final-year optional course in a management subject to the BA economics program. These activities led, in 1961, to the establishment of the autonomous Industrial Division within the Department of Economics and Commerce, with Galvin Whitaker as its director—Whittaker having earlier, in 1955, failed to gain the Montague Burton Chair of Industrial Relations at Leeds due, at least in part, to his lack of experience. By 1965 the division had grown from a director, a lecturer, two part-time lecturers, and a part-time assistant lecturer at its formation to 16 individuals engaged in both teaching and research.

Over the early years, as highlighted by Whitaker, "Professor A.J. Brown, to whom the Director of the Division has been formally responsible, has advised on the development of the Division and has established liaison within the University at critical periods in the Division's development." [19]

Moving forward a little, the development of business studies at Leeds may be seen by some economists as perhaps being too successful. Although only marginal to our account of Brown's contribution to economics, but perhaps indicative of some of the challenges that economists over the past

20 years have had in making their work relevant to the world, economics at Leeds has now been subsumed into the Leeds University Business School. This is a fate many other economics departments have suffered.

In December 1965, and just after Brown had ceased to be head of the school in October and Maurice Beresford had taken over, the School of Economic Studies, as it then was, was renamed the School of Economic Studies and the Department of Management Studies. The change was not without friction, with the economists feeling that management studies was no more separate than were economic history or accountancy. Further, despite being large, the division had no professor, Whitaker not being seen to have adequate academic credentials.

Brown's role seems to have been one of smoothing the transition, and especially the challenges involved in positioning subjects such as industrial relations and accountancy, the industrial relations–management problem being a particularly irksome one for Brown. His experiences in the US in 1950—where he found "connections between American Universities and industry and commerce [were] closer than here"—indicated to him that here was clearly common subject matter.[20] But approaches and emphases differed, and this led to the two groups viewing themselves more in terms of conflicts than synergies. Brown was a member of an *ad hoc* school committee to try to reach some workable compromise. The notion of a Department of Management and Industrial Relations emerged; but the main advocate, Thomas Lupton (the Montague Burton Professor), at that point took up a professorial post at the University of Aston. The outcome was that management remained a department within the newly titled school with a non-professorial head.

In later years, the focus switched very much towards the marketability of management and business school titles, and towards the perception of the vocational value of MBA degrees. Thus, in 1988 the School of Economics Studies and Department of Management Studies were integrated and renamed the School of Business and Economic Studies and, ultimately (in 1997), the Leeds University Business School. It now in 2017 has over 200 academic and 120 professional staff.

THE CENTRE FOR TRANSPORT STUDIES

While Brown's view on economic policy and development at the local and regional levels was largely Keynesian in orientation, as seen in his later writings, he saw demand stimuli as germane to any short-term unemployment problems, with infrastructure policy being a longer-term issue and only relevant when regions have a comparative economic advantage that they could exploit. But his local involvement with West Yorkshire, the upsurge of interest in modernizing the UK's transportation infrastructure, and the growing urban problems of handling local traffic brought the recognition by Brown and engineers at the university that there was the need for more research and education into transportation matters. This was also stimulated by the concerns of the local, metropolitan public transportation service providers and planners in Leeds over mounting traffic congestion, and the willingness of it, and several other undertakings, to provide some seed money to establish a suitable research/education unit at the university.[21]

Brown had first mooted the idea of a center to the vice-chancellor in the summer of 1964, and provided detailed thoughts on the form it might take, together with information regarding his contacts with the industry.[22] These thoughts were subsequently refined in terms of detailing what the Economics Department might contribute to such a unit.[23] In particular he emphasized the importance of the traditional element of studying the cost structure of the transportation industries in the context of a sector prone to monopoly forces and, perhaps because of the composition of the department's faculty, the need to consider the role over time of public policy, and especially its successes and failures, more generally. He also, probably because of the ongoing program to expand the nation's motorway network and the publication of the Beeching Report in 1963 that had laid out the need to rationalize the activities of British Railways, highlighted the role economics has in terms of cost-benefit analysis. But within this he made it clear that there should be no strong focus on any specific mode of transportation as was common elsewhere; teaching and research should be "very broadly described."

A Senate Committee on Transport Studies established at Leeds in 1965 included Brown, as well as other members of the Economics and Engineering Departments. The concept received support from the UK Ministry of Transport for "research studies of a multi-disciplinary nature, engaging the attention principally of economists, statisticians, engineers and specialists in operations research."[24] Brown, when asked for possible candidates for a professorship in transport economics, suggested Christopher Foster (then at Jesus College, Oxford), Alan Walters (Birmingham), Gilbert Walker (Birmingham), and Michael Beesley (LSE).[25]

It transpired that Brown's suggestions turned out to be non-trivial individuals. While none moved to Leeds, all went on to distinguished careers in academia and public service. For example, Sir Christopher Foster, besides holding academic posts at LSE, Oxford, and MIT, advised government on poll tax and rail privatization and has sat on the Audit Commission, the

Economic and Social Research Council (ESRC), the London Docklands Development Corporation (LDDC), and the Megaw Committee on Civil Service Pay. Sir Alan Walters was a member of the Roskill Commission on the Third London Airport, Sir Ernest Cassel Professor of Economics at LSE, an economic advisor to the World Bank, and Chief Economic Advisor to Prime Minister Margaret Thatcher. Michael Beesley became Reader in Economics at LSE, the UK Department of Transport's Chief Economist, advisor to the electricity regulator (OFFER) and economic advisor to the gas regulator (OFGAS), and a founding Professor of Economics at the London Business School. Gilbert Walker had been a professor at Birmingham since 1947, having built up both the department there and its reputation in industrial economics.

Ultimately, Kenneth Gwilliam, a graduate of Magdalen College, Oxford, was appointed Professor of Transport Economics in 1967 (Coleman O'Flaherty had been appointed to a Chair of Transport Engineering the previous year).[26] This was in many ways an ideal appointment. Gwilliam, although essentially an industrial economist, approaches economics in a similar way to Brown, with an emphasis of ensuring empirical analysis takes due account of the institutional context in which it is set, and the inevitable subjectivity that accompanies many valuations is clear. He was also continually engaged in the transportation industry and its policy-making, being an assessor for the Layfield Inquiry into the Greater London Development Plan, a director of the National Bus Company, engaged in policy debates within both the UK and the EU, and ultimately became principal transport economist at the World Bank.

The gradual spreading of economics into a multidisciplinary unit focusing on transportation matters along the lines Brown supported has been a manifest success. The early years saw the creation of an MSc in Transport Engineering and an MA in Transport Economics, and the engagement in research projects in low-cost highway construction materials and the economic impact study of the M62 motorway. Physically and institutionally, the Centre initially remained within the parent departments. During its first five years, it grew gradually, seeking to gain recognition whilst reconciling its separate identity within the continuing interests of the parent departments.

In 1971, the Science and Engineering Research Council (SERC) invited bids for the establishment of four "centres of excellence" in transport. The unit's bid for the largest of these centers, in Transport Planning, was successful and funded about 20 research posts for five years. The Institute was unashamedly interdisciplinary at a time when that was not fashionable. Also, as a basis for gaining recognition it was necessary to encourage, liberalize, and attempt to reward true academic initiative. At a time when the number of tenured posts was limited, rewarding was not always easy; but, as a sign of the quality of the effort, more than a dozen of the staff and students in the early years subsequently became professors. In 2009, the Institute received royal recognition by winning a prestigious Queen's Anniversary Prize for Higher and Further Education; the associated citation read it was for "sustained excellence—40 years' impact in transport research and teaching."

Brown clearly felt that his role in establishing the Centre, later the Institute, was one of his major achievements at Leeds:

> The Institute can claim to be one of the University's most successful ventures into the field of specialized graduate education and externally financed research. I did a great deal in determining its original form as a "Centre," and think of it now as the most satisfactory bit of pure entrepreneurship with which I have been associated.

THE STRUCTURE OF ACADEMIC DEPARTMENTS AND THE ROLE OF PROFESSORS

While deviating perhaps even more from Brown's direct work in applied economics, some insights can be gained more generally into his approach to the subject by looking at his views on how an economics department should be managed, and the role of those within it. This provides some reflections on not just what he did at Leeds but also into the ways he would have liked to have done things. In this respect, when he ceased to be head of the School he produced some ideas for a university administration on how a more democratic administrative structure could be put in place while retaining the ability for the executive to govern. And remember this was in the context of someone who had almost complete authority over the running of the economics unit at a major research university for some 18 years.

When Brown first went to Leeds it was not unusual for a department to have just one professor who would be its head until retirement—there was some confidence in continuity. This was a system that continued in many institutions in the UK until the 1960s. Professors became more numerous as departments grew, but they usually held personal posts that, although as an individual they held tenure, disappeared when they left or retired. Readerships in the UK normally had no administrative responsibility associated with them, and were awarded for exceptional scholarship; these would certainly at the time be on a par with a full professorship in the US.

The 1960s saw something of a gradual change taking place in the role of universities as they expanded in number and form, and with this came changes in the ways that academic administration and leadership were viewed. The publication of the *Robbins Report* (Committee on Higher Education, 1963)—with its recommendations for the immediate expansion of universities, and that all Colleges of Advanced Technology should be given the status of universities—accelerated this process. More specifically of concern to Brown were ideas of greater academic democracy that were emerging with the Association of University Teachers (AUT) advocating, amongst other things, rotating headships of departments and majority voting of faculty.

In this context, Leeds's Senate sought the views of its staff. The economics department came down in support of the broad AUT approach, a head elected for a given period by the entire faculty and voting on issues by the entire staff. This was against the views of Brown and one or two other senior faculty. Brown's objection was mainly that the diversity of views in the department, and given the argumentative nature of economists probably in all economic departments, made it too large a body to perform the role of a cabinet. Secondly, he had doubts that a head of department appointed for a short period would be able to develop the continuity in teaching and research required for a successful unit.

In terms of Brown's position, the late 1950s had seen the department change as he devolved more duties and as the nature of the academic environment shifted with fewer research assistants and a gradual growth in full-time faculty. This tended to result in a sense of "something like arithmetical equality was the proper, and attainable, aim." But this did mean that the position of professors, who tended to be left to set their own agendas, would change with them having tasks assigned to them. This became an issue.[27] The fact that there was, after Richardson retired, only one permanent professor added to the control of that person. As more professors were appointed, with Beresford being promoted and the Montague Burton Chair being filled by Turner, Brown moved to weekly lunch meetings of professors, the head of accountancy, and Whitaker (as the Director of the Industrial Management Division) to discuss policy. This widened Brown's range of consultation and opened the opportunity of moving from a permanent head of department to one rotating amongst the professors.

Arthur Brown was a visiting professor from March to September 1963 at the Australian National University (ANU) leaving Beresford to run the department. On his return, and once more taking up the leadership of the department but also seeking to respect the views it had expressed to the Senate, he proposed reforming the department's management structure by formerly enlarging its governing body with two elected members: its chair (a professor) being appointed for three years, as its spokesman; and the

Executive, as in other departments, having to consult with other faculty but retaining the last word because it held formal responsibility. Brown did not see himself as the Executive, and by this time felt that change was required. In a paper sent to the vice-chancellor at the time, he explained his position as well as setting out his proposals:[28]

> Basically . . . my experience is that, if I do (taking one year with another) the amount of general University work that goes with being head of a biggish department, and the minimum of teaching that seems to me to go with being a Professor of my subject, I cannot at the same time write, read adequately and look after the Department properly. Whenever I have become at all deeply immersed in a piece of writing or a specific investigation I have found myself getting out of touch with my colleagues and my grasp of departmental affairs slipping. And, what is worse because it is more continuous and not so easily repaired, my acquaintance with current economic literature, even in my favourite bits of the subject, has steadily slipped below the level of respectability.[29]

His arguments supporting his favored structure involved looking at the pros and cons of alternatives, such as having "someone who is content to become academically *passé*, and to declare himself an administrator"—an internal head who would move to another unit after doing his/her "stint." The third option of a rotating headship fell away almost by default. The concept was accepted by the department, although with some concern expressed by those seeking an Athenian democracy. What the structure had not allowed for, as Brown records, was that, while the department subsequently had several excellent heads, it was not a position that was actively sought after.

This was not the end of Brown's involvement with the university's constitution, or that of the department. The arrival of Sir Roger Stevens, in part, as we later see, due to Brown's lobbying on both sides, as vice-chancellor in 1963 saw a renewed interest in change. Brown was appointed as deputy chairman of one of four committees established as part of the new machinery. Little, however, was done by the time, in 1967, when he had finished a major project for the National Institute of Economic and Social Research (NIESR) on regional economic development, and had been replaced on the committee. But whilst away Brown had begun lobbying to shift away from the situation that professors were now being treated as other faculty in terms of the time allocated for teaching and other tasks. The situation came to a head in 1969 when Brown was invited to take up the Chair in Applied Economics at Oxford—the initial suggestion coming from David Worswick, director of the National Institute and an assessor for the post, followed up by a formal invitation after positively replying to Worswick.

Brown went to Walter Newlyn, after talking to Vice-Chancellor Stevens, and told him his final decision would be influenced by the way he, and other professors, were to be regarded in the department. He was especially concerned that teaching loads for professors should be no worse than at Oxford, where it was a minimum of 36 lectures a session. While some of his motivation was obviously personal, he was also interested in making professional appointments more attractive in the department. The vote in the departmental board rejected Brown's proposal, despite the Executive Committee accepting it. Arthur Brown, however, decided to stay at Leeds, partly because he had considerable freedom anyway and partly because, as we see below, he would have had to resign his University Grants Committee (UGC) membership—an institution with which he had "already fallen in love."[30]

These events went on to have further consequences the following year. At a meeting of the British Association, Nicholas Kaldor approached Brown, saying he had been authorized to ask him if he would consider being a candidate for a chair at Cambridge that was being vacated the next year by Joan Robinson's retirement. Given the prior decision regarding Oxford, he declined the invitation.

Also in 1970, there were renewed efforts in the department to take up more completely the old AUT supported governance structure with the whole board having control. The unit was split again, with Brown strongly against the proposals being put forward. Nonetheless, in 1971 a proposal of a sovereign board composed of all full-time faculty and research staff plus four elected students, with the chair elected by full-time teaching and research staff, went to the University Senate. The report from the Committee on Constitutions on the proposal emerged in early 1972 and was not in support of the proposal—a decision that was not taken favorably by the school. The amended constitution saw Conrad Leser—who had arrived in 1968 as, by title, the first Professor of Econometrics at the university after Lomax's departure—becoming chairman and Brown vice-chairman.[31]

The outcome of all this, in terms of economic modeling, was later summed up by Brown as follows:

> The most conspicuous reason, however, for the School's failure to become a leading light of academic government was its 1970–1 bid for Athenian democracy, which alienated Senate (and much other opinion), and after the fence-mending of 1975, left it with a clumsy structure of effectively three-tier government, which, for a body of only forty people in all, would strike most observers as *prima facie* excessive. Given the atmosphere of the time, and given common human propensity to push most things beyond their long-term equilibrium levels, this was perhaps inevitable—though a little sad considering

that economists are supposed to understand more about long-term equilibria, trade-offs, and the rest of it, than practitioners of other trades.[32]

In sum, Brown did not enjoy these disputes about the constitution of the economics department, perhaps because some of the resultant changes were not always in his personal interest, but also because he seems to have taken a somewhat longer-term, pragmatic, and non-ideological view of matters than some of his colleagues. His inherent skills as an applied economist seem to have kicked into his thinking. He saw problems in seeking to move towards the collegial system found at Oxford and Cambridge with elected governments within a structure involving the integration of teaching and research. The Oxbridge system he saw as having more separation, with research conducted in specialized institutes requiring substantial resources under permanent directors rather than largely in teaching colleges.[33] His support for the Transport Centre at Leeds likely stems partly from what he had seen at Oxford before the War.

What Brown did find satisfaction in during the period after he ceased to be head of department was his administrative work at the UGC, which we move onto later.[34] But, reflecting, Brown clearly sees part of the problems of his later years as head of a department at Leeds lay in his desire to have cabinet responsibility rather than a single chairman for a fixed, once-renewable term of the form that has emerged in many universities subsequently. The latter both focuses responsibility and provides a degree of permanency in strategy. The lack of second professors at the time he took over at Leeds was an issue, however, and Brown's own personality in being initially attracted to a life-tenure as head complicated matters. The outcome was a clumsy structure of triple-tier and a Senate alienated by the efforts of much of the economics department to move towards an "Athenian democracy."

NOTES

1. St David's College in Lampeter, Wales, held limited degree awarding power from the mid-nineteenth century, but could only award BA and BD degrees.
2. These colleges were not mainly designed to meet the needs of the nineteenth-century northern industrial regions but did develop a strong economic tradition; for example Stanley Jevons taught at Owens College from 1863 to 1876 (Daniels, 1930).
3. *Interview with A.J. Brown, 25 May 1994, Headingley, Leeds*, p.12. Whales held the Chaddock Chair of Economics at Liverpool from 1945 to 1947, and then the Brunner Chair of Economic Science from 1947 to 1950. Brown also applied for an Official Fellowship at Nuffield College, but that went to John Hicks.
4. Meade to Registrar, Leeds University (17 January 1947, AJB C&P).
5. MacGregor to Registrar, Leeds University (9 January 1947, AJB C&P).
6. *Interview with A.J. Brown, 25 May 1994, Headingley, Leeds*. In her review Lynda Grier

(1926) describes Jones's textbook as "pre-eminently suited for those who are interested in business: it is not designed for the consumption of members of W.E.A. classes, nor [*sic*] primarily for such University students as are attracted by the more abstract aspects of Economics." She also "advise[s] those who desire to read this book in comfort to furnish themselves with a book-rest. It is, for its size and content, of prodigious weight."

7. The men's tailors, Burton, endowed chairs in industrial relations at the University of Leeds (where founder Montague Burton had his production facilities). Cardiff in 1929, and Cambridge in 1930. He also endowed chairs of international relations in Jerusalem (1929) and at the University of Oxford (1930), LSE (1936), and the University of Edinburgh (1948).

8. After two years, he moved to Liverpool to take up the Brunner Professorship of Economics. Brown was, ironically and to his embarrassment, the external assessor for the position!

9. *Interview with A.J. Brown, 25 May 1994, Headingley, Leeds*, p. 12.

10. Brown later provides an account of how he viewed the economic characteristics of the region and an account of what had been done at Leeds in the 1950s and early 1960s; and, looking forward, he argued that: "It is, however, to the economies of our own region and of its constituent parts that we can best look in the long run as our largest single field of research interest." *A Note on the Regional and Local Economic Research* (30 April 1965, AJB C&P), p. 2.

11. *Interview with A.J. Brown, 25 May 1994, Headingley, Leeds*, p. 22.

12. Goodwin's presentation was subsequently published as Goodwin (1953).

13. Letter from A.J. Brown to Christopher Waller, 14 December 1994 (cited in Waller 2013).

14. The UK was behind Continental Europe and the US in establishing business schools; the School of Commerce in Birmingham was the first, set up in 1902.

15. For example, "A course of lectures has been given this year on various British industries, in which Maurice Beresford contributed on films and Denis Sargan on fish." Brown to Whitaker (3 April 1951, AJB C&P).

16. Brown, *The Department of Economics and Commerce/School of Economic Studies: A Personal Memoir* (August 1979, AJB C&P), p. 9.

17. Brown to Whitaker (3 April 1951, AJB C&P).

18. Brown, *Division of Management Studies in the University of Leeds: Revised Proposal June 1960* (28 March 1961, AJB C&P).

19. Whitaker, *Memorandum on the Industrial Management Division of the School of Economic Studies* (26 October 1965, AJB C&P), p. 5.

20. *Interview with A.J. Brown, 25 May 1994, Headingley, Leeds*, p. 23.

21. When established in March 1966, it had £25,000 (over ten years) from Shell Mex and BP Ltd, £22,500 (seven years) from British Petroleum, £7.500 (10 years) from Dunlop Rubber, £7,000 (seven years) from the Cement Makers' Federation, and £500 from Leeds City Council (Leeds University press release, 21 March 1966, AJB C&P).

22. Brown to Leeds vice-chancellor (7 August 1964, AJB C&P).

23. Brown to Leeds vice-chancellor (25 February 1965, AJB C&P). Brown also provided a first draft of the vice-chancellor's subsequent approach to industry for funding, a request couched very much in multidisciplinary terms (20 August 1965, AJB C&P).

24. Minutes of the Leeds University Senate Committee on Transport Studies (3 February 1966, AJB C&P).

25. Letter from Brown to G.G. Williams, Assistant Registrar, Leeds University (11 January 1966). Brown was subsequently appointed as the Senate representative to any committee established to appoint two professors to the new transport center (Registrar to Brown, 8 March 1966, AJB C&P).

26. Brown's view on O'Flaherty was expressed in a letter to the University Registrar (8 August 1966, AJB C&P): "The fact is, however, that we have no other candidates in mind for this particular Chair who have been at all well recommended and that the choice seems to be between a speculative appointment of Dr. O'Flaherty and a total collapse for the time being of our work and plans in the transport field. In these

circumstances I think that we have to be prepared to take a risk and other members of the Committee who know Dr. O'Flaherty will probably agree that on grounds of energy, enterprise and personality in general he looks a good risk, while the evidence of those correspondents who know something of his work seems to suggest, when taken as a whole, that the same may well be true in regard to his academic promise . . . In other words, while recognising that O'Flaherty's appointment to a Chair would be a risk I should be prepared to take it."

27. Brown was not at all happy with the idea of professors having their activities limited by a department committee, and on his return from Australia toyed with the idea of being put up for a Professorial Fellowship at All Souls, although he later learned that the position had only been advertised to provide a veneer of competition for a post that was aimed at honoring John Hicks (Brown, *The Department of Economics and Commerce/School of Economic Studies: A Personal Memoir*, p. 21.

28. Brown to vice-chancellor Leeds University (7 August 1964, AJB C&P). Brown to Standing Committee of Senate Business, *Future Organisation of the Department of Economics and Commerce* (4 December 1964, AJB C&P).

29. Brown, *The Government of the Department* (1964, AJB C&P), p. 1. He, tongue in cheek given his own background, also suggested: "Perhaps heads of departments would be better appointed at fifty, after 20 years of mature reading and peaceful writing?"

30. Brown, *The Department of Economics and Commerce/School of Economic Studies: A Personal Memoir*, pp. 26–7.

31. Leser is best known for his work on the Engel curve, and proposing what has become known as the Hodrick–Prescott filter.

32. Brown, *The Department of Economics and Commerce/School of Economic Studies: A Personal Memoir*, p. 32.

33. Brown, *On a Different Sort of University* (19 March 1971, AJB C&P).

34. He was also pro-vice-chancellor at Leeds from 1975 to 1977, although his various commentaries say little about this time.

5. African decolonization and world disarmament

INVOLVEMENT IN INTERNATIONAL AFFAIRS

The 1960s saw Arthur Brown, besides attending to matters in Leeds, heavily engaged in a series of committee and advisory activities in the international arena. UK Prime Minister Harold Macmillan's "Wind of Change" speech given in Cape Town in February 1960 had confirmed a continued and accelerated trend towards the winding down of the British Empire. Clement Attlee's Labour governments of 1945 to 1951 had started a process of withdrawal, most notably involving India following independence in 1947, but the Conservative governments of Winston Churchill and Anthony Eden from 1951 had halted this. Macmillan confirmed a reversal of the latter policy, and by 1980 most colonies had gained their independence. The challenge was to ensure an efficient transition, leaving the colonies, with their often rather arbitrary boundaries and limited physical and institutional infrastructure, able to move forward (Judith Brown, 1998).

This was also the time when ideas of economic integration were being pushed in Europe following the Treaties of Paris in 1951 and of Rome in 1957 that had begun to create common markets in primary products and manufactured goods respectively. The latter was also intended to morph towards a customs union. These sorts of "experiments" were under trial in British colonial Africa, and a concern was that, where successful, their institutional structures should be reformed and strengthened in preparation for the member colonies' ultimate independence.

At the same time, the Cold War, which had begun in 1947—the year of the Truman Doctrine, a US policy pledging to aid nations threatened by Soviet expansionism—had reached a crisis stage after the Hungarian Revolution of 1956 had been stopped by the Soviet Union, which had then also got involved in the Suez Crisis of the same year. These events were followed in 1961 by the Berlin Crisis and in 1962 by the Cuban Missile Crisis. These actions took place at a time when the relatively newly established United Nations was seeking to clarify its role in world affairs and in the maintenance of world peace. To this end there were initiatives to slow down, if not reverse, the arms race. There were, however, serious economic problems seen in doing this.

Brown became involved in both the efforts of Britain to ensure an orderly withdrawal from Empire and in the UN's efforts to temper the effects of the ongoing Cold War. The former has clear economic implications: the ex-colonies should be left with viable internal and external institutional economic structures.

The actual role of an applied economist in the UN's efforts to bring about disarmament are less immediately clear; after all this seems more of a matter of agreement on the parts of the US and Russia regarding a downsizing of their respective armed forces. Although President Dwight D. Eisenhower's convenient term, "the military-industrial complex," did not become part of the vocabulary of political economy until 1961, it was clear in the late 1950s that disarmament would have serious economic implications for the nations involved, and that a strong economic case would be needed, in addition to that of reducing international political tension. A transition to a peaceful use of resources was feared to have serious short-term consequences for structural unemployment, and longer-term possibilities of demand deficiency. This was not quite the same thinking that went with the end to the Cold War in 1989, when all the media spin was on a peace dividend.

THE RAISMAN EAST AFRICAN COMMISSION

The post-World War II period not only saw huge changes within Britain but also in the country's foreign policy. The latter was accelerated in Asia with the loss of prestige after the initial successes by Japan in the war. The conflict had significantly reduced Britain's role as an international power, but had also accelerated a trend towards reassessing its colonial role. Furthermore, Britain had been left essentially bankrupt, with insolvency only averted in 1946 after the negotiation of a $4.33 billion loan (in current prices) from the US, the last installment of which was repaid in 2006.

The reassessment of Empire and how to handle transition was a major concern. The scale of the challenge was enormous, and complicated by both the onset of the Cold War and the upsurge of various independence groups, most notably in India but also in some parts of Africa. In 1922, the British Empire held sway over about 458 million people (one-fifth of the world's population) and covered more than 13 million square miles (almost a quarter of the Earth's land area). Early efforts at decolonization, and most notably that involving the Indian sub-continent, was not Britain's finest hour—with the loss of many millions of lives in the process.

Other colonies, especially in Africa, were given independence somewhat later, largely because they were less well developed in terms of institutions, infrastructure, and in their abilities to compete in what were becoming increasingly global markets. It was following Macmillan's "Wind of Change Speech" in 1960 that the sea-change began for the African colonies, the timing being to some extent brought about by halo effects associated with events in French North Africa where a *de facto* colonial war had developed. Thus, while the Sudan and the Gold Coast had already gained independence in the 1950s, nearly ten times that number of British colonies did so in the following decade.

The UK authorities sought guidance from several committees and other advisory bodies as to what exactly the situation was in the colonies and in what ways independence could be carried through. Brown served on two of these: the East African Economic and Fiscal Commission in 1960, and as First Secretary of the State's Advisory Group on Central Africa in 1962. His contributions were supplemented with external, academic thought on some of the important issues, for example regarding the advantages of economic unions—something he came back to very much later in the context of the European Community.

It is obviously useful to look at Brown's intellectual inputs to these activities and to examine his influence, and indeed that of the advisory bodies more generally; but, in addition to this, Brown provides commentaries on some of the travels these commitments undertook—their field work. These "diaries" offer insight not only into exactly how such bodies operated on a day-to-day basis but also the interactions between Brown and others engaged. The focus, however, remains on economics.

Brown was not at that time an expert on African affairs, but his experience with the Foreign Office during the war and the diversity of memos and articles produced, combined with his networks, would have made him a logical choice. There was also a relative shortage of expertise; the deconstruction of the world's largest empire does not, after all, occur every day. Brown had prior commitments both at Leeds and as external examiner at Manchester University, but the necessary trip to Africa, reduced from three to two months, could be squeezed in during the summer vacation.[1]

Kenya, Tanzania, and Uganda have cooperated with each other in various ways since the early twentieth century. But the cooperation had largely been brought about by the colonial power rather than by agreement. As Jacob Viner (1950: 70–71) put in his seminal work on customs unions:

> The Tanganyika–Kenya Customs Union provided a striking instance where a territory was brought into a customs union by external authority to provide an

expanded field for the tariff protection of industries of another territory . . .
The customs union operated to create a protected market in Tanganyika for the
produce of a small colony of British planters in Kenya, for whose welfare the
British Government has shown a constant and marked solitude.

In historic terms, the common market had been formed linking Kenya
and Uganda in 1917, into which Tanganyika—the share of German East
Africa which the British took under a League of Nations Mandate in 1922—
had been gradually integrated between 1922 and 1927. Inter-territorial
cooperation between the Kenya Colony, the Uganda Protectorate, and
the Tanganyika Territory was subsequently formalized in 1948 by the
establishment of the East African High Commission. This provided a
customs union, a common external tariff, currency, and postage. It also
dealt with common services in transport and communications, research,
and education and their method of financing.

The coming of independence, when foreseen in the late 1950s, raised the
question of whether this economic union should continue. Those in favor
of essentially maintaining the *status quo* argued that it had been successful
in the expansion that it had brought about in the market for manufactures
and the wider increase in wellbeing that had been generated. Opponents
of continuation maintained that while Kenya had manifestly gained economically from the union, the other two members had not done so well,
and could possibly do better in the future if Kenya did not enjoy unfettered
access to their markets. Walter Newlyn had been on leave of absence from
Leeds as economic advisor to the government of Uganda in the late 1950s
and had talked to Brown about the grievances there regarding Kenya,
and especially regarding the lost revenues from duties on imports from
around the world that resulted from them now being substituted by duty-
free imports from Kenya. This, Uganda claimed, resulted in import duty
revenue that it would have enjoyed by buying in the world market going to
Kenya whose duty-free sales to Uganda were at higher than world market
priced manufacturers.[2]

Such was the background against which the UK Secretary of State
for the Colonies—on behalf of the Governors of Kenya, Tanganyika,
and Uganda—and the Administrator, East Africa High Commission,
establishing in 1960 a commission to examine agreements in place in East
Africa for a common market area; and to look at the economic coordination between the countries and fiscal conformity.[3] In a sense the idea was
to conduct a general cost-benefit assessment of the existing arrangements
and to make suggestions for any adjustments or modifications that would
make them fairer and more economically efficient (East Africa Economic
and Fiscal Commission, 1961). Sir Jeremy Raisman chaired the three-man

Commission, with Brown and Ronald Tress as the other members. Tress was, at the time, Professor of Political Economy at the University of Bristol. He had earlier served on the Nigeria Fiscal Commission (1958) with Raisman, and later became Master of Birkbeck College, London, Secretary-General of the Royal Economic Society and Director of the Leverhulme Trust. His career also further entwined with Brown's, as discussed later, when they worked together on British university costs.

Raisman was a highly distinguished civil servant in pre-independence India, where he was, amongst other things, Finance Member; he was effectively responsible for organizing India's finances during World War II, and led the Indian delegation at the Bretton Woods Conference (Chandavarkar, 2001).[4] He was also, following his retirement from the civil service, a highly successful executive, notably with Lloyds Bank. Importantly for the East Africa Commission he had led similar exercises, albeit with somewhat different remits, chairing the Fiscal Commission for the Federation of Rhodesia and Nyasaland (in 1952) and the Nigerian Fiscal Commission (in 1957–58), as well as advising the government of Pakistan on its distribution of central and provisional revenues. All these had a common thread with that for East Africa: they involved not only economics but also constitutional law and politics in the different countries concerned. This led to a strong team, with Brown and Tress supplying more relevant economics, and Raisman, with his extensive experience in the Indian civil service, providing the political and institutional skills, not to mention an extensive network of contacts.

Given the paucity the good data, and of more general information, together with getting a political feel for the situation, fieldwork was required and the trio spent from 14 July until 9 September in East Africa. Brown subsequently produced an unpublished detailed travelogue of this trip.[5] The account provides not only a mass of information about how these sorts of commissions functioned at the time, the importance of the dynamics of their members, and the limited information that they often had to try to draw policy recommendations from, but also administrative and political constraints that had to be brought into the making of economic policy recommendations—the standard *ceteris paribus*.

While the "Brown Travelogue" is insightful regarding the political-economic situation in East Africa and the role Brown played in the drafting of the ultimate report (East Africa Economic and Fiscal Commission 1961), it was his subsequent academic writings on economic unions that provide his more enduring contributions, including his much later commentaries on, what was at the time, the European Economic Community (EEC).

It was initially agreed by the group that Brown would undertake two main tasks.[6] One was to sort through the available data to get a much clearer picture of the growth rates of the three colonies involved, their terms of trade, the importance of trade in their economies, and their trade with the rest of the world. The questionable data on price levels and inter-territorial trade in imported goods, on which customs revenue was calculated, proved a major challenge. The second task was to assess the effects on the national incomes and governments of Uganda and Tanganyika of import-replacing developments in Kenya. And to this latter end Brown initially developed ideas founded upon foreign-trade multipliers based on the assumption that effective demand limited output and public expenditure constraints limited public expenditures. This requires estimates of the marginal proportions of additional income in each territory that were taken as direct and indirect taxation, that were saved, and that were spent respectively in the rest of the Economic Union and outside, and the proportions of Kenya's extra import-replacing productions that were sold there and in the other territories.

Brown's initial estimates were tested at a talk to the Uganda Economics Society at Makerere University that effectively, and with some diplomacy as an academic exercise, looked at how much Uganda was affected by tariff-protected development of Kenya. The multipliers he had estimated to that date were presented to what apparently was a decent sized audience, and applied these to a crypto-Kenya and a crypto-Uganda. Using reverses of his estimated values saw the less developed country come out rather well. The implication of this for the Union was that Uganda would seem to gain rather than lose even in this extreme case. According to Brown the ensuing debate saw some questioning of his assumption that demand only depended on demand within the Union and putting forward ideas that primary producing countries for the world market would find extra demand from within the Union would likely divert earning from exports rather than add to earnings and output in total.[7]

Ultimately, when it appeared, the Raisman Report provided support for a strengthening of the East Africa Economic Union institutions and for the creation of a fund that would help redress regional imbalances. It found that while Kenya had grown faster than the other two members of the Union for several reasons, not least of which were its geographical advantage and its larger white population that had reinforced its growth, neither Uganda nor Tanganyika would have done better as independent economies. The big problem was that the growth of Kenya's industries protected it from outside tariffs; but free trade with its Union associates had resulted in growth in intra-Union trade at the expense of trade with other countries, and thus a loss of customs revenue for Uganda and Tanganyika. There were therefore gains from spread effects within the Union, but

Uganda's and Tanganyika's public finances suffered from negative trade diversion effects.

The Raisman solution was that 40 percent of the income tax collected on manufacturing and financial undertakings and six percent of customs and excise revenue should be paid into a Distribution Pool of revenue. Half of this would go to the High Commission to finance non-self-contained common services, with the remainder split between the three territories.[8] The idea behind this was to provide a relatively stable source of funding for the non-self-contained common services of the East Africa Customs Union. The report argued that this would:

> assist these services in their activities by providing them with greater certainty of funds and that it would also promote a more efficient use of funds between services enabling the High Commission to function as a single authority, able . . . to administer its services from the point of view of the whole of East Africa rather than as an agency of territorial governments. (East Africa Economic and Fiscal Commission, 1961: 65–6)

The Pool was put in place in 1961–62 and in the fiscal year 1962–63 Kenya transferred £320,000 to Tanganyika, £285,000 to Uganda, and £143,000 (at current prices) via the Pool.

As for the impacts of the Committee's work on the East African Union, after the completion of the report, the East African Common Services Organization (the Commission had recommended the title of "Central Commission for East Africa") was established in 1961 in the lead-up to the territories gaining independence. The hope was that this would lead to a political federation between the three territories. The new organization, however, ran into difficulties because of the lack of joint planning and fiscal policy, separate political policies, and Kenya's dominant economic position. There was some initial effort on the part of the three colonies to pursue this with a joint declaration in 1963 that pledged them to form a political federation of East Africa, and a draft constitution was drawn up. Ultimately, the independent states could not accept surrendering any of their newly acquired national authorities; nor was the imbalance in trade in manufactures to be politically sustained.

The Commission also took a longer view of the situation in East Africa and at the small scale of manufacturing in Uganda and Tanzania. The Report argued that "as development tends to bring increased specialization and increased reliance upon activities in which the minimum efficient scale of operations is large, the contributions which the Common Market arrangements can make to economic growth are likely to be greater in the future than in the past" (East Africa Economic and Fiscal Commission, 1961: 62). This, however, was not something the leaders of the colonies considered when planning and acting on independence.

This was an important report, and not just for immediate issues of decolonization in East Africa. Peter Robson (1968: 313), in his later, wider geographical analysis of African integration, for example, described it as: "A classic on East Africa, and of interest for students of common markets in less developed countries generally." In fact, its approach to evaluation of the implication of economic unions provided a basis for a series of further refinement, and not only regarding less developed countries. The basic methodology was later applied to the questions raised when the issue of the UK entering the European Economic Community (EEC) was resurrected in the early 1970s.

From the academic perspective, Brown's input into the wider debates on common markets extended beyond his contribution to Raisman. On his return, he published papers in the *Yorkshire Bulletin of Economic and Social Research* (Brown, 1961a, b). (The second also led subsequently to him being even more involved in African policy.) The first article lays out in very straightforward terms, the economic implications of an economic union on the various stakeholders. It makes use of his East Africa experiences to compare the implications of an economic union for a developed country such as the UK and a developing one, making use of Kenya and Uganda as examples. In doing so he highlights that:

> there is a tendency for industrial countries to do a higher proportion of their trade with each other, and a lower proportion with the rest of the world, than is the case with the non-industrial countries. Development, therefore, seems in general to make for a trade pattern which, according to static theory, promises substantially greater benefits from customs unions than does the pattern of trade of countries at low levels of development. (Brown, 1961a: 35)

In the longer term, developing of manufacturing can allow economies of scale within a union to lead to internal trade replacing that with the outside world.

The second paper is more technical, and provides methods for putting hard numbers on many of the key economic parameters that determine the outcomes of the common market as was done by Raisman Committee. The article applied Brown's reasoning to East Africa based on his best-guess assumptions regarding the size of the key parameters.

Put briefly, Brown's analysis is essentially in terms of Keynesian multipliers assuming there are unused resources within the common market. It focuses on the economic spread effects within the union of the development of a common market, and on the extent that this offsets the higher import costs of a common external tariff. The modeling involves two countries,

A (basically Kenya), with some industrial production and spare resources that could be used for import substitution, and *B* countries (Uganda and Tanganyika). The model makes use of: the marginal propensities of *A* and *B* to import from other members of the union and from external suppliers; the amount of import substitution, both in terms of its consumption in *A* and *B* following a union and levels of customs duty in *A*; and the marginal propensity to save. Developing this within a multiplier framework for *A* provides both a primary multiplicand, based on the primary increase in *A* sales to *B* plus the value of its reduced imports from the rest of the world, and a second multiplicand relating to the spread effect: the change in *A*'s exports due to the rise in *B*'s income. Savings and imports from *B* are the leakages. The implications for *B* are similar without additional exports, other than those due to *A*'s higher income. There are higher imports due to its own rise in income, but these are partly offset by increases in its own production. The duties formerly collected on imports from outside the area now vanish and appear as higher incomes in *A*, which is producing the import substitutes.

Using estimates of the key parameters, Brown (1961b: 90) concludes: "with these values the country in which manufacturing arises to displace imports into the free trade area experiences a rise in income equal to twice the new manufactured output, the rest of the area experiences a rise in income of about a tenth of the new manufacturing output." Sensitivity analysis suggests that while it is possible for *B* to lose if *A*'s marginal propensity to import from *B* is less than 0.024, in the reality of the East African Customs Union, Kenya's propensity to import from Uganda and Tanzania was about 0.05 at the time.[9] There is also a matter raised by Robson (1968). While Brown's analysis indicated that the income generated by Kenya's extra imports from Uganda and Tanzania compensates them for the higher costs of their import substitution from world market suppliers to Kenya, this may not mean the latter would not be better off having independent economies. This is because some of the industry that may go to Kenya to benefit from the Union may have moved to Uganda or Tanzania without it. Brown is aware of this, but thinks this situation unlikely and does not allow for it in his analysis, for example in the context of Uganda: "Uganda is too small a market to support a plant of economic size in most industries" (Brown, 1961b: 94).

Brown's academic work resulted in several re-estimations by others using different assumptions and measures of protection. Robson (1968), in addition to adding insights of his own, provides a good summary and only a flavor of what Brown's paper stirred up is offered here. Walter Newlyn (1965), Brown's colleague at Leeds, for example, took the actual situation and compared it with a counterfactual of the Union being broken into three separate national markets. He then considered the gains and losses for Uganda and Tanzania, as Tanganyika had become, using comparative static assumptions. He divides industry into that which is viable in Uganda and Tanzania with protection and that which is common market based. Ending of the Economic Union would cause shifts in the form and the ending of the latter. The challenge here is in dividing up industries. He arrived at the conclusion that there would be gains to Tanzania from leaving the Union and insignificant losses to Uganda.

Whilst most of the other contributors to the debate essentially modified Brown's methodology and used different data, D.P. Ghai (1964) approached the topic from a different angle. He used margins of protection as an indicator of economic gains and losses for each member participating in a union. This involved using a weighted measure of each country's categories of inter-territorial exports by the relevant nominal degree of protection. The losses incurred by each country are measured in terms of their imports weighted in the same way as exports. He found, unlike Raisman, that Kenya was the main beneficiary of the East African Union, with Uganda gaining somewhat but Tanganyika suffering a major loss. The limitation of this approach is that it assumes that all inter-territorial trade in the Union requires protection; but, as Hazlewood (1966; 1967) shows, much of this would have taken place without protection.

THE ECONOMICS OF DISARMAMENT

In the 1950s and early 1960s, the UN sought to reduce the tensions of the Cold War by renewing its initiatives on disarmament. The Secretariat set up a ten-person Consultation Group on Economic and Social Consequences of Disarmament in 1960 that the General Assembly had requested be formed the previous December. Brown was invited to join.[10] The politics behind the establishment of the Group was that previous attempts at disarmament had failed, in part because the communist governments had refused to provide details of their existing forces. Khrushchev had in 1959 appealed to the Assembly for total disarmament within four years. A ten-nation Disarmament Committee had subsequently met at the UN's European headquarters in Geneva in March 1960, only to be stymied by the same problems as before. Added to this, the U2 incident whereby a US spy-plane had been shot down over Russia, led to a planned summit being abandoned. The scene got even murkier when relations between Russia and China deteriorated.

In terms of perceptions regarding disarmament, setting aside the probable objections of the armament industries, the Russians felt that the West was unwilling to disarm not only for security reasons but also because it feared a return to pre-World War II economic depression.[11] There was something of a superficial convergence of Keynesian and Marxist thinking in this respect. Brown, however, argued that the more sophisticated thinking of Keynesians in the 1960s would have led to the belief that enhanced civilian public and private expenditure could be brought into play to sustain aggregate demand. Brown's view was that the Russians sometime in 1960 realized that disarmament would only be accepted in the west if it were shown that a major economic depression would not ensue. To this end, Oscar Lange, then chairman of the Economic Committee of the Policy Council of Ministers in Poland (presumably with Soviet support), proposed a UN study of the economic implications of disarmament, although the proposal for such a study ultimately came from Pakistan. Russia was otherwise engaged at the time, having encountered another slight problem in the Congo, and effectively had to accept the position of the Secretary-General of the UN.[12]

Brown had not at first been keen to join the enterprise that was initially meant to report by spring of 1962, later pushed back to July, after some resistance. This was because of his Leeds commitments and the prospect that it might prove "tedious." The change of heart came about after receiving a letter from Jacob Mosak, director of the Secretariat's Division of Economics and Policies, and someone who *de facto* kept the subsequent wandering of the Consultative Group in check. Brown had known Mosak, an eminent mathematical economist, since his visit to Columbia University in 1950 and "in the course of a little investigation which [he] had done for the Secretariat in 1959–60."[13] The group of ten, in addition to Brown, consisted of a powerful set of economists. From the US there was the Russian émigré and subsequent economics Nobel laureate Wassily Leontief, who, among other things, had developed the input-output methods widely adopted in national income accounting.[14] Another émigré to the US, in this case via the UK, was the Polish-born Oscar Lange, who was an academic before becoming the first post-war Polish Ambassador to Washington. He made important contributions to both Keynesian and socialist economics (most notably with a model of market socialism).

There was a good mix of economic expertise in the Group. As the other European there was Alfred Sauvy, the director of the French National Institute of Demographic Studies.[15] And, besides Lange, the more physically planned economies were represented by the Russian V.Y. Aboltin, the Deputy-Director General of the Institute of World Economics and International Relations of the Soviet Academy of Sciences, and by the Czech Ludek Urban, a member his country's Economic Institute. From the less developed countries were Aftab Ahmad Khan, Chief Economist of the Pakistan Planning Commission who also subsequently wrote some commentary on the Group's work; Mamoun Beheiry, an Oxford graduate in PPE, Governor of the Bank of Sudan, and later first President of the African Development Bank; B.N. Ganguli, Head of the Dehli School of Economics; and Antonio Mayobre, Venezuela's Ambassador to the US.

The Group's final consensus—*Economic and Social Consequences of Disarmament: Report to the Secretary-General Transmitting the Study and its Consultative Group*—was published in 1962 (United Nations, 1962). The format was very much in line with the general issues listed in Brown's initial statement at the first meeting of the Group in Geneva.[16]

> I said that we should first seek to discover what resources disarmament would release, and how quickly, then consider how adaptable these resources were to non-military kinds of production, and how far the kinds to which they were most adaptable were those most likely to be expanded. Further we should consider whether world demands for any primary materials were likely to be severely reduced by disarmament, and by the cessation of military stockpiling, and whether international disposal schemes, like the post-war Commonwealth wool-disposal scheme might be called for.

The methodology that Brown favored, probably because of Leontief's membership of the group, was input-output analysis, and this was what was used for large parts of the analysis. He also suggested that, for the developed economies, the experiences of the US after 1945 should be examined to see how changes in the objectives of public expenditure could be accommodated without any reduction in employment and output. The subsequent contents of the report covered, in turn:

- the resources currently expended on arms (estimated in current prices at about $120 billion a year and directly involving about 50 million people);
- the purposes to which the resources may be diverted in civilian use;
- the impact of disarmament on employment and production;
- the structural problems of disarmament; and
- the effects of this on international relations, economic development and social life.

It offers optimism in the sense that the Group felt all the macroeconomic challenges of complete disarmament could be met by appropriate national and international measures, although there would be difficulties that would vary between countries.

The argument was that the communist countries could manage the change by adapting their economic capacity through their use of material balance planning. The Group showed optimism that this could be achieved quite smoothly in the Soviet Union, Poland, Yugoslavia, and China. The Western, essentially free-enterprise, economies could make use of fiscal and monetary policies, although there was appreciation of the political problems likely to be encountered and the vested interests that would need to be overcome. However, when reflecting on the post-World War II period, "huge armies were quickly demobilized without a significant rise in unemployment in most countries" (United Nations, 1962: 48).

However, it would be the less developed economies, albeit to different degrees, that would benefit most from disarmament. In terms of manpower, disarmament would release scarce, and in particular skilled, labor resources to the civilian production sectors for civilian production and provision of social services. Because less developed countries were also mainly meeting their requirements for military equipment by importing them, disarmament allowed for retention of foreign exchange rather making munitions- and arms-based industrial workers redundant. Resources would be more plentiful for infrastructure investment—a point subsequently reiterated by Khan (1962). There is always an inevitable caveat to these things, and in this case it is that some of these less developed countries would suffer from a temporary loss of mineral exports currently going to make munitions elsewhere.

In addition to the report of the Consultative Group, in April 1962 Volume II of Appendices was produced in mimeograph form rather than printed. This contained the replies of 17 governments and specialist agencies as *notes verbales* that had been circulated by the Group; and, as Brown later put it, the Appendices made very interesting reading, but "it is perhaps not surprising they were little commented on except by specialists in the economics and disarmament."[17] Brown took a particular interest in the Russian contribution, which, as he put it:

> was a statement, in some 24 pages, of the infinite desirability of disarmament, particularly to stave off the threat of mass destruction, of the Soviet devotion to that aim (traced back as far as Lenin's disbanding of the Russian Army in 1917), of the absence of any economic difficulty of achieving it in a socialist country (or even, seriously, in a capitalist one), and of the benefits to the standard of living and growth rate."

To sum up the outcome: "The Consultative Group is unanimously of the opinion that all the problems and difficulties connected with disarmament could be met by appropriate national and international measures" (United Nations, 1962: 52). Of course, the problem is that countries did not have the political will to enact "appropriate national and international measures," as subsequent reviews, often with hindsight of subsequent events, pointed out (for example Gray, 1962).[18] The conclusions were also not altogether in line with a parallel study by the US Arms Control and Disarmament Agency (1962) and led by the Columbia University business professor Emile Benoit that looked specifically at the possible implications of disarmament on the US economy.[19] This study was far more sanguine about the ability of a market-based economy such as the US to adjust to a disarmed world, and in particular for the country to maintain its position in research and development without a significant defense budget. An advanced, profit-driven economy was considered too complex to rapidly adjust; in addition, the concentration of military spending locations would make local economic depressions difficult to handle.

As with all reports, the roles of individual members of a group are not altogether clear. Indeed, there was an explicit "decision not to print personal submission."[20] In this case it was transparent that Leontief was responsible for the thinking behind the input-output work, although this was supplemented by analysis of the UK economy by Richard Stone using embryonic static computable general equilibrium modeling. It was also clear that he set the overall tone for the first meeting in Geneva on August 5, 1960. Basically, Leontief said they should accept that disarmament was to be desired on economic as well as other grounds, and that they should devote their time to their main business "to initiate a systematic and comprehensive study of the shifts that would be brought about in all countries by the redeployment of resources away from military uses."

At Geneva, he had been "brigaded" into drafting group two that was to focus on national and social issues. Drafting was seen as important if a consensus document was to emerge, and each group had a member from a Western, a less developed, and a central planned economy. Initially, in Geneva he was tied with Lange and Ganguli to work on national economic and social problems, which, because of Lange's expertise, posed no significant problems for the trio. The group all being English speakers, albeit with diverse accents, also seemed to have helped.

The main problems were with the group involving Leontief, Aboltin, and Kahn dealing with the quantitative information to be collected. The Russians had never released the sort of data required for economic analysis, and they would not supply detailed information on military expenditures; the country had only ever published annual data on the total defense expenditure in the State Budget. Aboltin could not very well ask for data that he knew his government would not give; this would make it appear as if Russia was being unreasonable. He argued that there was no point in asking for details of the disarmament package being envisaged, and after that the information was not needed for planning purposes.

Brown recalls that Mosak came up with some solutions for allowing the process to move forward to the second meeting, partly motivated by the need to ensure UN deadlines regarding the first report were met. The outcome was that hard data matters were to be tempered with a request for assessments (as opposed to estimates) of such things, and much more focus was to be put on qualitative analysis of where the released resources after disarmament would be redeployed (including, at Sauvy's insistence, some hypothetical cases) and on issues of international relations, trade, and social welfare.

The UK's input regarding the existing situation was a combined document from Brown and the Treasury (seemingly largely in the personification of Bryan Hopkin because Alec Cairncross, then the main economic advisor to the UK government, was heavily engaged in domestic economic matters)—with Brown, as we see later, doing much of the drafting of the *note verbale* and the Treasury much of the editing. Brown's own view of the respective workloads was:

> I soon found myself obliged to find out about the current military use of resources . . . I could not afford to wait for the Economic Section to produce its account of military absorption of resources before I started work. The consequence was that my practical course was to set about drafting the "country" study for the United Kingdom, including a first shot at the "assessment" of military absorption which was asked for under the first, general heading of the *note verbale*.[21]

This involved Brown in making a round of visits to the various responsible government ministries and agencies. He also consulted, although gaining little additional information, with the Economist Intelligent Unit that, with assistance from the Ministry of Defence, was gathering information on a similar theme that resulted in 1963 in the publication of *The Economic Effects of Disarmament*.

He was also concerned that the then most up-to-date input-output tables for the UK for 1954 were not adequate to capture the effects of disarmament. As he said later, in static terms, for example:

> From the Defence Estimates, expenditure on weapons and supplies can be classified under broader headings—aircraft and equipment, electronics, guns, armour and ammunition, motor transport, shipbuilding and ship repairing, and a miscellaneous engineering category. Unfortunately, these headings do not correspond closely with the product-classifications for which the direct and indirect import-contents are available from input-output tables (notably *Input-Output Tables for the United Kingdom*, 1954). (Brown 1967: 116–17)

In the dynamic context, the static nature of input-output coefficients could also seriously distort the estimates: "If, for instance, people spent more on consumption because of reduced taxation, the pattern of this extra consumption would presumably be different from that of the whole body of existing consumption, to which the relevant art of the input-output tables referred."[22]

Brown sought to correct this with a set of "back-of-envelope calculations and judicious verbal reservations." It was now that he also contacted Richard Stone, whom he felt had more up-to-date input-output calculations within his "Rocket" model, albeit with less sectorial delineation than did the official UK tables. Brown initially asked in late September 1961 for some key parameters used in the model regarding capital/output ratios for different sectors of the economy and marginal propensities to consume the products of different industries. Stone, however, went further and offered to run Rocket taking out defense outputs and making some plausible assumptions about the substitutions in expenditure that would occur.

There was something of a debate at about this time, albeit inevitably one-sided, involving Brown and HM government about how the UK's contribution to the Group should be presented. Much of this was ultimately Brown's work, but the issue was whether it would go in under his name, as a UK official document, or as a kind of hybrid paper.

In January 1961 the Foreign Office freed Brown to submit some of his work under his own name, with the caveat this was not an official UK document—"in particular, any figures, and especially those relating to balance of payments problems."[23] The subsequent official UK *note verbale* was 15 double-spaced pages that, as Bryars (a Treasury official), put it to Brown, "You will find some parts of the text easily recognizable."[24] In fact, it was a condensation of the first two parts of Brown's paper, coupled with his third section on looking at multiplier effects on the marginal efficiency of capital stemming from redirecting savings from armament reductions to reducing taxes or the debt on higher investment. The regional economic implications of disarmament were omitted. There was additional material on specific cases relating to the impacts of closure of overseas military bases in Gibraltar, Malta, and Kenya, and some movement in the geography of text in the document; but Brown felt that, "my text was pretty faithfully summarized, including the Cambridge contribution, mainly in my own words . . . I found this outcome rather amusing at the time. . . . I did not feel disposed to complain." In fact, no personal submissions were included in Volume II of the final report.

Returning to the workings of the Group, there was Sauvy's requirement of hypothetical studies mentioned earlier to contend with. Although not strictly taken up after the first meeting—largely because "when it became clear that only he would be willing to meet it or, indeed, understood quite what he wanted"—this was partly met.[25] The Cambridge Department of

Applied Economics provided Stone's analysis at Brown's instigation to the Group as an unpublished study. This involved hypothecating that UK military expenditure would be replaced in equal parts by increased private consumption, increased domestic capital formation, and increased foreign aid, output would be reduced in only two of the 19 sectors of the economy and would need to expand by between 3 and 6 percent in others, textiles and motor vehicles being exceptions (where expansion would have to be 9 and 14 percent respectively).[26] Brown seemed rather proud, "That the results of the Cambridge calculation and my rough reckonings broadly supported each other, though on further inspection it seemed that this agreement owed something to compensating errors (or differences of inter-pretation) in our respective data sources."[27]

The idea of some hypothetical analysis was also met indirectly in an ongoing US study by Leontief and Marvin Hoffenberg (1961) that became available to the Group. This was based on 1958 demand data, and assumed that the reduced US military expenditure would be replaced by increased expenditure on civil goods and services spread *pro rata* across the economy. The outcome of an $8 billion cut in US military expenditure, and its transfer to civilian uses, would result in 253,815 jobs being eliminated in 19 civilian industries and 541,855 new jobs being created in the other 38 industries–a net gain of 288,040 jobs. Brown's (1962b) estimations for the UK was that between three-and-a-half and four percent of the occupied population would need to find non-military work, or change the civilian sector they worked in. Handling this, he felt, would not impose a major burden on government finances, especially compared to the costs of post-war demobilization, given the savings in military outlays.

The Group, after its initial meeting in Geneva, had a second meeting in New York in January/February 1961. Some of the various national *notes verbales* were now available, including that from Russia, as was a preliminary draft of Part 1 of the report.[28] Three, effectively re-drafting groups were again formed, with Brown staying with his original colleagues, although other groups involved some reshuffling. Since there were to be six chapters, this gave each group a week to work on each of the two allotted to it. Consideration of the impact of disarmament on national produc-tion and employment went to the Brown–Lange–Ganguli trio in the first week (finally being Chapter 3 of the report), with structural problems of conversion (Chapter 4) being the subject of the second week.

The first round went well for the Group, a fact Brown partly attributes to Lange's familiarity with both the "languages and susceptibilities of both Marxist and capitalist worlds." The chapter was also rather descriptive in its design and generally made use of readily available data. The second task also posed only limited difficulties, mainly because of Stone's work and that of Leontief and Hoffenberg. The sorts of disagreement were minor, for example:

> We were reflecting on the differences of direct and indirect industrial input into some category of construction suggested respectively by the Leontief–Hoffenberg and British Studies. Someone looked out of the window and pointed to a newly-built skyscraper. "There," he said, "steel, frame aluminum panels, electronics in every room. If you filled it up with liquid oxygen and paraffin, it would probably go into orbit. Not quite like the typical product of the British building industry."[29]

At this point time was pressing, and there were still three main sections to complete, plus a chapter on social costs that Aboltin had insisted upon to be developed and was ultimately short and drafted with Lange and Urban. There were also the Introduction, Summary, and Conclusions to be drafted, elements of which the Secretariat were not prepared to take full responsibility for. Brown's drafting group took on the latter task in addition to its other commitments and he, in effect, drafted the Introduction that was taken by the group "like lambs"—and gave Brown time for a weekend trip to Troy State University! The other two groups found their tasks more of a struggle.

He then offered to also take on the drafting of the Summary and Recommendations. As he puts it:

> It was a different kind of task from the Introduction; the safe, established UN method of doing things is to string together, as far as possible, strategic sentences lifted from the text, a process which directs one's attention ruthlessly to the extent to which these sentences fail to say what they mean—or either of the things that two contending parties meant about them.[30]

The initial draft, however, had a "slightly bumpy passage," not least because Lange described Brown's English as too good. Brown subsequently concluded this meant "British English is a minority taste among readers of UN documents."[31] But they were largely adopted with "euphoria."

All members of the Group signed the Report on Friday, 16 February 1962. Volume I was published in March, followed in April by Volume II containing the *notes verbales* from national governments and specialist agencies. The message is, as Gray (1962: 908) subsequently puts it: "the UN analysis unanimously, and without reservation, concludes that the transition [to disarmament] can be made with appropriate national and international cooperation." Khan (1962, 179), in his own semi-retrospective on the Group's work, is also happy with the outcome: "This is very heartening in a world where it is very difficult to get agreement on anything between the adherents of the two blocs."

The impact of the Report, given the timing of the study and the turn in world affairs following its acceptance, was very limited. The Berlin Wall had gone up during the Group's work; the UN Secretary-General, Dag Hammarskjöld, had been killed in a plane crash in Africa; and the Cuban Missile Crisis followed about six months or so after its publication. It also appeared in a competitive market: the US Arms Control and Disarmament Agency's work was published in the same year, and the Economist Intelligence Unit's study a year later.

While Brown mused over his experiences with the Consultative Group in his later, unpublished personal recollections that provide retrospective insights, there is also some additional, more contemporary technical material contained in two speeches from the 1960s, both conveniently subsequently published. The first was his 1964 David Davies Memorial Institute Lecture, given at a House of Commons meeting chaired by Philip Noel Baker, the 1959 Nobel Peace Prize recipient. In this lecture, Brown focused much more on the long-term growth effects of disarmament rather than the short-term, transitional challenges of demand management and unemployment. But by then, however, his main interests were reverting back to UK domestic matters (Brown, 1965).

Second, sometime later Brown (1967) did return to the subject of the economic impacts of disarmament in the context of its possible effects on the UK's balance of payments. This was in a speech to the Conference on Economic Aspects of World Disarmament and Independents held in Oslo in 1995. The Program of Research on International Economics of Disarmament and Arms Control and the International Peace Institute organized this. Emile Benoit, he who had earlier led the US Arms Control and Disarmament Agency's work on the economic impacts of disarmament, subsequently brought together the papers from the conference. A diverse range of topics were covered at the meeting, which was attended by an array of eminent academics and senior officials involved in the field. They included: Abba Lerner, Imre Vajda (who presented), Alec Nove (who presented), and François Perroux (who presented); future Nobel Prize winners Alva Myrdal (for Peace), Trygve Haavelmo (Economics), and Jan Tinbergen (Economics, who also presented); Leif Johansen, Alexander Eckstein (who presented), and Abram Bergson, as well as Lüdok Urban, who had been a member of the Consultation Group.[32]

Brown's subject at the conference was an update of material he had submitted to the Consultative Group regarding trade balance effects of disarmament, and may be seen as a case study of the UK's situation.[33] The published version also contains Brown's derivation of multiplier links stemming from reduced military in the context of no changes in exports or private gross investment that was omitted from the UK evidence in the Consultative

Group's report. The presentation and the subsequent chapter contain a detailed account of how the UK's balance of payments would be altered if there were disarmament. The impact on the economy turns out positive although the implication on the balance of payments would be more complex. Brown concludes from the work that, "Perhaps the paper's chief message was that the effects of disarmament, as indeed of many hypothetical changes, on the British balance of payments are highly complex and problematic."[34]

Unlike Leontief, who produced several other academic publications and reports for government, Arthur Brown did not engage in any further work on disarmament after 1967.

ADVISORY GROUP ON CENTRAL AFRICA

Brown's involvement with Central Africa began after his stint on the UN Consultative Group, with an invitation in early 1962 to present a paper to a Ford Foundation-sponsored symposium in the then Nyasaland on "Economic Development in Africa," focusing on the pros and cons of economic unions.[35] This was clearly a spill-over effect of his work on the East African Union, and the two-part paper he had published in the *Yorkshire Bulletin* in 1961, that had come to the attention of Dunduzu "Gladstone" Chisiza, the Parliamentary Secretary of the Ministry of Finance in the new Nyasaland government.

The idea Brown came up with was to extend, in a more specific manner, the arguments of the Raisman Report regarding the advantages of large markets as opposed to tendencies towards the potential spread effects of local concentrations across geography. The talk would be something of a response to a recent survey paper by Richard Lipsey (1960a) that had argued the advantages of unions largely in terms of scale economies. Brown, however, felt that the underlying assumptions of this prevailing view were, at least in the short term, much less valid in the African context than for wealthier regions.

Basically, as Brown (1961a) had written earlier, the African economies as they stood were more complementary to outside markets than to each other, and thus mechanisms fostering trade outside were what development policies should emphasize. Such arguments, however, Brown was to emphasize in his talk, would decline as education and infrastructure quality improved in the African countries and as economies of scale developed, but this would take time. This was not quite a full-blown infant industry argument perhaps, because trade with selected countries may well be advantageous, but more a refined version focusing on the specifics of trade. He was to provide arguments, following his drafting, seeking to establish conditions where unions, "the economic criteria for judging what kinds of economy are most likely to gain from economic associations of various sorts –carefully noting that 'specific proposals for inert-territorial union, like proposals of marriage, have to take account of many factors other than economic ones.'"[36]

His thought processes were disrupted by a call from the Home Secretary, R.A. (Rab) Butler.[37] Given his background it was not altogether surprising the Home Secretary felt it appropriate to directly contact an academic. Richard Butler had been born into a family of academics and Indian administrators and had enjoyed a brilliant academic career before entering Parliament, where, as a junior minister, in 1935 he had helped pass the Government of India Act. Having served as Education Minister (overseeing the Education Act 1944) and Chancellor of the Exchequer, Butler had become Home Secretary in 1957. He went on to be Deputy Prime Minister and Foreign Secretary and, after retiring, was appointed Master of Trinity College, Cambridge.

Butler was concerned at the time about events in the Federation of Rhodesia and Nyasaland (or the Central African Federation)—a union that Brown subsequently described as "one of the world's most improbable political entities"—and wanted Brown to become an advisor. The Federation consisted of Nyasaland (broadly, in geographical terms, Malawi from 1964), Northern Rhodesia (from 1964, Zambia), and Rhodesia (from 1970 the Republic of Rhodesia and from 1980, Zimbabwe) and was in a state of near breakup as Nyasaland was moving to leave. The members of the Federation each had about 3 million black inhabitants. Southern Rhodesia had 210,000 white inhabitants that had ruled it through a parliamentary system since 1923 with a convention that Westminster could not initiate legislation governing the colony. In contrast, Northern Rhodesia and Nyasaland were protectorates ruled through governors reporting directly to the Secretary of State and then the Central African Office. The former's white population had grown to about 72,000 by the early 1960s and there were pressures for government along the lines of Southern Rhodesia with probably long-term designs of merging with it. There was also concern in the UK that the apartheid movement in South Africa would move north.

Historically, the federation was the UK's response to concerns that economically none of the territories were considered viable as individual entities and some form of union would help resolve this problem. Such an entity was formed in 1953, largely leaving "native policy" unchanged but giving a federal government responsibility for such things as defense, electricity supply, economic policy, currency, customs, white education, trunk communications, and federal income tax. White Rhodesians accepted this as well as Nyasaland as, if not ideal, a workable compromise mainly because it seemed more financially attractive than any federal system. Black Southern Rhodesians saw advantages in Colonial Office protection and remaining linked to large black populations. The problem was that the black populations of Nyasaland and Northern Rhodesia were naturally hostile to being tied in with Southern Rhodesia, with its pass laws, partial segregation, and land apportionment.

It was not long before it was clear that Southern Rhodesia was not changing fast enough to meet the expectations of an evolving, less racist world; the French and Belgians had already dismantled their sub-Saharan empires. Despite changes to the constitution that would allow proportionate growth in black representation (albeit with no clear timetable), the expectations of the black populations were for majority rule much sooner. In the northern territories things had begun to move faster, with Nyasaland, while technically having a governor in charge, had an African majority legislative council. There were proposals in 1961 for Northern Rhodesia to move from a white-dominated legislative council to a black majority controlled council.

Regarding the Federation, there was to be a review after seven to ten years, and in preparation for this the UK government had in 1959 established a two-stage enquiry process. The Monckton Commission (Advisory Commission on the Review of the Constitution of Rhodesia and Nyasaland, 1960), as the second part of this, had concluded that despite being a success economically because of the complementarity of its members and that the Federation could borrow more cheaply than any of the individual countries, political pressures meant that the "Federation cannot, in our view, be maintained in its present form." For it to survive would require considerable force or massive changes in racial legislation. Roy Welensky, the Prime Minister of the Central African Federation, rejected the report and the subsequent Federal Review Conference (after making little progress) was abandoned.

The economic analysis of the Federation, however, was more qualitative than quantitative. Brown's view was that, "In particular, The Monkton Commission's economist, D.T. (afterwards Sir Daniel) Jack of Durham, whom I remember mainly for his absence whenever I visited his university, had shown no sign of recognizing that there are strains as well as advantages in a common market, or that quantification is important."[38] The more rigorous analysis that was available at the time by Hazlewood and Henderson (1960) found that the territories differed not only politically, but also economically in terms of income, with Southern Rhodesia having the highest, Northern Rhodesia following, and Nyasaland some way behind.[39] The proportion of whites in the populations was a major factor in this. Northern Rhodesia, however, raised considerable tax revenues from its copper mining, which meant in the federal system it subsidized the other members; e.g. Nyasaland's government revenue was augmented 70 percent. The other main effects of the Federation, namely trade creation, were less clear. The three territories all exported more to countries outside of the Federation than to others within it. While much of the internal trade in coal by Southern Rhodesia to the copper belts would have occurred anyway, there appeared to be some growth in internal export of manufactures from Southern Rhodesia that was at least partly associated with the external federal tariff structure that was de facto being paid for largely by Northern Rhodesia in terms of higher prices and reduced customs revenues.

The idea was that Brown, along with Sir Ralph Hone and David Scott (with Roger Stevens as chair), would provide advice on the future of the Federation. The team was a powerful one, as was probably needed given the nature of the challenges at the time. But, unlike the East African Commission, Brown was the sole economist. He was also probably included in the group to bring a fresh mind to the issues.[40] The latter Scott (1981: 114) implied when outlining their local briefings: "Much of what we heard was new to Stevens and Brown, but for Hone and myself it was the third time around the course: occasionally I felt that if one of our witnesses forgot his lines I could complete his evidence word for word."

Stevens, who was to play a significant role in Brown's later career, had done consular service in Buenos Aires, New York City, Antwerp, Denver, and with the Foreign Office in London, and had been British Ambassador to Sweden and then Persia. In 1958, he returned to London as Deputy Under-Secretary of State (Foreign Office) and then, as we have seen, took up the position of vice-chancellor of the University of Leeds, whilst at the same time being advisor to the First Secretary of State on Central Africa between 1963 and 1970. Ralph Hone—whom, like David Scott, Brown did not know prior to the establishment of the group—had been in colonial service in Uganda, Zanzibar, and Tanganyika, and then Attorney General of Gibraltar and Uganda. Following a period at General Headquarters Middle East, he moved to the War Office dealing with South-East Asia, the handover to civilian rule of Malaya, and serving as Secretary-General to the Governor-General. He had later been Deputy Commissioner-General in South East Asia, Governor of North Borneo, and head of the legal division of the Commonwealth Relations Office. David Scott had been chief radar adviser in the British Military Mission to the Egyptian Army and then assistant private secretary to the Secretary of State in the Commonwealth Relations Office. From 1951 to 1953 he was in the Cabinet Office in Cape Town and Pretoria before becoming Secretary General of the Caribbean and Malaya Constitutional Conference. He served in Singapore in the mid-1950s and was on the earlier Monckton Commission on Central Africa, in 1960. At the time the Advisory Body was set up, he was Deputy High Commissioner to the Federation of Rhodesia and Nyasaland.

The Advisory Group left the UK to start their mission on 15 July. Work began upon arrival, and visits with the relevant national and federal parties took place with some fluidity and frequency. But as a diversion, on this initial trip, Brown (1962a) also gave his paper to the Nyasaland symposium on the 20th in his capacity as an academic. In addition to Brown there was an impressive array of economists at the symposium, including Nicholas Kaldor (from Cambridge), Eugene Staley, Edward Jackson and Gerald Meier (Stanford University), Rudolf Rhomberg (IMF), and K.N. Raj and V.K.R.V. Rao (Delhi). "The paper was received well in the sense that nobody reacted to it with marked hostility, and several, including Teddy Jackson, said nice things . . . I was not aware, at least in Zomba or in Salisbury, of any awkwardness for the Team arising from my symposium activities."[41] It did, though, make headlines in the *Rhodesian Herald*, and especially a remark about an Africa of 50 separate economies made no economic sense.

The Advisory Group did not take long to each bring conclusions about, and then the challenge became the recommendations. As Scott (1981: 113) puts it:

> In the light of what was presented to us we could not fail to endorse the view that in the last, Nyasaland could not be kept in the Federation by force. We also accepted that if the two Rhodesias were to be kept together there would have to be an extensive redistribution of power from the Federal to the territorial governments.

Arthur Brown's initial thrust into providing something constructive was to collect relevant data and, specifically, prepare a statement on the economic implications for Nyasaland of secession from the Federation in the context of a Federal Treasury paper on the subject. The latter calculated that federal expenditure benefitted Nyasaland by about £5 million above the territory's contribution to the budget. Further, it argued that most of the capital formation in Nyasaland had been by the Federation and that Nyasaland would be responsible for servicing some public debt if it left, and for assets created by the federal government. Leaving would also deprive Nyasaland of some federal markets, and deprive it of the advantages of common marketing and of remittances from its workers who would no longer work in the Rhodesias. Added to this was an unspecified loss of taxable income.

Brown's approach to the document was an immediate recognition that leaving the Federation would allow the country to collect import duties from Northern and Southern Rhodesia, as well as elsewhere, or to bargain for some revenues in lieu of this. Also, there was a need to substantiate the assumption that it would cost more for Nyasaland to maintain its public services after breaking away, notably in terms of the responsibilities currently with the Governor General and the Royal Rhodesian Air Force. To get at the various primary effects of public finances and other external changes on Nyasaland's tax revenues and future gross domestic product (GDP), Brown basically adopted the multiplier framework he had developed whilst on the Raisman Commission.[42] But this needed data and judgments.

The first challenge for Brown was the data. He initially gave a verbal account of his estimates in Salisbury on 28 July and then produced a written version. The former had raised problems because Brown had not fully understood the different accounting conventions in Salisbury and Zomba, and especially so regarding debt interest and repayment. The learning process, involving Henry Phillips from the Nyasaland Treasury, was a difficult one and both Brown and Hazlewood, who was also there, were somewhat bemused even after long discussions with the officials. Part of the problem, as Brown put it, was that "The federal and territorial finance officers clearly did not often talk to each other."[43] The issues that remained after these discussions did not, however, materially affect the general picture Brown presented in the written draft.

He had found that the initial impact of succession on Nyasaland's current account budget would be of the order of £3 million before taking account of the defense and diplomatic costs that would be incurred. Keeping the existing battalion of the King's Rifles would add at least £1 million to the cost. He factored in additional secondary costs on national income and taxable capacity, and the likely problems of maintaining the existing investment base. Hazlewood's presentation seems to have offered similar conclusions.

The Commission chair, at a meeting shortly after this, raised with Hastings Banda—the de facto Prime Minister of Nyasaland who, as early as 1953, had called the Federation "stupid"—questions regarding: the possibility with secession that Southern Rhodesia would discriminate against Nyasaland labor and goods; the impacts of loss of federal help in promoting tobacco sales; the difficulty of retaining doctors and nurses and of replacing the specialized medical facilities in Salisbury (Banda was the first black doctor to qualify in the country); and the problems of maintaining adequate air services and of running a national currency system. Brown's observation recalls Banda's oft-cited position that he would take

Nyasaland out of the Federation even if "we have to eat roots." But, as Brown said, "It's one way of disposing of economic difficulties, at least until you actually meet them."[44]

A second visit to the Federation began on 4 September and at once tried to reconcile the data issue with some help from another Phillips (this time E.M.), but at the Treasury in Salisbury this time. A revised paper was produced and circulated that included some introductory notes on changes in taxation that may have helped with Nyasaland's problems. While quite well accepted in Nyasaland, it was not so well liked by the Federation Treasury:

> Professor Brown's appreciation of the budgetary and economic situation in Nyasaland in the event of secession is careful and fair. Given the assumptions upon which he has based his appreciation, there are, in the Treasury's opinion, only a few points in his appraisal over which issue could be taken. The assumptions, however, are a different matter.[45]

Brown argued that some of the concern was really a misunderstanding of how scenarios were presented: they were regarding investment effects being taken as assumptions. Of more substance were concerns about the level of the assumed increase in tax revenues and of output, especially in agriculture, that would off-set subvention. There was also the criticism that Brown had ignored monetary and balance of payment difficulties that he had subsumed within production and foreign borrowing problems.[46]

Butler largely rejected the proposals in the report, and particularly the idea of a Commission to replace the Federation, because it would "shoot the Federation dead." As it transpired, the elections in both the Rhodesias in December 1962 were the death knells of the Federation; and, despite Butler visiting Africa early the following year, the break-up of the Federation was not smooth and there was no fallback position for the UK government to adopt.

Upon return to the UK, Brown had the expected meetings with Butler and the Central Africa Office, to discuss the final report that had been produced. It was also meant to have been sent to the Federation authorities and regional governments, but this does not seem to have been done. The Committee seems to have drafted separate sections, and Brown admits to having not read it in its entirety. Brown's own responsibilities lay in drafting two appendices: Appendix B on the economic effects of secession on Nyasaland, and Appendix K on the desirable ingredients of a future union between the territories. He added to this a section entitled "The Central African Marshall Plan" outlining ideas for conditional aid.

While the report of the Advisory Group was not published, David Scott (1981) provides some details in his autobiography, *Ambassador in Black and White: Thirty Years of Changing Africa.* Basically, the conclusions, that extend beyond the economic assessment were: that the secession of Nyasaland from the Federation was inevitable unless the UK government was willing to use a great deal of force; that Nyasaland's leaving would impact on Northern Rhodesia, leading it to leave; and that a conference should be called after the forthcoming Rhodesian elections to put forward the Group's proposals. As a transition mechanism it was suggested, along the lines Brown had set out in Appendix K, that a new, looser body be established to replace the federal government with the remit of carrying on functions that could not quickly be transferred to the territories.

The report contained Brown's third round of estimates of secession on the Nyasaland economy based upon both Nyasaland's responses to earlier rounds and the work of Hazlewood. The Nyasaland government had broadly accepted Brown's estimates of the impacts on a first secession budget of £5 million, basically Brown's first estimate with another million to account for the current annual deficit. The government was also optimistic about continued access to the Southern Rhodesian labor market and in its ability to get loans and grants to make up for investment now made by the Federation. Added to this it would raise revenues from taxes and fees over five years to bring the total to about 40 percent of GDP, amounting to a 95 percent rise assuming GDP grew by 35 percent over this time.

Brown's reaction to this is in Appendix B. Here he agreed that Africa's agriculture would improve; that foreign grants and loans were perhaps high but not out of line with what other African countries had enjoyed; and that the tax increases would bring the revenue–tax ratio up to that of Uganda and Tanganyika. The challenge would be the £15–20 million of budgetary aid needed for growth that would need to come from the UK in the first five years of secession.[47]

Regarding Appendix K, Brown drew heavily on his experiences in East Africa. He argued ideally it would be advantageous for the territories to have common markets in goods and labor, common public services, and a common currency. But, excepting the labor market, there were serious difficulties, not least of which is that such a structure of internal trade would favor more rapid growth in Southern Rhodesia and this would not be acceptable to the other members. Ways around this were discussed, including the Marshall Plan concept. The idea of this plan was that the UK would continue with support for the Central African Territories on condition they coordinated and integrated certain policies; the latter, it was suggested, could be drawn up with the assistance of a World Bank mission.

In his later memoirs, Rab Butler reflected both on the quality of the report and of the use that he made of it given the political situation of the time:

> Looking back, I feel I may not have paid enough tribute to this distinguished body of men. Roger Stevens was decidedly the best of the Foreign Office could provide, and Brown's lucid and imaginative plan for an African Common market was my constant study. Yet such constructive ideas were, alas, engulfed in the torrent of racial nationalism. Although I could not accept my advisors' advice, this is no reflection upon their idealism, industry or contribution. They performed an invaluable service in keeping the atmosphere hopeful in 1962. And although the more constructive hopes were disappointed, their report, particularly with its documentation notably on Nyasaland, was of greatest assistance when it came to arranging an orderly wind-up of the Federation. (Butler, 1971: 217)

Brown later reflected that despite the "kind words" the report basically was lost without trace, and that Roger Stevens was asked not to admit the report was "complete or submitted" because he wanted to "keep things fluid."[48] Brown wondered whether the strategy was a success given that Welensky knew the report had been submitted.

Perhaps of more relevance here than these largely political outcomes' terms are the accuracies of Brown's predictions. Following Nyasaland's (by then Malawi) independence in 1964, a year after the Federation was dissolved, the first year's budget deficit was £7 million in current prices, £2 million more than predicted. Allowance, however, must be made for high levels of inflation in the country between 1963 and 1965, and adjustment for that provides a deficit of £4.5 million in Nyasaland 1962 prices or £6.3 million in 1962 UK prices, the amount the UK paid. The aim of the Nyasaland government to raise tax revenues by 40 percent over five years was almost achieved, with revenue being 10.5 percent of GDP in 1965 and 14–15 percent in 1969–70. The GDP growth target failed to be met, but not by much. Taking triennia between 1953 to 1955 and 1961 to 1963, to allow for the inevitable fluctuations of a mainly agricultural economy, saw an average annual growth of about 3 percent that rose to about 6 percent in 1961–63 and 1969–71; not the 90 percent forecast but still of the order of 75 percent over five years.

Inflation and the taking over of federal functions led to government expenditure rising in money terms, although not by enough in Brown's view to maintain the real level of territorial and federal expenditure of 1962. Despite this the budget did not come into balance until the early 1970s. The UK met budget deficits amounting to £21 million in 1962 Nyasaland prices (£7 million in UK prices) between 1965 and 1972, a figure slightly above Brown's prediction of £15–20 million at 1962 prices over five years. This budgetary help facilitated Nyasaland to borrow £16 million between

1965 and 1969, half from the UK, which also gave a development grant of £3.5 million in 1965—a figure higher than the Federation had predicted.

Overall, because of the Keynesian multiplier effects Brown had estimated, real GDP did not fall despite the decline in public expenditure. Additionally, real fixed capital formation increased—as did aggregate real demand, real exports, and aggregate output. As Brown put it 26 years later, "In the end, neither the Malawi minister's optimism about their ability to borrow, nor my estimate of their budgetary problems, nor their, and Arthur Hazlewood's, plan for meeting it turned out to be too far off the mark."[49]

NOTES

1. Besides, Brown was also keen on participating for personal reasons: "It was an exciting invitation. Far as far back as I could remember, such things as I had read about East Africa, from the great nineteenth century explorers to 'Maneaters of Tesvo' and 'Snow on the Equator', had appealed very powerfully to my imagination." Brown, *East Africa, 1960* (May 1988, AJB C&P), p. 2.
2. *East Africa, 1960*, p. 3.
3. There were other studies conducted about that time of the community, or of its individual member states, of which a Rand study appearing slightly after the report of the Raisman Commission (Massell, 1963) was perhaps the most complete, and provides a succinct history of the Union.
4. While much earlier than Brown's time, Raisman had coincidentally also spent a short period as a student at Leeds University, having been born in the city.
5. *East Africa, 1960*.
6. *East Africa, 1960*, p. 22.
7. *East Africa, 1960*, p. 26. Sometime later, Brown heard from Conrad Lesser, the econometrics professor at Leeds University, that David Walker, who had been a colleague in Dublin, had told him it was one of the two best lectures he has ever attended.
8. As Brown admitted later, these divisions were essentially based on political expedience, and the maximum the Kenya government would consent to rather than any detailed scientific assessment, *East Africa, 1960*, p. 40.
9. The longer-term issue of backwash effects, and the possible movement of skilled labor moving from the slower to the faster growing countries, is also raised by Brown (1961b: 95). This he sees as an institutional matter of financing tying in with Raisman's idea of a Distribution Pool. The loss of labor is not the problem *per se*, but rather the loss of skills and experience, and this could be compensated for by a common pool of resources that can be drawn on and by the more advanced economies extending their services to the slower growing ones.
10. Brown, *Economic and Social Consequences of Disarmament*, mimeo, undated (AJB C&P), p. 1. (Note: after p. 13 of the mimeo Brown starts numbering at p. 1. Here, for simplicity, the numbers are run on after p. 13.)
11. Khan (1962: 177), a subsequent member of the UN Consultative group, provides the less objective view: "there is a lurking suspicion that very powerful vested interests, specifically in the wealthy countries of the West, are interested in maintaining armaments at a high level so as to ensure that their profits are sustained." Khan gives the fear of recession second place to the arms race.
12. The UK Foreign Office's response to this was implicitly that Brown should have asked about it before getting involved, as can be read into the FO's reaction: "The Secretariat

have asked us to let you know that Her Majesty's Government have no objection to your participation. Please be assured that we welcome it." *Economic and Social Consequences of Disarmament*, p. 3.

13. *Economic and Social Consequences of Disarmament*, p. 3.
14. Leontief (1944: 290) had effectively summed up the quantitative challenge confronting the Consultative Group much earlier, although in the context of a disarmament that would take place at the end of World War II: "How will the cessation of war purchases of places, guns, tanks, and ships—if not compensated by increased demand for other types of commodities—affect the national level of employment?"
15. Brown felt that he "showed a good background in economic training, and expressed himself in French of a majesty and sonority which made his contributions sound more important even when, as sometimes happened, the rest of us could not quite gather quite what they were." *Economic and Social Consequences of Disarmament*, p. 5.
16. *Economic and Social Consequences of Disarmament*, p. 4.
17. *Economic and Social Consequences of Disarmament*, p. 13.
18. To help widen accessibility to the findings of the Group, Brown produced a subsequent summary pamphlet produced for the United Nations Association almost immediately after the publication of the report (Brown, 1962b).
19. Brown had had prior contact with Benoit during a visit to *Economist Research* on 19 July 1960, and he turned out to be the husband of his former editor at Chatham House, Atta Fleming.
20. *Economic and Social Consequences of Disarmament*, p. 10.
21. *Economic and Social Consequences of Disarmament*, p. 14.
22. *Economic and Social Consequences of Disarmament*, p. 15.
23. Wire from HM Foreign Office to the UK Mission in Washington, 29 January 1961. This was circulated as document ST/SG/AC.3/R.18 to the Group. A copy is in Brown's papers.
24. *Economic and Social Consequences of Disarmament*, p. 23. Bryars had initially written to Brown a few days before the UK response was sent that it would be a paper "which will not be just a reproduction or adaptation" of his work.
25. *Economic and Social Consequences of Disarmament*, p. 12.
26. As the UN report points out, however, Stone's calculations were based on very rapid disarmament, and that, "If the operation were to extend over a number of years, the change per annum would be only a fraction of the total" (United Nations, 1962: 29).
27. *Economic and Social Consequences of Disarmament*, p. 16.
28. This had been drafted by Sidney Dell, a UN economist and a near contemporary of Brown at Oxford.
29. *Economic and Social Consequences of Disarmament*, p. 16.
30. *Economic and Social Consequences of Disarmament*, p. 24.
31. *Economic and Social Consequences of Disarmament*, p. 25.
32. Perroux was a French economist who had founded the Institut de Sciences Economiques Appliqués and who later worked on regional economic growth developing growth pole theories, ideas not unlike those Brown later became interested in (e.g. Brown, 1969d).
33. It was originally Appendix III of the paper Brown circulated to the Consultative Group, and the part that was completely omitted from the UK's *note verbale*.
34. *Economic and Social Consequences of Disarmament*, p. 16.
35. Brown, *Central Africa, 1962* (February 1988, AJB C&P). The subsequent presentation was Brown (1962a).
36. *Central Africa, 1962*, p. 2.
37. Brown, on initially being asked to take the call by the Home Office, later thought it was about "one of my colleagues had done something terrible (the same colleague who, two years later) got himself into gaol in Nigeria)" (*Central Africa, 1962*, p. 2).
38. *Central Africa, 1962*, p. 8.
39. Arthur Hazlewood, besides being like Brown an "Old Queen's man," became actively associated with the advisory group, and coordinated empirical work with Brown when it

was decided he would look after the interests of Malawi's elected ministers in Nyasaland (*Central Africa, 1962*, p. 15). Hazlewood was a Fellow of Pembroke College, Oxford at the time of his involvement.

40. Brown boned up on the subject a little by talking to another Old Bradfordian, Duncan Watson, then a chief ex-colonial official at the new Central African Office.

41. *Central Africa, 1962*, p. 16. Brown also remembers that "Kaldor, whose rather stormy career as a fiscal advisor had recently reached a climax in apparently provoking bloodshed in British Guinea, felt moved to deliver an apologia, which was unstoppable and consumed most of the allotted discussion time."

42. When he discussed his initial calculations in Salisbury with Henry McDowell, Federal Secretary to the Treasury and a contemporary of Brown's at Queen's College, Oxford the latter told Brown that as far the Keynesian calculations went, "you may not find anyone to take that up in Salisbury" (*Central Africa, 1962*, p. 21).

43. *Central Africa, 1962*, p. 22.

44. *Central Africa, 1962*, p. 24.

45. *Central Africa, 1962*, p. 24.

46. Part of the latter problem lay in the Treasury's thinking that Brown's multiplier analysis was to be taken up separately. Brown, on request, gave a copy of his equations to A.G. Irvine, McDowell's deputy—and who had just published a book on the Federation's balance of payments (Irvine, 1959)—who in turn not only read over them but also sent Brown back a model of his own.

47. Roy Welensky (letter to Butler, 22 October 1962) did feel "particularly anxious about Professor Brown's proposed budget for Nyasaland because it was believed to be an underestimate." The Federal Government later got a special version of Appendix B.

48. *Central Africa, 1962*, p. 49.

49. *Central Africa, 1962*, p. 52.

6. The "Phillips Curve" and inflation

INTRODUCTION

Arthur Brown was involved in one of the more challenging elements of immediate post-World War II economics: explaining the causes of inflation and providing an understanding of the information needed to design anti-inflation policies. The need for maximizing wartime production had pushed matters of inflation into the background and, mentally, the Great Depression had earlier suppressed it as a problem in society's collective memory. This is not to say that Keynes had not considered the problem, indeed he had advanced ideas for containing both wartime and post-war inflation. But inflation was not a core theme within the *General Theory* and much of his thinking on inflation during the war was largely context specific and disseminated through newspaper articles and internal, official memoranda.

As we have already seen, the period immediately after World War II saw considerable shifts in emphasis in the economics discipline. The traditional approach, with its focus on exposition and prose, was being transformed by the likes of Jan Tinbergen pushing forward for more explicit quantification; of Paul Samuelson (1947) bringing the language of mathematics to the core of the subject with the publication of more explicit quantification through both the publication of his PhD thesis, *Foundations of Economic Analysis*, and by his gradually increasing the analytical rigor of university syllabi through successive editions of his widely used textbooks. None of these changes were new in themselves—Stanley Jevons, Léon Walras, and others, for example, had been involved in encouraging more explicit formalization in the late 1800s; but the early 1950s saw a shift in the mainstream.

What was perhaps more important from an intellectual perspective was the gradual adoption of the Keynesian ideas that the national economy may constitute more than the aggregate of its microeconomies. This possibility had been around even before Ragnar Frisch came up with the distinct concept of macroeconomics in 1933, though strictly he used the term "macrodynamics." Keynes, however, as we saw earlier, offered a systematic framework in which to treat it. The Great Depression was a driving force, but Keynesian economics deploying new concepts such as the consumption function, marginal efficiency of investment, liquidity preference, and so on, provided formalization and the prospects for quantification.

As the study of the aggregate had gained ground, Keynesian economics, with its novel concepts, cried out for more formalization and quantification. The inflations suffered in many countries during the immediate post-World War II period, however, highlighted an area where Keynesian theory was proving deficient: namely understanding the forces that cause rises in aggregate price levels. To help tackle these types of problem, electronic calculators, and later mainframe computers, began to provide the necessary powers of estimation, econometrics the link between data and theory, and mathematics the tools for formal hypothesis setting. The political desire to have more control over national economies provided the stimulus for systematic data collection, and measures such as gross domestic product (GDP) emerged as the result of the work of Colin Clarke and Richard Stone at Cambridge and Simon Kuznets at the University of Pennsylvania. Institutionally, this led to a period of shifting "power" within the academy, with an overall rise in the perceived importance of economic research and education resulting in new research centers and departments being formed, existing ones being expanded, and some established ones losing influence.

But this took time, and in the 1950s, while there had been movement, the tools of analysis and the sets of data in use had only moved from the Stone to the Bronze Age. While it was true that electronic calculators, and computers were beginning to help in data handling and manipulation, econometrics in providing quantitative economics with a sounder statistical basis, and mathematics in ensuring more rigorous theoretical analysis, these were not the battery of sophisticated instruments we take for granted in the twenty-first century. As David Laidler (2002: 224) points out regarding dynamics and the work of Bill Phillips looked at later:

> [He] was . . . working on problems that required the estimation of continuous-time dynamic models in an era when the state of the econometrician's art extended only (and only just) to systems of simultaneous equations in discrete time, and when most empirical work even in leading U.S. universities was still carried out with electric-mechanical calculators.

Against this background, our broader interests here are several. One is in the transition process in economic methodology, and examining just how messy it was. It was neither a rapid change nor a very clean one, and certainly there was questioning of whether the speed at which some of the results thrown up was useful. To give context, the focus here is on the wage-rate change/unemployment relationship that was heavily discussed in the mid- to late-1950s and the approaches adopted to look at it by Brown and his contemporaries.

Second, individuals inevitably play a role in change. The ideas of having economic forces shape inflationary pressures engaged not just Brown, but many of the leading economists of the mid-twentieth century, but the publication in 1958 of Phillips's famed (and perhaps notorious) paper, and the subsequent moniker of the Phillips Curve (hereafter the "Curve"), unquestionably attracted the most attention. Here, beside looking at Brown's approach to matters of inflation, we focus on the extent to which Phillips's findings were interlaced with those of Brown's (1955) book *The Great Inflation, 1939–1951*, and consider whether the prequel in some respects offers a superior piece of analysis: see also Button (2018).

There are not many economic concepts that are named after individuals; the Phillips Curve is one. Whether, as Bernard Corry (2001) argues, the Curve is actually "Phillips's Curve," Phillips's general formulation of a measurable wage-rate change/unemployment relationship is still often found in textbooks, referenced in the media, and seen as a useful pedagogic device for public discussions.[1]

The question here is one of whether due credit has been given to Brown's work on inflation and unemployment. Both Anthony Thirlwall (1972), a student of Brown's in the late 1950s, and John Brothwell (1972: 57), a colleague, favored the "Brown Curve."[2] Away from Leeds (at what was then Queen Mary College, London), Corry (2001: 171), co-founder of the economics department at Queen Mary College, London University, posited, "a case can be made for referring to Brown-Phillips curves." Louis Dicks-Mireaux and Christopher Dow (1959) and Edwin Kuh (1967) also give Brown at least joint credit. In their seminal survey paper on inflation theory for the *American Economic Review*, for example, Martin Bronfenbrenner and Franklyn Holzman (1963: 631) argue that "Perhaps the most widely discussed and applied methodological innovation of inflation theory during the 1950's [*sic*] has been the Phillips curve, used originally by A.J. Brown and B. Hansen." There are few rewards in academia, but recognition is one, and Brown may well have not got his fair share.

One should note that there have been prior claims to the sorts of findings of Brown and Phillips.[3] The first relates to the claims of the editors of the *Journal of Political Economy* that empirical evidence of the inflation–unemployment relationship underlying the Curve is to be found in the work of Irving Fisher (1926), and indeed the paper was reprinted, with due American understatement, by the journal as "I discovered the Phillips Curve" (Fisher, 1973).[4] The second relates to claims by Amid-Hozour et al. (1971) that Paul Sultan's (1957) text, *Labor Economics*, contains a theoretically-based diagram that is in essence the Curve. As Corry, Robert Gordon (2011), and others have pointed out, however, neither of these works fits with the underlying argument of the Curve, and indeed they take inflation to be the causal variable.[5] Fisher, for example, explains this relationship over a relative short period (1915 to 1925) in terms of business receipts rising faster than expenses during the beginning of inflation, thus stimulating employment. Further, since Fisher sees this as a short-term effect it is suggestive of a vertical long-term curve of the Brown type. Sultan's book came out after Brown's, and so any claimed precedence must relate only to Fisher's work.

The concern here is not to dwell on claims made for prior developments of the Curve other than those of Brown; these are anyway largely dismissed in Forder (2014). Instead it is to position Brown's 1950s work on inflation more centrally in a world when the academic focus was more geographically concentrated than today, and when there were major changes in the methodology of economic analysis taking place. In the latter context, it also provides something of a contrast between two alternative approaches to the same issue, and raises some questions about the current focus on cardinal analysis, speed of publication, and the style of presentation. Brown may well have been unlucky in that his methods, expositional style, and medium of dissemination were moving out of fashion when he undertook his work on inflation perhaps resulting in it missing the headlines.

THE ECONOMIC BACKGROUND TO THE CURVE[6]

By historical standards, World War II and its immediate aftermath witnessed considerable inflation in many countries; Brown describes the inflation of 1939 to 1951 as "in any sense one of the greatest, if not the greatest, in the history of the world economy." One of the challenges he highlights in understanding its causes, and then ultimately to ensure there would be no repetition, "arose from the unsatisfactory and rapidly changing nature of the theoretical framework at [our] disposal" (1955: v). And he focuses on the embryonic nature of dynamic economic models of the time.

The problem at the time was very much one of too many ideas without the methodology to separate out the salient ones. One reason behind this vacuum was the focus put by Keynes and his followers during the Great Depression on comparative statics, whereas inflation is a dynamic phenomenon. Added to this was the problem that institutional economics was still considerably underdeveloped, focusing more on description and criticizing neo-classical analysis than bringing forth its own positive analysis; the latter had to wait for Oliver Williamson (2000) and others. In a nut-shell, economists lacked not only the element of Keynesian economics that provided anything but an elementary model explaining inflation, but also the data and institutional understanding to operate such a model. To follow Brown, this was a time "large enough for one of the rare master-pieces of broad economic interpretation, or for several lesser works with more modest pretension."

The economic and social problems associated with inflation in the 1940s and early 1950s were not unique to the UK. For example, Australia, Venezuela, New Zealand, South Africa, and Norway had experienced price rises of between 70 and 86 percent over that time; and even more extreme were the cases of Canada, Switzerland, Costa Rica, the United States, the UK itself, and Ireland, where inflation lay between 116 and 130 percent. As Brown highlights in his subsequent analysis, the latter group contained the two main trading countries of the time, and countries largely tied to them.

Following the publication of Keynes's *General Theory*, the view that demand conditions may lead to an equilibrium entailing high levels of unemployment led almost automatically to fears that the conditions of the pre-war Great Depression would return in peace time. But the Keynesian framework, and as depicted by John Hicks' (1937) Keynesian-cross diagram, was lacking in satisfactory explanation of how labor markets may link with inflation, or more generally how output linked with prices.

From a political perspective, employment and inflation were gradually gaining attention among UK politicians as World War II progressed. In 1941 James Meade, Brown's predecessor as lecturer at Hertford College, had proposed to the War Cabinet that a series of public works and social services would be necessary, together with greater labor market flexibility and a wages policy, to prevent inflation accelerating as unemployment was reduced. In 1942, the ex-director of the LSE, William Beveridge (1942), produced his *Report on Social Insurance and Allied Services*, which recommended the post-war establishment of a social security system embracing child allowances, unemployment benefits, and health services based on an assumption of 8.5 percent unemployment. Subsequently, Beveridge (1944a) wrote *Full Employment in a Free Society*, proposing an unemployment target of three percent, with Keynesian demand management targeted on employment. The Treasury, concerned about the cost of the scheme, countered with a compromise employment policy target with a long-term budget balance.

The 1946 Labour government, with the Chancellor—another ex-LSE economist, Hugh Dalton – following a more orthodox line, saw inflation not as a symptom of excess demand but as an inevitable consequence of full employment, to be moderated by price controls and production subsidies. But this all raised the joint question of "What should be the target level of unemployment, and the tools used to mitigate inflation?"

While this is not the place for an extensive history of efforts to close the circle on this matter, there are already several excellent accounts. It is worth noting that some of the leading economists of the time, notably Pigou (1945)—who explicitly wrote that trade unions "must choose between high rates of wages and lower rates of unemployment"—and Lerner (1951), made significant contributions to the inflation debate immediately prior to Brown's work.[7]

THE CAST

As discussed earlier, the academic world of the early 1950s was significantly different to that of today. Communications between economists was slower (generally conducted by mail or word of mouth), there were no photocopiers to mass produce papers, computing was in its infancy, and there was no cheap air travel. Intellectually, networks were necessarily smaller and tighter. World War II had seen the university system disrupted both for students and academics as the wartime demands for intellectual inputs expanded. Most individuals of student age were enlisted into some form of national service, as were the bulk of university buildings.

Also as we saw in Chapter 4, the post-war period with demobilization of tens of thousands of military personnel, saw a surge in demand for university places, which were partly met by expanding existing institutions but also by upgrading the status of former colleges.. Importantly, for Brown as we have noted, this offered him his opportunity to head the Department of Economics and Commerce at Leeds University, but it also afforded the opportunity for Phillips to remain at LSE after completing his PhD. But in addition, the situation led to a dispersion of many of the pre-war "teams" that had gathered together (particularly at Oxford, Cambridge, and LSE in England). New groupings formed, although the wider "college" of economists remained small and relatively well connected.

In broader terms, the general outcome of this was the formation of new academic networks but still within an established communications system. Nevertheless, without the "advantages" of email, texting, and blogs, ideas spread more slowly and audiences tended to be more focused given the challenges of joining an information network. Hence those involved in the wage-change/unemployment debates of the 1950s were few, largely geographically concentrated, and personally acquainted. In this environment, personalities and context were important in understanding how ideas were developed, and which ideas ultimately gained most traction in economic policy debates.

Bill Phillips

The characters, backgrounds, and circumstances of Brown and Phillips were significantly different. Bill Phillips was, by all contemporary accounts, something of a polymath but with few academic pretensions, Brown much more of a conventional scholar. They were indeed very different people, and perhaps this is summed up in two anecdotes:

> At meetings, having explained the economic theory, Brown would produce a small slide-rule that he carried in his top pocket and carry out rapid calculations to give some quantitative basis for argument. In his hands this simple tool kit could be devastatingly effective. (Bowers, 2003)

> Bill's office was near mine. He heard me and came to my office. He pulled out (much to my surprise) an electrician's screwdriver, opened the thermostat in my office and fixed my heating.[8]

In contrast to the almost mandarin-style progression of Brown's career, Bill Phillips (1914–75) was more a man of physical action—hence the greater need for a screwdriver rather than a slide-rule—with entrepreneurial tendencies, who arrived in the realm of academia relatively late in life.[9] Born and brought up in New Zealand, he became an apprentice electrician, and then spent time travelling around Australia before going to England in 1937, where he became a graduate of the Institution of Electrical Engineers (IEE). He signed up at LSE, where he took courses in local government administration, geography, and banking, but then war intervened.

His wartime service in the Royal Air Force Volunteer Reserve saw him made a Member of the Order of the British Empire (Military Division) for bravery and spending three years as a prisoner of war. With peace, he returned to LSE, where he just managed to obtain a degree in Sociology with Economics, but only after failing both the Applied Economics and Economic History examinations and passing Economic Principles by a single mark—apparently with a little help from Lionel Robbins, Dennis Robertson and Nicholas Kaldor, who saw considerable potential in him (Blyth 1975: 305; Sleeman, 2010).[10] The fact Meade (2000) considered Phillips a genius must also have helped.

In 1950, Phillips began with Walter Newlyn, who moved from LSE to Leeds University in 1948 to build a physical hydraulic Keynesian model of the national economy based around his work on economic dynamics (Phillips, 1950; Newlyn, 1950, 2000). This was MONIAC (the Monetary National Income Analogue Computer). The prototype was completed only three years after ENIAC (the Electronic Numerical Integrator and Computer), the world's first large-scale, general-purpose digital computer. Meade had him make a machine for LSE, and Abba Lerner, as his agent, got some sales in the US (Barr, 2000). Brown not only bought the prototype for Leeds University, he also provided the funds from the Economics Department's budget (£100 then, or £3,000 in 2016 prices) for the initial hardware costs, and loaned the prototype to LSE for marketing purposes.[11] Brown also occasionally met Phillips when he came to work on the Leeds machine (Brown, 2000, 2011). The "model" formed the basis for Phillips's PhD thesis, which was supervised by Meade and for which Dennis Robertson was the external assessor.

Phillips became an assistant lecturer at LSE in 1950, being promoted to Reader in 1954 and to the Tooke Professorship in 1958. His major contributions in the early 1950s, and a subject he frequently returned to, being on stabilization conditions (Phillips, 1954, 1957). The birth of the Phillips Curve, which Alan Sleeman (2011) describes as "a rushed job," was possibly stimulated by the need for *vitae* enhancement prior to seeking the Tooke Professorship.[12] But it also reflected an element of Phillips's main academic interests whilst at LSE, that of stabilization policy (Schwarzer, 2012). As Arthur Brown later reflected, "Bill's first love was certainly the conditions of stability of activity . . . In the 1950s there seemed to be hope that 'full' employment could be maintained if only the frequency to inflation that went with it could be controlled."[13] He goes on to add that Phillips was probably more concerned with unemployment than the price level when thinking about the Curve.

Following his 1958 publication, Phillips, save for Phillips 1959a, b, 1961, did little more on the Curve, and subsequently moved to a professorship in economics at the Australian National University (ANU), where he spent most of his time studying the Chinese economy. While Robert Leeson (2000: 10–11) offers several broad possibilities regarding why Phillips's interests changed, Kelvin Lancaster (1979: 634), focusing specifically on the Curve, argues that he became "increasingly aware of the difficulties of estimating the relationship [between wage changes and unemployment] he considered necessary for policy design and of the fact that the necessary techniques were beyond his grasp."

The Supporting Cast at Oxford and LSE

For any concept to gain support there is normally a set of influential people in the background providing sounding boards, as well as networks facilitating dissemination. In this case most of these had, at some point, Oxford or LSE connections in some way or another. While the London School of Economics and Political Science in the 1950s and 1960s was a powerhouse in economics, Leeds University was a "redbrick" institution steeped in the industrial needs of the textile industries of the region; indeed, it still attracts the highest level of industrial funding of any university in the UK. The Department of Economics and Commerce in the 1950s had little of the intellectual social science pedigree associated with the likes of Sidney Webb, Beatrice Webb, Graham Wallas, and George Bernard Shaw at LSE.

The economists at LSE when Phillips was developing the Curve represented one of the strongest groupings in the UK, and with an international academic network to match.[14] Many had close ties with Oxford, and had interacted with Arthur Brown since the 1930s. They included Robbins from 1925 until 1961; Meade from 1947 to 1957 (when he moved to Cambridge); Basil Yamey, who was editor of *Economica* when Phillips's paper was published; Richard Lipsey, who subsequently offered a critique of Phillips's work; and Ralph Turvey, who subsequently wrote a review of Brown's book. Richard Sayers, who had earlier taught with Brown at Oxford and offered a critique of Brown's work on liquidity preference, had been at LSE since 1947 as Cassel Professor of Economics, and later served on the Radcliffe Committee that looked at the working of the UK monetary system and to which Brown gave evidence.

Of considerable importance in the inflation debates there was Henry Phelps Brown, who had been working on similar topics to Phillips since the late 1940s and was an advocate of the cost-push theory of inflation. One output of Phelps Brown's work was a five-nation study of inflation covering much the same period as Brown's and Phillips's work and that provided a systematic set of data widely used in later studies by others, including Phillips (Phelps Brown and Hopkins, 1950). Indeed, he, together with Meade and Lipsey, is acknowledged in a footnote by Phillips (1958: 285) for their "index of hourly wage rates."[15] Phelps Brown was, as we have seen, very much steeped in the Oxford economics tradition developed by Roy Harrod (Besomi, 1998; Lee, 1991; Hancock and Isaac, 1998), as was Arthur Brown.

Phillips (1958: fn1) indicates that Phelps Brown read early drafts of his paper, although Phelps Brown (1996: 136) suggests he interacted little with other academics: "At the London School, though I was surrounded by experts, I did not engage in discussion with them, and worked in greater isolation than I had done even under the College system in Oxford." Another possible factor in the story of the Curve, and certainly if true (and it may well be apocryphal) not a trivial one, was Phelps Brown's supposed suggestion "one Friday" that Phillips could apply his data for wage rates and those of Beveridge for unemployment to explore the price–income relationship (Lipsey, 2000: 234–5).

There was also Frank W. Paish, the Sir Ernest Cassel Professor of Economics, who in the 1960s became an ardent supporter of an extreme interpretation of the Curve when arguing that a small amount of spare capacity, involving a level of unemployment, was needed to prevent inflation and increase capacity (Paish, 1962)—the so-called Paish theory of economic management. In a minority at LSE, Paish did not have an

Oxford background, but studied at Trinity College, Cambridge. Like Brown and Meade, he later became President of Section F of the British Association for the Advancement of Science.

Added to this was Abba Lerner, who—besides being Phillips's American marketing man for his "machine" (Nicholas Barr, 2000, 317–18)—was a graduate of LSE, interested in links between wages and prices, and, importantly for the subsequent transatlantic uptake of the Phillips Curve, well known to Samuelson, not least because of their works on factor price equalizations. Kelvin Lancaster, who subsequently wrote a short biography of Phillips, arrived at LSE as an assistant lecturer in 1953 and was a contemporary of Phillips while completing his PhD.

Brown's Support Group at Leeds

In contrast, Brown at the time was building up the Department of Economics and Commerce at Leeds; and, although it had Newlyn (but who was away for extended periods working on African matters) and Denis Sargan (who subsequently anticipated a Friedman (1977) style expectations-augmented Phillips curve; Sargen, 1964), they were at the beginning of their careers in the early 1950s. There was also Hermann Hillmann, an expert on the German economy—and who is explicitly acknowledged by Brown (1955: vii) in *The Great Inflation*—and John Brothwell, initially an industrial economist who subsequently became an expert on monetary studies, who joined the faculty in 1953 after graduating from Leeds.

THE GREAT INFLATION, 1939–1951

Brown became involved in the inflation–unemployment debate as part of the UK's Royal Institute of International Affairs initiative to explore more general issues of inflation. He already had extensive ties with Chatham House through his wartime work and that had involved, as we have seen, some basic examination of inflation issues. Brown had also published a more detailed piece in the *Yorkshire Bulletin* (1949a) looking at "inflation and the flight from cash." This was an examination of the causes of hyperinflation, focusing largely on case material from before the war; although to the modern reader the idea that Syria and Iran were stable economies may seem a little unexpected. It was also, by dint of its using velocity of circulation as its core transmissions mechanism, a subject not that distant from his D.Phil. thesis.

Broadly, he found that the "monetary behavior of mankind" was at the root of hyperinflation but admits that this, "like other aspects of its behavior, possesses certain regularities which are useful as tools of empirical analysis, even though they fail to inspire the confidence which one would require to make them bases of prediction" (Brown, 1949a: 41–2).[16] Indeed, his findings were extremely modest:

> In the first place, the increase or decrease in velocity in accordance with the previous rate of change in prices is seen to hold good in most countries, despite violent changes in velocity due to other causes . . . Generally, it seems to be true that the sensitiveness of velocity to price-change is less in hyperinflation than in countries not suffering from that extreme disorder. (p. 42)

Essentially, as he concludes from this work, we really have little idea of what causes the different patterns of behavior in inflation. With this perhaps at the back of his mind, and the fact he had earlier been interested in looking at the holding of different classes of money holder, he began the much larger study.

The intention of the Institute was that Brown should conduct a comprehensive study of the causes of inflation in the 1940s over two or three years. In fact, for practical reasons, the work took much longer. As Brown put it in his Introduction to *The Great Inflation* (1955: vii), "To the Royal Institute also I owe profound apology for the slowness with which the work proceeded, in competition with the rival claims of academic administration and teaching." The initial time frame of the analysis was also somewhat different to that initially envisaged, as can (with some simple arithmetic) be deduced from a letter he sent in late 1951 to Max Hartwell, who had just moved to New South Wales University of Technology after a period at Oxford:

> So far as my own was concerned I made some progress with "inflation," but not as much as I had hoped, though I am now, I think, at least very near the end. My lack of progress was largely due to the very large administrative burden that happens to come my way last year.[17]

Added to the burden of running a large and evolving department, Brown was also a very meticulous writer, and took inordinate care over his work before it formally saw the light of day; there were no "rushed" papers.[18]

Arthur Brown's Keynesian leanings were clearly reflected in his approach in *The Great Inflation*. He saw the work as focusing on "one of the greatest, if not the greatest [inflation], in the history of the World Economy" (Brown, 1955: iii); and, while much of the analysis relates to the UK, he sets this within an open economy in which producers enjoy levels of market power. In doing this his aim was to explain the underlying forces leading to inflation, on the premise that merely characterizing it as "a propensity of the community to spend more than its current income . . . does not throw much light upon the causes of inflation" (Brown, 1955: 16).

Brown set about his analysis in a world where many Keynesian economists were encumbered by a model that assumed an "inverse L-shaped" aggregate supply curve that assumed the economy worked significantly differently at full employment than at less than full employment.[19] In the former case, and following the Fisher quantity theory, output was fixed and any expansion to the economy was felt through monetary variables, and most notably prices. At less than full employment, prices were fixed in the economy and expansion effects were seen in changes to real variables. One could, one supposes, in terms of contemporary econometric modeling, say there would be two fixed effects, one for each situation. This is hardly helpful, however, in understanding things, or for developing economic policy.

Brown's main objective is that of quantification, not in a strict econometric sense but rather in terms offering support for a relationship between inflation and unemployment, and to provide empirical evidence of the general form that this takes.

He also saw a role for policy discussions, and not simply a retrospective assessment of what had gone before. Chapter 9 of Brown's book, for example, provides a critique of monetary policy as a cause of or cure for inflation, and provides both a foretaste of Brown's evidence to the Radcliffe Committee (Committee on the Working of the Monetary System, 1959b) and the conclusions of the Committee's subsequent report itself.[20] This influential analysis of the UK's post-World War II economy established the dominance of fiscal policy to steer the county's economy, and the basis for the essentially Keynesian foundation for economic thinking in the 1960s and early 1970s (Laidler, 1989).

The broad conclusion of *The Great Inflation* thus supports the Keynesian ideas of causality, in that business cycles are driven by fluctuations in effective demand: during periods of strong growth, an excess demand for labor increases the bargaining power of unions and reduces unemployment, leading to an increase in the rate of money wages growth; meanwhile when the expansion stops and unemployment begins to rise, the rate of growth in money wages declines. This relationship between wage changes and the unemployment rate, however, is non-linear with wage changes being larger when unemployment is low than when the unemployment rate is high. The implied curve is thus very flat at high unemployment rates, becoming much steeper, if not vertical, at low levels of unemployment.[21]

In terms of his approach and method of analysis, Brown was someone in the tradition of the applied economics of the 1930s through to the mid-1950s. He was far from innumerate, and his pre-World War II papers contain analysis using the econometrics of the time; but he was someone more interested in presenting the numbers and ideas rather than the symbols of abstract economic theory. As said in the Introduction (Brown, 1955: v), his objective was to explain the theory "not as a solid body of doctrine, but rather as separate introductions or frames of reference for each aspect of inflation which are discussed, the main objective of the discussion being to find how well the facts of experience fit the framework." As to the intended readership, this is explicitly stated on the flysheet to *The Great Inflation*: "No previous knowledge of economic theory is required by the reader. The theoretical ideas which are thought to be necessary to an understanding of the various matters dealt with are expounded in non-technical language as the need arises."

Thus, we find the early chapters setting out the theoretical thinking of the time and providing factual, historical, and international context for the subsequent critiquing of this, including detailed coverage of the effects of wartime expenditure on price levels. Chapter 4 is really the guts of the book, and the one that provides much of the basis for the claims that Brown's analysis was, at the very least, a prequel to the Curve. The remainder of the book is primarily focused on the 1939 to 1951 inflation, and, unlike Phillips, treats this as having little relationship to the pre-World War I situation.

Chapter 5 is important in that it considers the role of income distribution on inflationary processes, something that Brown comes back to in his later works on regional economics, and largely forms the basis of William Mitchell and Joan Muysken's (2008) observations about Brown's insights into what became known as the conflicting claims theory of inflation.[22] Basically, Brown considers the case that workers negotiate real wage targets via money wage demands on firms, who are themselves pursuing a target markup to achieve a desired rate of return. If the costs of price adjustment prevent prices adjusting in time, then the sum of the claims will exceed national income. Either or both parties may use their price-setting power to achieve their targets, but, in aggregate, inflation is the outcome of the conflict.[23]

The policy implications of his findings, and commentary of the way anti-inflationary policies have been deployed in the past, are found in Chapter 7. Given its focus on prices and wage controls, this part of the book (although seemingly sensible at the time), in retrospect, seems somewhat misplaced after the efforts of Presidents Richard Nixon, and later, Jimmy Carter in the US, and the actions of the Labour governments in the UK from 1960 to 1979, to apply forms of prices and incomes policies.

Other chapters highlight Brown's view that there are no discernible patterns to the various inflationary spirals found in different parts of the world, whether in their speed, duration, or cause. There are also chapters looking at hyperinflation (Chapter 8), with a specific emphasis on expectations, and the role that price control and subsidies can play in offering "insolation against temporary excesses of demand, internal or in the world market." In supporting the latter, he argues that 'a wage policy is [also] needed" (Brown 1955: 171). In this way, Brown's analysis extends the positive evaluation of the data he used to embrace partially normative, policy suggestions.

BILL PHILLIPS'S ADDITIONS

The period immediately after the publication of Brown's book saw two major public enquiries, both heavily influenced by LSE economists. The first was the Radcliffe Committee on the Workings of the Monetary System, established in 1957 but reporting two years later (Sayers was a member and Paish and Robbins testified); the second was the Cohen Council on Prices, Productivity and Incomes (with Robertson, and Phelps Brown involved). What this showed was that there was no consensus at LSE on the principal cause of UK inflation: demand-pull factors were supported by Frank Paish, cost-push factors by Phelps Brown, social factors by Robertson, and excess money supply by Robbins. The only thing they did agree on was that import prices had also been an important contributor in the post-war years. Despite this, and a paucity of in-depth empirical analysis, there was some agreement that unemployment of around two–three percent was needed to stabilize prices.

It was generally by both cost-push and demand-pull advocates that the behavior of the price level was largely driven by the behavior of wages (hence Brown's focus on changes in wage rates), while unemployment was seen as being a proxy for capacity utilization. Further, in the 1950s, the UK economy was often described as on a 'labor standard' whereby trades unions exerted a considerable influence on wages, and thus ultimately on prices. Brown's work put flesh on these relationships, but did not provide the degree of exactitude some had hoped for or that met the needs of the embryonic macro-models that were emerging.

The underlying question addressed is: What were the additions of value that Phillips made to Brown's analysis? In many ways, Phillips's paper follows Brown's Chapter 4. Both used similar data sets related to union-agreed wage rates—although Brown's time frame was 1881 to 1951 and Phillips's from 1861 to 1957—and to unemployment for their respective periods. The two key diagrams depicting their data plots and Phillips's subsequent curve are reproduced in Figure 6.1 directly from the originals.

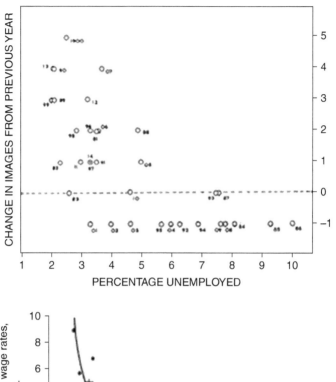

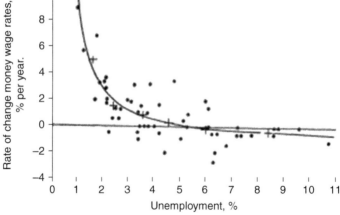

Note: The number of points plotted by Phillips is less than those he says were used; this possibly reflects either some coincidence of points or an error in the drafting that would have been done manually in 1958.

Sources: Brown (1955: Diagram 13, reproduced with the permission of Chatham House, the Royal Institute of International Affairs) and Phillips (1958: Figure 1, reproduced with permission of Wiley Global Permissions).

Figure 6.1   The pre-World War I Brown (upper) and Phillips (lower) wage-rate change unemployment data plots

While the *Framework* makes no effort to exact any hard relationship from Brown's data, Phillips, and possibly this is why the Curve gained the fame it has, did so with his (Lipsey, 1978). The Curve is fitted in a way that many may find rather awkward today in the age of ubiquitous computer power and econometric software.

The exercise saw the data divided into six unequal tranches according to unemployment levels roughly corresponding to trade cycles. The average unemployment rate was used for each tranche to capture the rise and fall in unemployment over each cycle; these are the crosses in the figure. A hyperbolic curve was fitted though the lower four crosses and close to the upper two.[24] He also looked at a number of trade cycles (in his Figures 2–8, not reproduced), each of about eight years' duration (1861–68, 1868–79, 1879–86, 1886–93, 1893–1904), and found supporting evidence in the general pattern for his Curve.[25] As to the scientific exactitude of this work, Phillips's drafting and estimations are in his collected archive at the University of Auckland's Economics Department. He plotted the data by hand in pencil on graph paper, probably using nothing much more than a flexible ruler and logarithmic tables. There was little examination of the data quality other than a recitation of various historical events that might have affected it, and no statistical tests were carried out on the estimated curve.

It was not just the estimation method that subsequently came into question, but also the data. Given the time frames, and particularly that prior to the 1920s, both the wage and the unemployment data inevitably embraced considerable synthesis of various time series, not to say inventiveness, in their construction (Nancy Wulwick, 1987). This was not the best of data. As Phillips pointed out, they covered only a small part of the labor force, and related to the standard (or "wages," in the terminology of the day) not the actual wage rates ("earnings")—the former often being negotiated to cover several years Brown (1955: 93) also points out that the bases of wage agreements changed after World War I, with sliding scales increasing in importance compared to the standards that had been the previous norm. Additionally, the data on wages was not for the same industrial set as for unemployment.

One also gets somewhat different results by taking Brown's data and deploying Phillips's methodology and unemployment groupings. The resultant six crosses do not have the appearance of a smooth downward-sloping function, but rather a rough-hewn inverted-J curve (Figure 6.2). As Guy Routh (1959: 299), who had been a pupil of Phelps Brown and had also tried to refute the Curve, says after conducting a similar but slightly different exercise, "different wage and unemployment series will yield significantly different results."

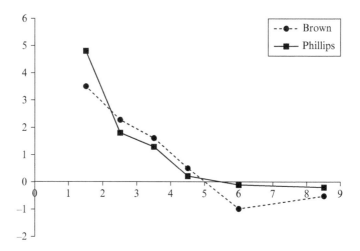

Figure 6.2   Phillips's Curve using his data and that of A.J. Brown

Both looked at changes in wages and unemployment levels in the pre-World War I period (Brown to 1914 and Phillips to 1913), and related these to various later periods. Further, they had essentially the same quest. For brevity I quote only Brown (1955: 90):

> The probability of a relationship of this kind [an inverse relation between wages/prices and unemployment] has . . . already played a considerable part in economic discussion . . . It seems, however, that empirical investigation has not hitherto been directed towards verifying the existence of such a relation, or to finding the level of unemployment beneath which the price-wage spiral seems to come strongly into operation in any one economy.

In Phillips's case, it may have also entailed the more practical matter of helping get a better supply model for MONIAC (Yamey, 2000: 338).

Where they differ is in their approaches to the data and in some of their conclusions. As summarized by Malcolm Sawyer (1989: 102):

> The approach of Brown can be contrasted to that of Phillips in three respects. First, Brown places the statistical relationship into a much fuller discussion of the process of inflation . . . Second, Brown did not attempt to draw any curve through his data . . . Third, Brown did not argue that the wage change-unemployment relationship observed for the pre-First World War period held thereafter.

Compared to Brown's detailed examination of the causes of inflation, Phillips provides very limited explanation of what he finds.[26] While in the

"Hypothesis" opening section to his paper there is a rather broad discussion of the forces that may underlie rates of change in the UK's money wages, this is never really integrated into the statistical analysis, and there is limited discussion of the underlying rationale of his findings. James Tobin (1972: 9) later commented on the Curve that it was "an empirical finding in search of a theory," while Worswick (1979: 37)—who was at Oxford in the 1950s and subsequently director of the National Institute of Economic and Social Research—described Phillips's analysis as "stark."[27] James Forder (2010: 331) perhaps sums things up best: "The significance of Phillips finding is that it amounts to a claim that the relation is independent of any of the extensive institutional or political changes that took place over the period."

Brown, in contrast, offers a more complete and integrated explanation for his findings, fitting them within an institutional and industrial organization framework, as well as a Keynesian explanation.[28] His basic view is that:

> though it may be possible to give a generally valid formal description of what constitutes inflation, the causal mechanisms by which it happens are various and their roots may go deep into the market institutions and the social and political structures of the communities concerned. For this reason it is not profitable to approach the events of the inflationary-period treated in this book with a single theoretical scheme into which they must be fitted. (Brown, 1955: 17)

Put simply, he sees no curve.

Given that data used by Brown and Phillips are remarkably similar, why did Phillips then see a consistent relationship between wage-rate changes and unemployment? First, Brown felt that any historical relationships prior to 1939 were not overly useful in explaining inflation between 1939 and 1951 (p. 90), the subject of *The Great Inflation*, given the scale of the military conflict from 1939 and its aftermath. Then there is the matter of the challenge of fitting the Curve.

As Meghnad Desai (1975) points out, the fitting of the "relationship" would not be deemed very satisfactory even allowing for the state of econometrics and the computing facilities available in the late 1950s.[29] Phillips's procedure did not allow for any genuine significance testing, and extrapolation into future periods saw deviations from the Curve explained in ad hoc terms. Wulwick (1989) did elicit from one of the "anonymous" referees of Phillips's papers that the R^2 for the four-point regression was 0.96, but this is not the same thing as the fit to the full data set. The breaking down of the data by trade cycles was a common practice at the time to handle computation challenges and to cope with serial correlation, but tests for the latter are not reported despite work at LSE on the subject by

James Durbin (one of Phillips' PhD supervisors) and Geoffrey Watson (1950, 1951).

Subsequent fittings using more modern regression methods by Lipsey (1960b); Leeson, 1994b, who was appalled at the scientific approach of Phillips and tried to refute it, found that 64 percent of the variation in the wage growth was explained by variations in unemployment. Further, Lipsey found that fitting a curve to data for 1862–1913, as Phillips did, provides a somewhat different picture to that using 1923–39 and 1948–57 data—the latter being above the earlier period for unemployment rates under three percent, and below it for unemployment rates above three percent.

The methodology favored by Phillips also provided neither short- nor long-term equilibriums but rather, as Desai (1975: 2) puts it, "a locus of long-run equilibrium points for U and $\dot{W}$ thus making the common distinction between short-run and a long-run 'Phillips curve' unnecessary and erroneous." Brown, in contrast, sought to look for explanations of a temporal relationship between unemployment and wage-rate changes, because he was interested as much in the dispersion of results over time periods as in any sets of long-term equilibriums. It is in this context that Brown probably did not see the Phillips approach as useful.

But the reason Brown did not, at least in print, attempt to fit a relationship seems to have had more to do with the data than the lack of computing power or any personal inadequacies in terms of econometrics skills. He simply did not feel the quality of the data justified any efforts at detailed curve fitting. His approach to the pre-World War I data, besides reporting it, was to look for time series effects, and for differences in business cycles.

> One is tempted . . . to look at the year-to-year changes in wage rates that have occurred in the past along with the levels of unemployment prevailing at the time. In the United Kingdom, between 1880 and 1914, the index of wage rates was strongly influenced by certain industries—most notably coal mining—in which (especially for the early part of the period) wages were related to the price of the product. This clearly reduces the probability that experience over these years will throw light on the present problem, but a glance at the data is, nevertheless, not entirely unwarranted. (Brown, 1955: 90)

In doing this, he did find some consistency regarding the booms breaking in 1890, 1900, 1907, and 1913: "money wages usually continued to decline at a fairly-steady rate of about one percent per annum until the onset of recovery, to the accompaniment of a steady increase of unemployment. During the upswing, the *rate* of increase of wages rose steadily as unemployment fell" (Brown, 1955: 90).

What may have made Brown's approach appear more rigorous in the mid-1950s is if he had applied regression analysis to the data incorporating dummy variables, basically fixed effects in modern econometrics parlance, to isolate cycles. Dummy variables, however, did not enter applied economics until after the publication of Daniel Suits's (1957) paper. They would have been available to Phillips as a device to isolate cycles around the Curve, but he did not use them. Even though dichotomous variables only differentiate changes in slope coefficients, without providing intellectual rationale for the changes, they would have allowed Brown to confirm and provide quantification of the magnitude of the shift in wage-change/unemployment functions.

Brown also provides an explanation of the quite dramatic changes after turning points—c.g. especially after the booms of 1900 and 1907 when the rate of wage change became negative the following year. He introduces the importance of expectations that is largely absent from Phillips's paper, most notably in terms of its asymmetric implications for the wage-change/unemployment relationship in the upward and downward phases of a cycle. In addition, he highlights the "floor" of wage changes that is observed in the pre-World War I period, although this is less pronounced in Phillips's data. Brown argues (1955: 92): "In a society in which labour is organized with any considerable degree of effectiveness, there is probably an absolute limit to the rate at which wage rates can be reduced—unless something remarkable is happening at the same time to the cost of living." He does not, though, provide an explanation of what determines the critical level of a "considerable degree of effectiveness."

In sum, Brown did not consider it worth expending much energy on the pre-World War I period as a guide to the timeframe he was focusing on. Relationships essentially change with circumstances. In a way, Phillips also accepted this when he argues that the Curve breaks down on occasions, and most notably at times of major wars and "in or immediately after those years in which there is a sufficiently rapid rise in import prices to off-set the tendency for increasing productivity to reduce the costs of living" (1958: 298).[30] This, however, he treats as irrelevant for a full analysis.

In terms of the later periods, again while Brown is content to just plot points, Phillips joins them and highlights the way they seem to fit the Curve. It is quite clear that the Curve breaks down between 1919 and 1923—a period Brown (1955: 93) describes as "quite unlike any experienced at other times." While both agree that the pattern in 1919 to 1920 was due to cost of living rises, the fall in wages after 1920 were, following Brown, because "By the time the slump came, sliding scales had become so popular that more than half of the recorded changes in wages in the years 1921–2 were made automatically in accordance with them" and one that Phillips (1958: 293) largely attributes to "a fall of 12.8 percent in the cost of living, largely a result of falling import prices."

For the subsequent period, Brown's findings reflect a broad Phillips Curve, but only up to a point:

> From 1924 until 1939 the relation between unemployment and rate of wage change was similar to that revealed in the cyclical movements of the generation before 1914; except that the level of unemployment throughout (as far as one can judge by comparing the post-war Unemployment Insurance statistics with the pre-war trade union records) was much higher. (1955: 93)

Considering temporal patterns, this would imply that there had been a shift in the Curve, which Brown partly attributed to the weakening of trade union power after 1926, but mainly due to structural changes in the United Kingdom economy, whereas Phillips saw a strict adherence to the Curve despite the gyrations about it.[31] Brown's position is clear, and relates both to changes in the types of industry and to their geographical concentration:

> It seems likely that at least half the unemployment existing in 1937, for instance, was of a structural character, and if that is so, one may say that, had there been no more structural unemployment than before 1914, the critical level of unemployment in the later nineteen-thirties would have been less than it actually was by something like 4 percent of the insured population. (1955: 95)

Brown also informally introduced the concept of the famed "loops," his spirals, essentially, as found later, associated with hysteresis in the labor market to account for this. Although he did not draw them, or at least offers no visuals in his book, he does talk of "roughly parallelogram-shaped cycles." More specifically: "The movement of both the variables were almost entirely of a cyclical nature, and the relation between them in their cyclical movement was fairly constant" (Brown, 1955: 90).

There was some difference in Brown and Phillips's interpretation of these loops, a fact the latter puts down to Brown not fully appreciating short-term lags in the system. Phillips, for example, finds that by introducing a lag of seven months into his analysis, the data for 1948 to 1957 fit well with the Curve (his Figure 11). He gives no explanation for the length of the lag; it simply seems to force the data onto the Curve. He does, however, discuss changes in the nature of wage agreements and bargaining, but in terms of the narrowing of his loops: "these agreements may have strengthened the relation between changes in wages rates and changes in unemployment in these industries [coal and steel]" (Phillips, 1958: 292). In contrast, Brown (1955: 93) emphasizes the importance of sliding pay scales, albeit in terms of shifting the wage-rate change/unemployment function.

Brown also observed that from 1939 to 1951, "In many of the countries most dependent upon international trade . . . the degrees of inflation experienced were not very different, though the stresses from which in the first place inflation arose—notably the stresses of war—bore very diversely upon them" (1955: 251). Phillips (1958: 296–7) focuses on the United Kingdom, which a critic could argue can offer little by way of a universal model, and just injects the idea that some of his spirals are influenced by import prices.

Brown's view that there had been a long-term shift in the wage-rate change/unemployment relationship after World War I was not subsequently changed by the publication of Phillips's paper:

> [T]he evidence is that the existence of unemployment alone, not accompanied by steady or falling costs of living, is not a very powerful reducer of wage-demands—or even of wage increases—in most modern economies. A generation or two ago when labour was less organized in most countries than it is now, and wages depended more upon competition between employers, it was somewhat more effective, but it seems that we must now reckon on rather a high rate of unemployment being required to produce a moderate reduction in the rate of wage-increase. (Brown, 1959a; 77–8)

Where Brown and Phillips do agree, however, is regarding the poor relationship between wage-rate changes and price inflation, or at least in the short run. This is clearly seen in Brown's Figure 17 (where he does join observations) and discussed in his accompanying text, although later Gordon mistakenly gives precedence to Phillips: "Phillips surprisingly debunks a third possible correlation, that between the rate of change of wages and the retail inflation rate ('working through cost of living adjustments . . .')." Equally, Gordon's statement—"Phillips was already thinking of a world in which demand shocks . . . and supply shocks . . . both mattered in determining wages and price changes"—seems to forget Brown's position (Gordon, 2011: 12).

What has attracted most of the policy debate concerning the Curve, but only scratched upon here—although Forder (2014) does a thorough job—is whether the Phillips's curve offered a menu of policy options involving trade-offs between inflation and unemployment. As we see below, Brown's essentially cost-push findings move more in the direction of the use of prices and incomes policies, which he looks at in some length in his book (Chapter 7). The debate over whether the Phillips Curve is "Phillips's Curve" is academically interesting and, dependent on the interpretation, has policy implications; but it really is a little beside the point when looking at the respective works of Brown and Phillips. The fundamental issue centers on whether the underlying causes of inflation are demand or cost pressures.

A.J. BROWN AND INFLATION POLICY

Unlike Phillips, who rapidly moved away from the wage-rate/unemploy-ment debate, Brown both returned to the subject on several occasions and, often, in a policy context. Brown's interest in the policy side of inflation had initially been stirred during World War II, and he had contributed several papers to the *Bulletin of International News* on the subject, most notably on wages and price control. His view on the subject then was, "the understanding of what [inflation] is (still less of how it is caused and how it can be avoided or remedied) has become as widespread as the fear of it" (Brown, 1945a: 11). But equally, and stemming from his extensive analysis in *The Great Inflation*, he still conceded a quarter of a century later, when reviewing John Dunlop's edited volume *The Theory of Wage Determination*, that, "The theory of wage determination is clearly one of the least satisfactory portions of economic theory, perhaps because it is less exclusively economic than many others, and as is only proper the contributions to this volume attack the problem from a number of widely different angles" (Brown, 1960: 78). This implies that while money supply may matter, as quantity theorists of the time argued, inflation policy should be looked at in a multifaceted and probably interdisciplinary way.[32]

Following the publication of *The Great Inflation*, Brown moved to explain its policy implications. He spoke on the BBC (Brown, 1956), gave evidence to government commissions (Brown, 1959b, c), and took oppor-tunities in his presidential addresses to section F of the British Academy and the Royal Economic Society (Brown, 1958, 1979) to reflect on infla-tion.[33] He also extended his analysis in his more academic writings.

In terms of defending his analysis against Phillips's work, Brown raises questions about the quality of the data used in their analyses of pre-World War II periods, pointing particularly to the revisions of unemployment data by Angus Maddison (1964: 221): "For 1950–1960 we have raised the registration figures [which Phillips used] by [one percentage point] because they do not cover all categories of unemployment, and the discrepancy from the 1951 census was of this size" (Brown, 1997b: 55). As Brown points out, this would imply that subsequent use of Phillips's calculations during what he calls the "Keynesian Golden Age" of the 1960s in the UK would have suggested that higher unemployment would have meant less wage inflation. The implication of this for Brown is that "it suggests a tendency towards local instability in the relevant part of the Phillips curve; that when unemployment is pushed down to some level at which recruitment difficul-ties are perceived or expected, the remaining available labour (or most of it) will be very quickly taken up for precautionary reasons" (p. 55).

Brown's later empirical work involving Jane Darby (1985), which is dealt with in more detail in Chapter 9, covered a range of developed and developing economies, and confirmed his view that any degree of wage inflation involves more than just demand factors and, in Friedman's sense, expectations (Friedman, 1968). Explicitly in terms of the Curve, the authors emphasize the ordinal nature of their findings (p. 381): "The simple Phillips relation between the tightness of the market and the *rate of change* of hourly earnings remains as a persistent, though not universal, constituent of wage equation." And, regarding the larger matter of inflation (p. 382), "Institutional and political changes contribute heavily to the complicated story of wage push."

While Phillips, excepting of his inaugural lecture at LSE (Phillips, 1962), eschewed any detailed discussion of policy—although subsequent adherents and antagonists of the Curve generally have not been so reticent—Brown, does venture into this, and particularly supports cost controls. His 1955 book contains a chapter on "Price Control" that reviews its prior applications and concludes: "in addition to price control and subsidies as measures of insulation against temporary excesses in demand, internal or in the world market, a wage policy is needed." The theme is returned to in a more popular way in a speech on BBC radio (Brown, 1956), when he argues for more public discussion and planning of "the proper absolute and relative sizes of wages, salaries, and profits" to prevent inflation. Later, his Presidential Address to the Royal Economic Society pushes the point further: "if I am right in believing that cost-push, and particularly wage- and salary push, plays a central part in reducing industrial profitability and competitiveness then it follows that incomes policy is bound to be helpful in breaking the vicious circle" (Brown, 1979: 11).

In one important sense, despite the widespread uptake of the term Phillips Curve, Brown's work may have been more influential, at least in the short term. Phillips's paper was timely in that the Committee on the Working of the Monetary System (1959b), especially since his LSE colleague Richard Sayers was a member, which cemented the notion of Keynesian and fiscal policy into the fabric of UK's macroeconomic policy, was conducting its enquiry at the time of its publication. But Phillips did not give evidence to the Committee, whereas Brown in 1958 gave both written and oral testimony. Brown, drawing on his book, spends time discussing monetary transmissions mechanisms:

> [I]t does not follow that a restriction of money supply is an efficient method of stopping inflation. If the latter is caused by a tendency of wages and salaries to rise through the collective bargaining process even in circumstances, which would not otherwise raise prices, then monetary restriction may be . . . an inefficient instrument for checking it. It is inefficient in the sense that it succeeds only at a high cost both in unemployment of labour and equipment and in delay in application of technical improvement. (Brown, 1959b: 50)

But, also reflecting on the wage-rate change/unemployment relationship in the later years of the interwar period:

> The wage changes between the wars are odd in all sorts of ways. For one thing they are negatively correlated with the growth of industry; that is very strange and seems to me to suggest that they have more to do with bargaining power, union activity and so on, than with the level of effective demand for labor in a particular industry. This seems to me to be rather symptomatic on the whole for the changes that have happened since about 1914. (Brown, 1959c: 593)

Clearly this is not a view consistent with Phillips's findings, and the policy implications are more in line with the concept of a "social contract" brought in by James Callaghan's UK government in the 1970s.

The academic up-take of the Curve foreseen by Brown was also seen in the US. Indeed, the term "Phillips Curve" was first coined there by Routh (1959), but really gained recognition in December 1959 when Samuelson and Robert Solow (1960) discussed it during a presentation to the American Economic Association (AEA).[34]

Samuelson and Solow, however, made no mention of Brown's work, despite the fact that his book contains a discussion, as well as a figure (his Diagram 15) virtually identical to their own Figure 1, and also uses hourly earnings data. These are reproduced as originally published as Figure 6.3. In fact, they seem to be unaware of it—"Strangely enough, no comparably careful study [as Phillips's] has been made for the U.S." (Samuelson and Solow, 1960: 187)—despite Brown's work being reviewed in the major US academic journals.[35] Leeson (1997) also mentions that he finds notes in Phillips's papers that also contain calculations locating a Curve for the US, and especially seeking the level of prices, and presents estimates of this (Phillips, 1962). This was of course well after *The Great Inflation* was published, and, in any case, they were not made public.

Regarding the overall picture, there are also strong similarities between Brown and Samuelson and Solow. The former (1955: 95, fn. 1) finds that, "It is . . . evident that the inter-war in the United States did not follow the same course as any of those in between 1880 and 1939." Brown also isolates a shift in the US wage-rate change/unemployment relationship between 1921 to 1932 and 1935 to 1941, with Samuelson and Solow (some five years later) noting a similar shift, albeit with 1933 to 1941 as the second period. Brown (1955: 96) attributes the change to "the New Deal, which greatly strengthened the power of United States labor, both by promoting its organization and by the introduction of relief and unemployment insurance." Meanwhile Samuelson and Solow (1960: 187–8) argue that: "One may attribute this to the workings of the New Deal . . . or alternatively one could argue that by 1933 much of the unemployment had

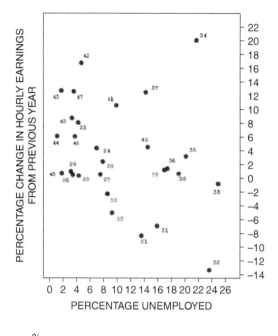

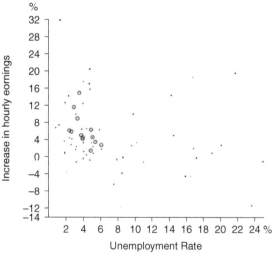

Sources: Brown (1955: Diagram 15, reproduced with the permission of Chatham House, the Royal Institute of International Affairs) and Samuelson and Solow (1960: Figure 1, reproduced with the permission of the American Economics Association).

Figure 6.3   US unemployment and annual change in hourly earnings; upper, Brown (1921 to 1948) and lower, Samuelson and Solow

become structural, insulated from the functioning of the labor market."
These latter arguments also have a remarkable similarity to Brown's rationale cited earlier for shifts in the post-World War I UK's wage-rate change/
unemployment relationship.

SO WHY NOT THE "BROWN-PHILLIPS" CURVE?

It is not unusual in economics to give dual attribution to advances that
help move debates forward when elements emerge sequentially or indepen-
dently. For example, there is in international trade the Hicks-Hansen synthesis for equilibrium in the closed macro-economy, and the Swann-Solow
and Harrod-Domar models of economic growth, or even the Newlyn-
Phillips machine.

In our context, this raises the question of why we have the Phillips Curve
and not, as Corry favored, the Brown-Phillips Curve.[36] It was not as if
there was an ocean between them: the works of Brown and Phillips were
known to each other, and of importance in the chronology of events; and
Phillips knew of Brown's book—indeed, Sayers (Phillips's colleague at
LSE) read over Brown's manuscript (Brown, 1955: vii).

There were also direct discussions between Brown and Phillips on the
Curve. Brown (2000: xii–xiv), reflects:

> I cannot claim to have known Phillips as well as his LSE colleagues for instance
> do, but our acquaintance, which was connected with the hydraulic model and,
> more fleeting, with the curve, made a deep impression on me . . . Before the pub-
> lication of his famous article which launched the curve, knowing of my earlier
> work on the same subject he invited me to discuss with him the results recorded
> therein. I think our discussion turned on the difference made by our having used
> slightly different time lags in our respective plotting of largely similar data.

In a set of comments by Phillips is a similar report of the meeting:

> [It] was a rush job, I had to go off on sabbatical leave to Melbourne; but in that
> case it was better for understanding to do it simply and not wait too long. A.J.
> Brown had almost got these results earlier, but failed to allow for the time lags.
> (Bergstrom et al., 1978: xvi)[37]

This latter statement, emphasizing the need for speed as a justification
for not even acknowledging Brown's work, seems rather strange given the
time frame involved.[38] But what is perhaps reflective of Brown's personality, and that he never seriously sought to claim precedence, is that he
clearly held Phillips in high regard, to the extent of having a photograph of

him and MONIAC hanging by his fireplace in his home (William Brown, 2011: 33).

So why did Phillips's paper attract the attention rather than Brown's work? The latter was certainly not unknown. As well as being discussed for a semester in 1956 at Robbins' LSE seminar (which was jointly organized with Phillips), *The Great Inflation* was reviewed by the LSE economists Ralph Turvey (1955) in *Economica* and Harry Johnson (1956) in the *Economic Journal*. It was also reviewed by Phillip Cagan (1955) in the *Journal of Political Economy*; John Gurley (1956) in the *American Economic Review*; Victor Morgan (1955) in the *Economic History Review*; Bronfenbrenner (1955) in the *Journal of Economic History*; and Edward Safarian (1957) in the *Canadian Journal of Economics and Political Science*. This fact of the diversity of the review venues is perhaps, however, indicative of the book falling between two stools in terms of the academic perception of its ethos.

Brown's work on wage-rate changes and unemployment was also part of a very much larger, international study of inflation, and thus his historical analysis stood out much less than Phillips's stand-alone, terse, and pointed article. Brown's writing was measured, and the work "evolved" with considerable feedback, rather than "appearing." Although the h-index and the like were well in the future, academic papers in journals were taking over from monographs; articles could be published more rapidly, and speed was certainly a feature of the publication of Phillips's 1958 paper. It should also be noted that many journals were institution based, and often a little parochial in their approach to content. Regarding Phillips's paper:

> I do not recall whether Bill gave me a copy of his paper for editorial considera-
> tion. I think I was given a copy by Lionel Robbins or James Meade. Anyway,
> before the day was over the paper had been enthusiastically recommended to
> me by several of the editorial board. I shared this enthusiasm after I had read
> the paper, and within a day of receiving it accepted the paper for publication
> in *Economica*—a speed of decision impossible for any refereed journal today.
> Yamey (2000: 336)[39]

The work of Brown was also probably too deeply grounded in the institutional literature (or too "descriptive," to use Meade's term regarding Brown's wider approach to economics) to be acceptable for the more technical orientation of textbook writers from the mid-1950s. Indeed, as mentioned earlier, the cover of *The Great Inflation* says that "No previous knowledge of economic theory is required by the reader ... It is hoped will give the general reader some insight into the way in which economist set about the analysis of current events." In fact, reviewers of the book specifically commented on its readability. For example, according to Bronfenbrenner (1955: 304–5), "Mr Brown has the gift, less rare among British than American economists, of disguising difficult and controversial propositions of economics as matters that any schoolboy can understand and all men of good will can accept"; meanwhile Gurley (1956: 190) says: "Brown writes exceptionally well." His later textbook, *Introduction to the World Economy* (Brown, 1959a), was written in a similar vein and manifestly diverges from the tomes of Samuelson and Lipsey that were then emerging. Clarity, however, is often not the best way to entrap readers.

The initial reception of Brown's book also offers some indication of the thought processes regarding its key themes. Turvey (1955: 261) found "The three chapters on the wage price spiral are excellent, Particles of fact, theory, and commonsense combined in Brownsian movement." Likewise, Morgan (1955: 254) talks of "the task of handling so much material would have daunted most writers, but Professor Brown does it with consummate skill and the result is a remarkably interesting and useful book." Indeed, the reviews in general were highly favorable, with critiques offering alternative perspectives; but certainly the book was taken very seriously. It was definitely not taken to be as trivial. So it cleared the academic review fence.

Timing is another factor in the adoption of ideas, be they sound or not. The mid-1950s was a time when wartime recovery was almost complete and, as Worswick (1979: 28) puts it, "*The Great Inflation* . . . was published . . . just at the time when it seemed the unemployment problem had been solved." By the later 1950s however, inflation was becoming an issue again and the Curve offered a way of looking at economic trade-offs, irrespective of Phillips's intent, for long-term policy formulation.

BROWN'S REFLECTIONS

Brown's view on the debates over the usefulness of the Phillips Curve, and that of his own analysis, can only be surmised; but his son, William Brown (himself a former chair of the Faculty of Economics and Politics and Master of Darwin College, Cambridge), commented in personal correspondence that he felt his father "Would he have liked it to have been called the Brown-Phillips relationship? Well, he would have liked the recognition; I have little doubt about that. But to be associated with all the subsequent over-simplified policy prescription, not at all." Elsewhere, in a draft in A.J. Brown's papers, his son says on the subject: "Dad never regretted that it was not his name that stuck to the 'Phillips Curve' which, by the 1980s, was to become a notorious economic relationship."

This was partly because he was a genuinely modest man, mistrustful of the simplifications associated with publicity. It was also partly because he never believed that the relationship he had unearthed should be a crude guide to economic policy. He was appalled at the propensity of later governments to throw people out of work as the easiest way of reducing inflation.[40] Equally, Brown did not feel that the way the Curve was adopted by many was Phillips's fault: "I agree that [Phillips] cannot be blamed for the excessively literal meaning attached by others (like Frank Paish) to his curve as a 'trade-off' indicator. But in the atmosphere of the time that sort of reaction to his work was inevitable" (Brown cited in correspondence; Leeson, 1997).

Brown was also not unaware of the influence of the visual in getting ideas across. Returning to a subject touched upon earlier in Chapter 3, in a commentary on the role of Roy Harrod's (1937a) "Mr. Keynes and traditional theory" in developing the IS-LM synthesis in parallel or, as Brown argued, in advance of Hicks (1937), Brown observed:

> I'd seen the Harrod equations and no doubt other people in Oxford had seen the Harrod equations some time before they were seen in the Hicks paper . . . It was clear to those who had a preview of Harrod that the equations used as a starting point were old friends . . . It's not Hicks-Hansen but Harrod-Hicks IS-LM . . . Hicks was a mathematician and this is what made the difference really, I think . . . He [Hicks] has the IS curve and the LM curve and the solution of the system, but Harrod did it in words. Having a picture is very important, since a picture is worth a thousand words. Hicks did a Marshall. The human mind is very receptive once it's got past its first year in university, it's very receptive of the idea of two curves intersecting. Anything more complicated is much harder to take in, and he got it down to two curves, that's why Hicks hogged the attention. (Brown, interview in Young, 1987: 89)[41]

In the case of the wage-rate change/unemployment relationship, Phillips got it down to one curve, and that is even easier for those who "got past [their] first year in university" to assimilate.

Mark Twain (1933) famously said: "It takes a thousand men to invent a telegraph, or a steam engine, or a phonograph, or a telephone, or any other important thing – and the last man gets the credit and we forget the others. He added his little mite – that is all he did." But in the case of the Curve, Arthur Brown's contribution can hardly be seen as a "little mite", even Phillips acknowledges this. His analysis was completed in advance of Phillips's, had more by way of theoretical justification, and many of his conclusions have proven to be much more robust. But Brown's *Great Inflation* had neither good "visuals" nor an appropriate sound bite. Samuelson and Solow, if not originating the term, certainly helped Phillips by popularizing the labeling of the Curve. Also, as Napoleon so often liked to point out, luck is perhaps the most important attribute of all: "All great events hang by a hair, I believe in luck." Phillips was lucky in his timing, his networks, his style of presentation, and in the changing fads in publication of his day.

NOTES

1. Forder (2015) critiques textbooks' uses of the Curve. The policy importance of the Curve in practice is more controversial; e.g. see Forder (2010) and Schwarzer (2013).
2. "[A]s a matter of historical fact, A.J. Brown's *Great Inflation*, published in 1955, ante-dates both Sultan and Phillips. Brown not only discusses in some detail the theoretical and institutional reasons why one might expect an inverse relation between the percentage level of unemployment and the percentage rate of increase in wages and prices; but more significantly, he plots a Phillips-type relation for the United Kingdom for the periods 1880–1914 and 1920–51, and for the United States for the Period 1921–48. I have often thought that the 'Phillips' Curve ought to be called the 'Brown' Curve—unless, of course, Brown himself had precursors" (Thirlwall, 1972: 325).
3. Mitchell (1999), Nancy Wulwick (1987) and Thomas Humphrey (1985) provide commentaries of the longer history of how others' efforts may fit with Brown's work on the subject.
4. Robert Leeson (1995) offers some observations on this publication regarding the fortunes of the two economists and the interpretations of their papers.
5. Donner and McCollum (1972) seek to integrate Fisher and Sultan's papers, or at least interpret their relative importance within their context.
6. These sections expand on material in Kenneth Button (forthcoming 2018).
7. See also, Santomero and Seater (1978), Mitchell (1999), and the important recent book by Forder (2014) for accounts of the pre-Brown literature on the wage-change/ unemployment relationship. It is also an issue that has not gone away, for example in newspapers—Paul Krugman (*New York Times*, 15 July 2014), Neil Irwin (*New York Times*, 24 October 2015), Justin Wolfers (*New York Times,* 6 November 2015), and Gavyn Davies (*Financial Times*, 19 October 2015)—and by officials. These included Federal Reserve chairwoman Janet Yellen, who, when giving the Phillip Gamble Memorial Lecture at the University of Massachusetts, Amherst, on 24 September 2015, acknowledged that "significant uncertainty attaches to Phillips Curve predictions, and the validity of forecasts from this model must be continuously evaluated in response to incoming data"; and Stanley Fischer, vice-chairman, to a dinner audience in Washington DC on 5 November 2015: "I believe we'll see it, The Phillips curve will come back." For more recent academic literature, see Mavroeidis et al (2004).
8. Meghnad Desai, correspondence with Robert Leeson, 26 December 1992.
9. For more details of Phillips's life, see Blyth (1975), Lancaster (1979), Leeson (1994a, 2000), Laidler, (2002), and Bollard (2011).
10. As Laidler (2002) points out: "universities were still run by senior academics rather than professional administrators," allowing some flexibility in decision-making. Brown (2000: xii) comments that the result was "partly because he had chosen a subject (Sociology) that did not really suit his ability, more certainly because the strains of war had affected his ability to perform in written examinations."
11. See Brown's letters to Meade—22 November, 15 December 1949, 19 January 1950—and Meade's letters to Brown 12 and 24 December 1949 (AJB C&P).
12. Sleeman (2011: 227) qualifies "rushed" by saying it related to Phillips's initial work on the Curve in 1956 rather than his reworking of the data and drafting between September 1957 and March 1958. Interestingly, Phillips wrote to Brown: "For some months now I

have been extremely busy in connection with a research project which we are hoping the Ford Foundation will finance. One of the things I had to do was work out some of the ideas on estimation. I have just finished the paper on the subject and enclose a copy" (28 February 1958, AJB C&P). Brown clearly gets the papers (Brown's letter to Phillips, 3 March 1958, AJB C&P). The intriguing question is whether this paper was that with the Curve in it and, if so, what were Brown's comments.

13. Correspondence, Brown to Leeson (Leeson, 2000: 17).
14. Lionel Robbins's (1971) autobiography adds more flesh to this.
15. Although Meade and Lipsey were also acknowledged (Phillips, 1958: 285), the latter subsequently said he did not see the paper until it was in proof.
16. Later he makes his position on this even more strongly:"Clearly, if there were no expansion of the supply of money, a hyper-inflation could not proceed very far" (Brown, 1955: 179).
17. Brown, letter to Max Hartwell, 21 September 1951 (AJB C&P). See also Brown's *Department of Economics and Commerce/School of Economic Studies: A Personal Memoir* (1979, AJB C&P) for an account of his commitments at that time.
18. Brown expresses the time pressures succinctly: "I was finishing my book on inflation—written, as I used to claim with only a moderate degree of exaggeration, in seven successive months of September" (*Department of Economics and Commerce/School of Economic Studies*, p. 7). I am grateful to John Bowers for the observation regarding Brown's working style.
19. Forder (2014: 22–6) critiques the concept of the L-shaped curve, and questions if a complete right-angled kink in the curve was ever in the minds of its advocates. Furthermore, it has been argued that one reason Phillips set about modeling inflation is that MONIAC, the innovative computer he had developed to describe the macroeconomy, involved flows of liquids and mechanics, could not easily handle dichotomous situations (Yamey, 2000).
20. Samuel Katz (1959) provides a contemporary critique of the report.
21. Brown's (1959a) later work, essentially a textbook, provides within it a more basic discussion of inflation in a world context.
22. See Rosenberg and Weisskopf (1981) for a more complete application of the approach.
23. Brown explains this for a later period in his *Framework of Regional Economics*: "It is in fact possible to 'explain' changes in male manual hourly earnings in each region (at six-monthly intervals) for the period 1959–69 in terms of the prevailing levels of unemployment, the contemporary rate of change of unemployment, the contemporary rate of change of retail prices, subject to a shift in the relationship in most regions from about October 1966" (Brown, 1972: 239).
24. To obtain his Curve, Phillips regressed the rate of wage change against the unemployment rate using the relation $\dot{w}/w + a = bU^c$, with w as the nominal wage rate, $\dot{w}$ the change, and U the unemployment rate. Because of the additive constant, a, and because several observations were negative for $\dot{w}/w$, the functional form is difficult to estimate. To circumvent the problem Phillips adopted a common procedure for the time. Unemployment rates are divided into six intervals—0 to 2, 2 to 3, 3 to 4, 4 to 5, 5 to 7, and 7 to 11—and the raw observations placed into them per which interval their unemployment rates fall. Within each group, the $\dot{w}/w$s are averaged and each paired with the midpoint of the unemployment interval defining the group. This average inflation–unemployment pair constitutes a composite data point, the cross in the lower part of Figure 6.1. Four of these points take positive average values of $\dot{w}/w$, and these are used to estimate b and c using least squares. The constant a is chosen by trial and error to make the fitted curve pass as close as possible to the remaining two composite points. The curve obtained was $\dot{w}/w = -0.9 + 9.638U^{-1.394}$. Wulwick (1987) provides some suggestions as to why this form of curve was adopted.
25. Two graphs are offered for 1879 to 1886 using alternative data sets on wages.
26. Brown's empirics explains inflation between 1939 as 1951 as resulting from the

aftermath of war and wartime shortages, higher import prices and changes in the composition of imports, and upward movements in factor prices of finished goods, most notably the nominal wage rate.

27. Away from the printing press, Worswick puts it more bluntly: "It seemed that he [Phillips] could get his results without knowing any economics at all" (letter to Brown, 14 December 1995, AJB C&P).

28. A full account of Brown's analysis is not offered; it is spelled out in his book, while Worswick (1979) and Mitchell (1999) provide truncated versions. Brown later provides an explicit and wide-ranging empirical, econometric assessment of the Curve from 1950 into the 1970s and covering a variety of countries. He finds little evidence for its existence (Brown with Darby, 1985).

29. Clive Granger and Yongil Jeon (2011: 52) explain Phillips's estimation process as stemming from "a clear shortage of computer power . . . the London School of Economics did not have an electronic computer in 1957 when the work was started." Phillips used an electric calculator, but this was not from lack of a mainframe machine: the University of London had a Ferranti machine that LSE could access (Wulwick, 1989). See also, Schwier (2000).

30. This is restated later: "the rate of change of money wage rates can be explained by the level of unemployment and the rate of change of unemployment except in or immediately after those years in which there is a significantly rapid rise in import prices to offset the tendency for increasing productivity to reduce the cost of living" (Phillips, 1958: 299).

31. Brown (1955: v) also questions whether the theoretical discussions had been misguided: "the institutional machinery by which prices and wages have been determined and changed have been quite largely different during the period of inflation from what had been assumed in the theoretical formulations, most of the theorists have not caught up with actuality." Whether "theorists" relates, at least partly, to Phillips's 1954 paper is unclear.

32. Brown (1966: 362) also scolds Pederson and Laursen when reviewing the analysis of *The German Inflation, 1918–1923*, arguing that their analysis "of the mechanism of inflation would be more helpful if the authors were not so anxious to escape from the Quantity Theory in any conceivable modification that they virtually leave money out of the picture altogether."

33. In his 1958 speech (p. 463) he mentions the potential of stagflation: "My own view, indeed, is that one of the less welcome marvels of modern times is the possibility, within limits, of enjoying inflation and depression at the same time." The tantalizing challenge is that he goes no further: "to discuss that would take me beyond the task I have set myself for this occasion."

34. While they offer a trade-off view, there is debate about whether they saw this as being in the long-run, and whether they adopt a menu approach to policy applications (Schwarzer, 2013; Hall and Hart, 2012).

35   There is also evidence that Brown was not unknown to Samuelson. They may have met during Brown's sabbatical at Columbia in the spring of 1950, but certainly had corresponded on other matters (Brown's letter to Samuelson 26 September 1950, AJB C&P).

36. There is an established literature examining the accreditation of ideas, and the aim here is not to add to this but rather to offer a few comments on the credit afforded Brown and Phillips for their work.

37. Phillips also regularly stayed with Brown: see, Phillips's letters to Brown 27 February and 10 March 1954; 28 February, 1 and 6 May 1958; Brown's letters to Phillips 12 March, 23 April 1954; 22 October 1957; 1 and 3 March, 2 May 1958 (AJB C&P).

38. He later also failed to mention Lipsey's (1960b) then unpublished work using quarterly data, lags, and regression analysis that he was familiar with (Phillips, 1959a).

39. The refereeing processes for the *American Economic Review* "in 2014 has declined to 82 weeks" (http://pubs.aeaweb.org/doi/pdfplus/10.1257/aer.1500001).

40. Draft by W. Brown, *Arthur Brown* (AJB C&P, dated 10 March 2003).
41. Brown (1988a), in his "A worm's eye view of the Keynesian Revolution," postulates that Harrod started to think in terms of an IS-LM framework as early as August/September 1935. Further, "I'm quite sure that an equation system purporting to represent the skeleton of the *General Theory* attributed to Harrod, was passed round Oxford within the month after the publication of the *General Theory* [Hilary term, 1936]. What I took to be the nature of the *General Theory* became clear when I first learnt of the Harrod equations, the four equations which I took to be its underlying structure" (Brown, interview in Young, 1987: 88).

7.   Domestic policy advisor

BACKGROUND

Brown advised on economic matters both domestically and, as we have seen, with respect to Africa and global disarmament, internationally. In terms of domestic "clients", advice was sought in a variety of forms by a diversity of bodies, committees, and commissions. He also covered a variety of subjects—monetary policy, nuclear policy, regional economic issues, de-colonialization, new universities, European Union policy, and so on. Much of his thinking and, to some extent, his approach to working on these topics can be traced to his wartime experiences and an appreciation of a need for clarity and relevance in what he produced. Advising government and the participation in groups with diverse backgrounds is considerably different to interacting with experts in your one field. Brown clearly recognized this, as did those seeking his advice.

He was also active at a time when national governments and international agencies were commissioning numerous outside studies and seeking advice from a variety of ad hoc commissions, advisory groups, and standing committees. In many cases the roles of these later became institutionalized as the UK professional civil service grew. The 1950s and 1960s represented a period of major social, economic, and political change. There was also an interest at all levels in seeking to ensure that policy decisions, and especially involving economics, should be made on the best possible advice. There was, in many cases, a feeling that Keynesian economics and the advances in data analysis that had taken place, allowed for a greater degree of micro-management of economies. It was also accompanied by major political changes in the capitalist economies necessitating, not just reforms of existing institutional structures, but also the creation of new ones; new economic approaches, for example, were needed to deal with the considerable shift of resources from the public to private sectors at the end of World War II.

One reason for the considerable demand for Brown's service as an advisor across a diversity of subjects is made clear by Tony Thirlwall (2003): "His skill was to take practical issues of public concern, and use economic theory and statistics to elucidate them in an intelligible, but rigorous way." This was a skill that had always been particularly valued in policy circles, but with the increasing formalization and mathematization of economics after World War II it gained an added premium. But this was his forte. It was stated about Brown later in his life: "This activity at the interface between the political problems of planning and the academic forefront of applied economics has proved to be the creative pattern of his life's work."[1]

Some of the rendering of advice justifies more specific coverage than is found in this chapter, for example regarding his service on the Hunt Committee that looked at UK regional policy and involvement with African economic development, so this has been done elsewhere. In other cases, more detail is offered, for example regarding advising the European Community on finance or in offering evidence to government committees more is provided in the wider context of what else was going on in Brown's life at the time, or with respect to his research. Here we focus more on the role of the policy advisor in the UK from the 1950s through the 1970s, and how Brown viewed his role within the framework. We also say a few things about some of his longer-term advisory activities, for example as a member of the UK's University Grants Committee (UGC), that does not easily fit into the other categories of activity set out above.

THE ROLE OF ECONOMIC ADVISORS IN THE UK

We have already seen that the role of the economist as advisor to government and industry had grown considerable during and after World War II; and although the legal necessity for a Council of Economic Advisors to advise the country's political leader had not crossed the Atlantic, it was clear after 1945—and particularly in light of the increased involvement of government in the economy—that economic advice would be useful, if not dominant, in the making of public policy.[2] But the issue was how this was to be injected; the case was not accepted by all.[3] There were already economists in the Treasury and Foreign Office in the UK during the war, but they were spread very thinly across what was, in any case, a small civil service in those days. In the short term, their number even shrunk, and by 1947 there were none in the Treasury (Theakston, 1995). When there had been major economic issues to consider in the past, there had been a tendency to seek outside advice from ad hoc committees and commissions, and this to some extent returned after the war. There was some injection of economists into the newly nationalized industries, such as the railways, coal mining, and iron and steel production, although these remained outside the civil service.[4]

One reason for the apparent shrinkage was a shift in definitions. The analysis of economic matter had become far more empirical, a fact that had become very clear during the war. The advent of National Income Accounting following the work of Richard Stone, Colin Clarke, and, in the USA, Simon Kuznets now provided the basis for determining trends in key economic variables that could act as lead indicators for a pre-emptive Keynesian-style strike before an economic recession set in. They also allowed an assessment of the success of various policies. The latter involved not only national trends but also economic sectors, as the newly nationalized industries after the war were seen by the Labour government as lead sectors to be used to stimulate and direct economic recovery and subsequently growth.

To this end, the Central Statistical Office (CSO) had been set up at the beginning of 1941 with the then purpose of handling the descriptive statistics required for the war effort and for developing national income accounts. Harry Campion, a member of the Central Economic Information Service in the Cabinet Office, was appointed its initial director. With peace, there was an expansion in the work of official statisticians resulting from the aim of managing the economy along broadly Keynesian lines using an integrated system of national accounts, and in 1962 comprehensive financial statistics were published for the first time. Many of those engaged in this work, although economists, snuck by under different designations.

The degree of coordination between the various elements of what subsequently became known as the Government Economic Service (GES) was initially limited, with individuals focusing largely on internal departmental issues. With the election of Harold Wilson's government in 1964, the GES was founded as a professional grouping of public sector economists working across the various departments and agencies of Her Majesty's Government and the Bank of England. The timing coincided with a renewed interest in national planning, but also a desire to have fewer Oxbridge generalists in the civil service. Although its institutional structure has changed somewhat over the years, the Service recruits economists on behalf of the departments, and is now the UK's largest recruiter of economists. It facilitates the movement of GES economists between posts in different departments, and maintains professional standards for recruitment and for existing members. It leads on the development of intellectual capital for cross-departmental issues. After its inception, the number of designated economists in the civil service grew from 21 to nearly 500 in 1990, the time Brown began genuinely to slow down (Allan, 2008).

Brown had developed a clear interest in active engagement in policy making during his time working for the Foreign Office during the war and through his extended ties from his time at Oxford; many of those he knew there went on to serve in the civil service. His experiences with advising government and its agencies obviously spanned the period when the modern civil service was being initiated through to its institutionalization into the core of the civil service after 1964.

ADVISORY COMMITTEES

Brown had been giving advice to various committees and to influential leaders throughout World War II and after. His applied skills inevitably made him a popular economist for government. He continued to do this after moving to Leeds, and later served on advisory bodies. He was, as we have already seen, involved in the decolonization of British Africa as a member of government advisory committees. As mentioned earlier, in the 1960s he was a UK nominee to the UN Consultative Group on the Economic and Social Consequences of Disarmament. And, as we see, later, in 1966, when the Wilson government launched an active regional policy, Arthur Brown—who had been director of a major project on regional policy based at the National Institute of Economic and Social Research (NIESR)—was the obvious choice to provide the missing analytical framework for the policy, and was appointed to the Hunt Committee on Intermediate Areas.

Importantly (and unusually), besides his contributions to policy assessment and development he also produced a variety of reflective pieces discussing his experiences. For example in 1940, well in advance of his "advisory career", he produced a historical piece laying out the use of the sorts of committees that he later served during the inter-war period (Brown, 1940a). While quite clearly hardly a mature perspective of an adviser, it does perhaps offer some indications of how Brown subsequently approached the advisory role, and indeed the advised role. It may well have influenced which committees he subsequently chose to sit on or to offer evidence to. Finally, looking at advisory committees could have provided some insights into the more generic features of the workings of committees that came in handy for dealing with the affairs of his department at Leeds.

His focus was on the Treasury, a body he would have been familiar with not only through current and past contacts at Oxford, but also in pursuit of his D.Phil. work on liquidity preference. This presumably gave Brown conduits into the way the Treasury treated advisors and the attention ultimately paid to their advice. There were also numerous reports available rendering advice sought by the Treasury, or by its political masters reviewing the actions of the Treasury and its implementation of policy.

Much of Brown's assessment entails detailing the workings of the Treasury, its role, and something of its history until World War II. Interesting though this is, its relevance for current macroeconomics is somewhat limited given the changes that have taken place in the functions of Her Majesty's Treasury. And this is especially so since 1998 when the Bank of England became an independent public organization wholly owned by the Treasury Solicitor on behalf of the government with independence in setting monetary policy. Thus fiscal and monetary responsibilities are now separated. Brown also discusses within this the more general role of standing and non-standing bodies that regulate government departments such as the Treasury; but again the situation is different now and specifics of the 1920s and 1930s, interesting as they are in setting historical context for the time, are largely peripheral to today's bureaucratic structures and machinations.[5]

Perhaps more germane to matters of economic policy was the Economic Advisory Council, set up in 1930 to advise the Cabinet. Chaired by the Prime Minister, it was comprised of non-ministerial members, of whom six were academic economists or economic journalist, with the rest coming from industry, banking, trade unions, and accountancy. The advice largely turned out to come from expert sub-committees reporting on "topical pests." Brown argues that any hope of it becoming an "economic staff" was stymied by the timing of its establishment, in the Great Depression, which gave little time for considered reflection regarding major expenditures. The consequences of this were not short term.

> The combination of inevitable failure to improvise what really needed years of preparation and propaganda with the crisis in national finances, which the depression brought, naturally produced the famous Treasury view that public expenditure as a depression policy had been tried and had failed well-nigh disastrously and—which perhaps mattered more—caused what should have been a permanent addition to the machinery of government to be regarded primarily as the instigator of this dangerous experiment. (Brown, 1940a: 91)[6]

Regarding the various specific committees established in the inter-war period, Brown pays attention to their composition (especially whether they were large or small) and to whether they consisted of largely disinterested parties, which for example he thought the Geddes Committee on national expenditure that reported in 1922 was, or whether they were composed of a balance of interested parties, such as the May Committee (also on national expenditure) that reported in 1931. He also finds their remits relevant to how successful they were in terms of affecting policy, with the more specific remits more likely to lead to recommendations that were adopted. The Macmillan Committee on Finance and Industry that reported in 1931 and the Colwyn Committees (the first the Royal Commission on Income Tax that reported in 1920 and the second, on National Debt and Taxation reporting in 1927), and were given "only general duties of diagnostics," were seen to be at the lowest end of the "effectiveness" scale.[7]

The composition issue was one Brown considered important, and he takes the time to footnote the composition of the main advisory bodies and to lay out in the text the expertise of members. He also offers some simple arithmetic on the numbers of witnesses called, their backgrounds, and whether they represented business, the civil service, or were there in their individual capacities. In addition to whether they were neutral groups aimed at offering an outside view on a subject or a balanced group aimed at compromise, Brown was impressed by:

> The fact that the Treasury committees of the period tapped the organized channels of opinion so thoroughly . . . [and it] . . . helps of course explain some of the difficulty in producing agreed and effective reports, but it also gives some ground for hope that, besides securing expert advice, they have done something to strengthen the democratic control of government. (1940a: 125)

These latter thoughts may have returned when he later drafted his report to the vice-chancellor of Leeds regarding the governance of the School of Economics.

ADVISING "NEW UNIVERSITIES"

Brown's experiences at Leeds in establishing a major academic unit led to him becoming involved in the setting up of the new wave of universities that emerged in the 1960s. These involved Colleges of Advanced Technology that were converted to universities following the 1963 Robbins Report on higher education, and the creation of what Michael Beloff (1968) called the "plateglass universities." In all cases advice was required on a range of subjects, and experienced heads were sought. There were also important economic considerations regarding finance as well as developing academic structures when there was an upsurge of interest in the social sciences. There was also the need for these institutions to meet the demands of a changing society requiring different skill sets to previous decades.

Brown was engaged in advising on the development of the University of Kent at Canterbury (a plateglass institution) and the University of Bradford (formerly Bradford College of Advanced Technology). He seemed much more at home helping with the development of Bradford than he did with Kent, and this familiarity extended beyond any cultural affinity to the Yorkshire area.

Kent, founded in 1965, was created along collegial lines very much akin to the Oxbridge and St Andrews model. It was originally envisaged as being a traditional collegiate establishment, with most students living in one of the colleges on campus, and one specializing in interdisciplinary studies in all fields, although this subsequently changed as government policy and other factors significantly modified the original concept. Brown was the only economist on the advisory board for Kent as the original concept was developed, but resigned before the university received its Royal Charter or a vice-chancellor had been appointed.

He changed institutions, as it were, just after being invited to join Bradford's Advisory Board. Any conflict of interest aside, his feelings about the Board's work at Canterbury were: "At Kent we sat around and had beautiful thoughts about what sort of ideals and profound principles the University might have. Then of course they appointed their first professors and the first professors did just what *they* wanted, which was only natural" (italics in original).[8] He was also not entirely convinced about the virtue of the institution trying to emulate the Oxbridge college system, despite some advantages one assumes he recalled from his own student days.

The practical problem in 1960, and one which goes a long way towards explaining the structures adopted by most other plateglass universities in the UK, was finance: the new universities had neither real endowments nor the central physical infrastructure that college-based institutions such as Kent and the University of York required. As Brown put it (and also likely drawing on his later experiences at the UGC): "The next thing you hear is they come along and ask the University Grants Committee for more money for departmental buildings, because all their buildings are colleges and not departmental buildings."[9]

There were three on the Advisory Board of the embryonic University of Bradford, plus a chairman. It emerged in 1966 from an established institution tracing its origins back to 1832, and thus the concerns were more of transition than of founding a university *ab initio*. It was also much more like Leeds than Kent, with a technology tradition tied closely to the needs of local industry and commerce. From 1956, government policy was that a number of technical colleges should concentrate entirely on advanced studies, undergraduate education, and postgraduate research Following the Council of Technological Awards, the body set up to oversee the policy recommendation in 1959, Bradford Institute of Technology was designate such an institution. The Institute's purpose was to provide a broad range and substantial volume of work exclusively at an advanced level, including postgraduate and research work under conditions comparable with those of a university (McKinley, 1997).

Brown's account of events suggests that the transition was not without problems, and part of these stemmed from some of the individuals involved. The first vice-chancellor of the university was the old principal of the College of Advanced Technology, where the internal structure was much more hierarchical than in most universities of the period. The Board had tried to "persuade him that a University isn't quite the same as a College of Advanced Technology." Despite this, things seemed to settle down into the university mold "fairly quickly."

THE UNIVERSITY GRANTS COMMITTEE

Brown was very actively involved for many years as a member of the University Grants Committee. While not entirely advisory, the UGC did have some actual power: it was responsible for the allocation of resources and advising the UK government on university planning and policy. It was also a committee that Brown served on for an extended period, and one on which he felt "very much at ease."

The UGC was first proposed in the report of a committee chaired by Lord Haldane, but was not created until 1918, becoming operational the following year. The initial Haldane principle was the idea that decisions about what to spend research funds on should be made by researchers rather than politicians. But by 1918, the expediency was one of addressing a need to find a way to channel funds to universities that had been neglected during the World War I. The UGC's initial role was thus to examine the financial needs of the universities and to advise on grants; but there was no remit to plan for the development of universities. Strictly, it was "To enquire into the financial needs of University Education in the United Kingdom, and to advise Government as to the application of any grants that may be made by Parliament towards meeting them."

This situation changed after World War II, when the Barlow Report of 1946 recommended that the UGC take on a planning role for the university sector to ensure that universities were adequate for national needs during post-war reconstruction. The Education Act 1944 had also aimed to increase the number of school leavers qualified to enter higher education, necessitating a period of expansion for the universities that needed planning by the UGC. The Committee's remit was therefore expanded "to assist, in consultation with the Universities and other bodies concerned, the preparation and execution of such plans for the development of the Universities as may from time to time be required to ensure that they are fully adequate to national needs." During the post-war years, the UGC thus continued to have a strategic role in the development of the university sector, acting as a buffer between government and the interests of the universities. In 1964 responsibility for the UGC was transferred from the UK Treasury to the newly constituted Department of Education and Science (Stewart, 1989).

It was shortly after the transfer that Arthur Brown was invited to join the UGC in 1969 and was active in it until 1978. His experiences at both Kent and Bradford added to his established credentials of working with university financial data. His initiation into the world of university finance began with a meeting with Thomas Balogh, who had been elevated to Baron Balogh of Hampstead a year before, at the House of Lords. Balogh, who had known Brown since before the war, was at the time a special advisor to the Prime Minister, Harold Wilson.[10] Brown was asked join the UGC in these comfortable surroundings.

In an extensive, unpublished retrospective Brown obviously thought engagement with the UGC was not only productive but also often intellectually highly stimulating.[11] It was not, of course a committee of economists and, although financial matters were often of considerable importance in its debates, its higher-level discussions, and ultimately decisions, were quite wide ranging. There were, however, sub-committees, and Brown was immediately given the task of chairing the one dealing with Social Studies. Equally, its composition was diverse (within limits), as Brown indicates when listing its members when he was first appointed:

> The balance between the main categories of university and the regions of Great Britain had also to be watched. At my first meeting, two of the academics came from the ancient English seats, two from Scotland, one from Wales, three from London, one each from a "new" (Shakespearean' or 'plate glass') university and an ex-CAT (promoted College of Advanced Technology), and five of us, including the Deputy Chairman, Sir Robert Aitken, who was in fact retired, from the English civics.

> Besides the university members there were . . . a Head Mistress (Miss Bradbury, a Leeds graduate), two industrialists, one of whom, Stephen Bragg from Rolls Royce, we evidently did not put off academic affairs, since he subsequently became Vice-Chancellor of Brunel, and a Chief Education Office[r], Dr. Cook, from Devonshire.[12]

Brown, besides his normal involvement with the affairs of the UGC, was specifically active in several areas. He took considerable interest in the way the Committee treated costs. The examination of university costs was not new to him. In 1956, he had been asked by the Committee of Vice-Chancellors and Principals to look at the effect of wage and price changes over the previous five years on university costs.[13] This was important in terms of funding because university costs did not move in line with the retail price index, and the necessary consideration of budgetary planning by the government and universities should ideally be based on real costs. This had been refined and, together with Ronald Tress at Bristol, he had created and maintained the Tress-Brown Index of university costs.[14] This has become today's Higher Education Pay and Prices Index.

In terms of usefulness to the UGC, Brown's view was that the vice-chancellors felt that if the Tress-Brown Index was accepted as statistically sound it should be used to help the universities defray these rising costs. The index specifically dealt with what may be described as the non-academic costs of universities, basically the wages and salaries of non-academic staff, national insurance, and the cost of books, maintenance, fuel, and lighting. There had been a constant movement in the costs of all these items, and the index provided a tracking mechanism. What happened was that if there was a change in the Tress Index the UGC considered it. It was then passed to the Department of Education and Science, which likewise considered it; and in due course the Department passed it on to the Treasury, which also considered it. So, far from there being an automatic increase to offset effects of inflation, there were three separate acts of judgment on any recommendation or any proposal—in other words, three additional delays.

The UGC's recommendation was thus that the Committee of Vice-Chancellors should deal with this, and that when they consider that rises in the index justify an increase in grant it should not then be a matter for further discussion with the UGC, the Department of Education and Science, and the Treasury, but that the recommendation of the Committee of Vice-Chancellors should be sufficient to activate the grant. The UGC's object was to insulate the universities to some extent from the erosion of their means by price increases, and so that at each quinquennium they could be evaluated fairly.

The only official reply the UGC got to that was: "The Government consider that it is one of the responsibilities of the University Grants Committee to advise them when, in the Committee's view, additional grants are required above increases in costs." "The comparative analysis available in future to the University Grants Committee will increase the value of this advice in this respect." But in Brown's view this missed the point of the UGC's recommendation, which was to try to give the index a very much more automatic effect than it had under the existing regime; and, without having such a regulatory effect, he doubted whether it served any useful purpose in convincing the universities that they were being protected against a rise in costs.

Brown's chairmanship of the social studies sub-committee brought up several issues, some of which he subsequently admitted he was not well equipped to handle but which required his managerial abilities to bring about reasonable outcomes. But there were also ad hoc working groups that he participated in that required his specific skills as an economist. One of these was that of library costs, a topic on which he also produced a paper of interest to librarians (Brown, 1980). This latter also reflected his continued membership of the working group even after he had left the main committee.

The topic at issue was essentially a cost-benefit problem of how to handle the annual costs associated with investment in book stock and storage capacity, and with operating them, weighed against the extra operating costs that would be involved in reliance on inter-library loans. Not perhaps quite the same operations challenge in the electronic information age, but a major one when information had a physical component attached to it. The issue had arisen in the mid-1970s when a serious scarcity of capital had arisen for university construction and the challenge of housing ever-growing amounts of literature came to the fore.[15] The UGC estimated that it had spent over £23 million (in current prices) on library buildings in the decade up to 1974—a rate of expenditure that could not be sustained; and yet it was faced with the problem that, out of 44 university libraries, 11 were virtually full and 18 more estimated that they would be full within four years.

A working group chaired by Richard Atkinson of the University of Wales (of which Brown was not a member) reported in 1975 that the time had come for universities to consolidate and focus much of their collections at remote locations rather than in campus libraries (UGC Committee on Libraries, 1967). Campus facilities would follow the concept of "the self-renewing library of limited growth." The inter-library loan system this entailed would play a key role in ensuring material was available when needed. The UGC commended the report and accepted its recommendations.

Brown's analysis, which was part of the remit of the working group chaired by Violet Caine, involved optimizing the length of time that books should be stored. Using estimates from a crude meta-analysis of the findings of others and from the Index of University Costs gave him values for the costs of an inter-library loan against that of purchasing a book (including selection, cataloguing, shelving, invoicing, and so on, and assuming it will last 70 years) and of the library building. Adjustments were made for a number of factors, such as the profile of a book's use over its life and where there is spare capacity for storage or when storage can be provided cheaply. From these calculations, Brown estimated a book must be borrowed once every 1.7 times to make a purchase worthwhile. On the principle that a bygone is a bygone and their costs are stranded, existing books should be discarded if not used about once every 13 years.

Overall Brown assesses the work of the UGC on the finances of universities during his time as depending on how one viewed the 8–9 percent worsening of student–staff ratios that emerged against the economies of scale that were realized. Essentially, he thought in terms of a social cost-benefit analysis.

Changes followed a little time after Brown left the UGC. In 1986, the Committee conducted its first "Research Selectivity Exercise" to decide the disbursement of funds for university research, which was a precursor to the Research Assessment Exercise and the Research Excellence Framework. The UGC was wound up on 1 April 1989, with its powers transferred to a new body, the Universities Funding Council, which was directly responsible to Parliament. The system had taken on at least a veneer of rigor in its work.

NOTES

1. Speech on Brown's award of an Honorary Doctor of Literature by the University of Sheffield in 1979 (no date, AJB C&P).
2. The US Council of Economic Advisers (CEA) was established within the Executive Office of the President that advises the President on economic policy in 1946 as part of the Employment Act. The aim of the CEA was to provide much of the objective empirical research for the White House, and to prepare the annual Economic Report of the President. Herbert Stein (1996) offers an insider's view on how it functions, or at least how it functioned when he served on it.
3. Although the situation was not as bad is in the interwar period, where one Bank of England article warned staff consulting economic material not to "become infected with the ideas or the language of an economist" (cited in Allan, 2008: 26).
4. Stewart Joy (1973), British Railways Board's Chief Economist in the late 1960s, gives some idea of the roles played by economists who went into the nationalized industries.
5. For example, there were such as the Tithe Redemption Commission that in the late 1930s was given responsibility for fixing compensation to tithe holders and the Arrears Committee on Statute Law Revision.
6. See Howson and Winch (1977) for a more more positive view of the history of the Council.
7. The MacMillan Committee, upon which Maynard Keynes sat, was, "A wide-ranging inquiry into how the banking system affected the economy, it was not intended to influence immediate policy" (Skidelsky, 1992: 343). The large number of Addenda by individual members was perhaps indicative of the task at hand and the varied interpretations that could be put upon it.
8. *Interview with A.J. Brown, 25 May 1994, Headingley, Leeds*, p. 21.
9. *Interview with A.J. Brown, 25 May 1994, Headingley, Leeds*, p. 21. Brown commented on the problems of financing collegial universities in his account of his time at the UGC, although no specific institution is mentioned:

   "I annoyed the Vice-Chancellor by pointing out that the college system in his University of which it was evidently proud, had a price, in the shape of certain difficulties of department organization, to overcome which requests for extra money were being adumbrated. He accused us of interfering, by implication, with a matter of organization which was the University's business. My colleagues nobly replied that

we, and indeed, the Main Committee, did not interfere with universities' choices—
that University's choice of a college system had been made without interference—but
that we did have a duty to advice the Main Committee on how different forms of
organization appeared to work in the field" [italics in original]. Brown, *The University
Grants Committee* (undated, AJB C&P), p. 22.

10. Balogh had known Brown at Oxford. Having immigrated to the UK, Balogh lectured at
University College London (UCL) from 1934, and in 1939 went to Balliol College as a
lecturer and to work at the Institute of Statistics. In 1945 he was elected to a fellowship,
which he held until 1973. He had earlier asked Brown whether he would be interested in
one of the special advisory posts then available in Whitehall, but Brown was then com-
mitted to the National Institute on UK regional economics.
11. *The University Grants Committee*. Brown not only describes the topics considered by
the Committee when he was a member but also, in short vignettes, the style and personalities of many of the individuals involved, and the ways in which it functioned. He
particularly seemed to like the fact "that it hardly ever voted on issues before it."
12. *The University Grants Committee*, p. 3.
13. Brown to Leeds Vice-Chancellor Eric Ashby (28 May 1956 AJB C&P). The motivation
for writing to the vice-chancellor was to inform him he was requesting data from the
Bursar for the exercise, making the point that it was easier to start the work by looking
at the institution he knew best.
14. The UGC called it the "Tress Index" when it first mentioned it publicly. The reason the
administration of the index had moved to Bristol by then was that Brown had acquired
a research assistant, John Tozer, who became his part-time helper. Tozer departed to
Bristol, where Tress was based, to become a lecturer in 1964.
15. The construction of university libraries since the publication of the Parry Report
(UGC, 1967) had tended towards modular, flexible structures with full air-conditioning
rather than more conventional fixed-function buildings, and this had provided something of an interim solution. The UGC (1976) subsequently provided a more comprehensive report on the capital funding of university libraries.

8. Regional economic policy and the Hunt Committee

SPATIAL ECONOMICS

All national economies have local and regional spatial aspects to them, if for no other reason than that economic geographers would be unemployed if they did not. Obviously, the physical geography of a nation is not homogeneous, and this affects the distribution of population, the availability of local raw materials, and the ability to interact between areas. But there are also human factors, with variations in culture and history affecting local tastes and inclinations to produce different outputs, and in the ability and willingness to interact with those living in other regions. These, and a plethora of more minor factors, lead to significant differences in the economic performance of regions. Arthur Brown was cognizant of this, and had explicitly discussed its implications for inflation in his 1950s book (Brown, 1955), and in his work on less economically developed countries and economic unions. Later, he became interested more directly in how to reduce spatial inequalities between regions, and especially those within the United Kingdom.

By the 1960s, regional economics had grown up in parallel with more mainstream threads of microeconomics, but with links to industrial efficiency, trade, and economic development. While Brown's interest was largely in the application of economics as a tool to gain a better understanding of the nature of divergent regional economies, and in looking for policy instruments to facilitate the removal of the worst of these differences, he was well versed in the theories of the subject. Much of this, as can be seen in John Meyer's (1963) excellent survey in the *American Economic Review*, was rather abstract in the 1960s, and a large part of the empirical analysis that had been undertaken was American in origin. The size, geographical diversity, and federal nature of the country provided many serious economic challenges for spatial economists. But Meyer openly admits that it was difficult in the 1960s to give a distinct character to regional economics in terms of the conventional sub-divisions of economics. This was largely because of its tendency to involve interdisciplinary methodologies and for the common vernacular in debates to be in terms of "regional science" or "regional analysis." Meyer spends five pages wrestling with definitional problems.

Added to this, because of the importance of scale economies (or more strictly those associated with agglomeration effects), there has often been a tendency to simply think of it in terms akin to industrial economics: a region is like a large firm or industry. Furthermore, much of the study of regions has been in terms of specific problems or study areas rather than in terms of theory, although there has been a tradition of theorizing about optimal location patterns.

Brown is somewhat less concerned in his work with the fine-tuning of exactly what regional economics is, and the fine distinctions between it and related areas such as economic geography or regional planning. He focuses instead on why people living in some locations are better off in terms of jobs and income than those in other locations. As he puts it in his own survey paper published in the *Economic Journal*, the issue of definition is really a pragmatic one:

> Regional economics is a field of study which has meant different things to different people . . . Regional economics starts from the diagnosis of regional problems . . . [A]ny economic circumstance that gives rise to regional sense of grievance, or any that give rise to a general, or governmental belief that the inter-regional distribution of population and economic activity is seriously wrong, may be said to constitute a regional problem. (Brown, 1969d: 759–60)[1]

He thus tends to look at the subject from a rather more political economy perspective than is often seen in some of the mainstream economics journals with a focus on regional economics, such as *Regional Science and Urban Economics* or the *Journal of Regional Science*. This is re-emphasized in his major book on the subject, *The Framework of Regional Economics in the United Kingdom*: "Regional economics starts from the existence of grievances that are identified with particular parts of the country, and from conflicts of economic interest between the predominant parts at least of different regional communities" (Brown, 1972: 1).

One problem with this is that of prioritization. There are scarce resources for tackling spatial differences in economic wellbeing, and inevitably there is unlikely to be a Pareto outcome to any policy initiative. But to select and prioritize actions there is a need to have some feel for the basis of grievances and for the costs of taking actions. The techniques for defining and measuring economic divergence, such as conditional beta-convergence, may have been understood in the 1960s but they were infrequently applied, if for no other reason than a paucity of reasonable data.[2] Indeed, much of Brown's efforts in regional economics involved trying to improve the empirical basis of analysis.

Regional accounts in the 1960s were generally incomplete and, when available, often structured in such a way as to provide limited information useful for economic analysis; e.g. inter-regional trade accounts being in physical quantities rather than values.[3] Brown and Vivian Woodward, in a subsequently published presentation to the International Association for Research in Income and Wealth, critique the situation in the UK. After somewhat understatedly describing the UK data as "neglected," and following two very short paragraphs on available Northern Irish and Scottish data, they conclude: "For the English regions, there is nothing known to us except the bold and exploratory attempt at a complete set of regional accounts by Phyllis Deane published in J.R.N. Stone's contribution to a survey of regional planning techniques" (Brown and Woodward, 1969: 336).[4] This is a point Brown re-emphasized in his extensive survey paper on regional economics published in the *Economic Journal* (Brown, 1969d: 764), while at the same time pointing to the practical advantages that those studying Scotland, Wales, and Ireland enjoy by dint of detailed Census of Production data being available.

The Standard Regions for which some data were collected were essentially designed for economic planning, but were not deemed very useful by Brown. Regarding the English regions, for example, he cites the Redcliffe-Maud Commission, which accepted them because, "we believe that the economic and geographical composition of the country falls broadly into the pattern of the eight economic planning regions" (Royal Commission on Local Government in England, 1969), and then questions this. He asks: what are the claims of the various UK regions to the internal economic cohesion that makes them good planning units, and are there other economic, social, or political qualities that mark them apart? Brown (1972: 51) concludes:

> The United Kingdom regions do not possess homogeneous characteristics either of natural or built environment, or of industrial or social structure ... That some of them ... do possess at least significantly widespread senses of their identity, history, and culture as communities, of the value of particular flavor of life, and of their claims as major components of the nation, is in fact to be reckoned with in considering regional policy.

In other words, Brown tends to view regions as much by their sociology as by their conventionally measured economic structures. See also Brown et al, 1968.

Despite this broad view, data was needed for analysis, and economic data was central to this. Although Brown did not actively develop new regional accounts, his work with Woodward for the Hunt Commission in intermediate or "grey" areas (on which he served from 1967 to 1969) and his later *Framework of Regional Economics* provide carefully thought through arguments of how such accounts should look and ways in which the data cells could be filled. This was not unimportant at a time when the UK was moving into the European Community.

As was highlighted earlier when discussing Brown's 1942 paper on trade balances, there was a widely held view up until the late 1940s that there were self-correcting mechanisms that would equate income across countries, and that this would also hold at the regional level. Much of the debate regarding regions in the post-World War II period centered on whether such automatic market mechanisms would, along neoclassical lines, bring about convergence in the performances of regions. Those who were skeptical, as much from a political economy perspective as from an economic modeling perspective, essentially felt that market imperfections of the sort associated with the macroeconomics of Keynes and the microeconomics of Joan Robinson and of Hall and Hitch, and later Nicholas Kaldor (1970), would lead to cumulative divergence: the endogenous growth theory. Basically, the labor constraints and high wages in the more prosperous areas would not encourage investors to put resources into regions with high unemployment and low wages because of the economies of scale and the ability to attract skilled migrant workers enjoyed by firms in the more flourishing spatial economies.[5] It was the possibility of the latter, its possible size, and what remedial policies might be needed to counterbalance these cumulative forces that Brown was concerned with.

UK REGIONAL POLICY PRIOR TO 1967

Background and experiences inevitably influence people to some degree. Brown grew up in the era of the Great Depression and, being from the North West of England and living in the North, he was witness to the severity of economic difficulties that were felt there, and to the quality of life in the shadow of dark satanic mills. Equally, the time spent in Oxford provided something of a counterbalance, it being geographically in relative proximity to London and the South East. He also grew up at a time when embryonic regional economic policies were being discussed and a few what in retrospect may be considered "experiments" were being conducted in economic intervention. Brown (1969d, 1972), for example, considers these exercises in regional economic policy in detail in his *Framework of Regional Economics in the United Kingdom*, his extended survey on the same subject in the *Economic Journal*, and elsewhere when focusing on specific geographic or policy instruments.

But it was not just the economic conditions that were important; it was also the inevitable interest of an economist like Brown in the success or failures of policies to tackle them from the 1930s. Following the economic depression from the late 1920s, the UK government recognized regional imbalances in industrial structure and initiated measures designed to reduce them. Unlike many other European countries, Britain's regional problems lay in the spatial imbalance of declining traditional industries that prospered in the nineteenth century, rather than a decline in agriculture that had occurred decades earlier. In quantitative terms, unemployment rose from 10 percent in 1929 to 23 percent by January 1933; but while in London and the South East it peaked at 15 percent, in parts of Wales, Scotland, Northern Ireland, and Northern England rates rose to between 27 and 37 percent.

There had been initiatives to reduce the severity and length of downturns in the UK business cycle in the past, but these had largely been actions to reduce market imperfections and to allow the forces of supply and demand to work more effectively. Basically, these recalled the older rural–urban problem of transferring farm labor to industrial jobs. The Labour Exchanges Act of 1909, for example, which created state-funded labor exchanges to help match the unemployed with available job opportunities, fell within this category. The post-World War II establishment of the Industrial Transference Board in 1928 was in a similar vein in seeking to remedy a mismatch of skills and job openings.

Brown argued that the idea of taking the workers to the work, which had some success before World War I, was not suited to the economic conditions of the late 1920s and early 1930s. He stated that:

> [What was] most needed was a full-employment policy of creating effective demand with a regional bias, rather than a policy concerned mainly with inter-regional movements of resources . . . It is hard to believe that the removal from those [depressed] areas of some of the more employable of the unemployed (in addition to those employed or unemployed, who removed themselves) had any serious effect in the short run on their attractiveness to incoming industry. (Brown, 1972: 284)

While much of traditional thinking had taken capital as considerably less mobile than labor, the gradual acceptance of Keynesian ideas, and mounting empirical evidence, shifted the focus towards moving the work to the workers. In his later writing, Brown attributed part of the long-term shift in policy thinking away from labor transfer to Jacob Marschak's work at the Institute of Statistics at Oxford, and notably to that of Helen Makower et al. (1939, 1940), which he inevitably knew about at the time.

Such an approach minimized social costs on labor and shifted incomes to areas where consumer demands were lowest. The Special Areas (Development and Improvement) Act of 1934 initiated the program by designating West Central Scotland, West Cumberland, North East England and South Wales as Special Areas. The caveat of not being able to provide funding for profit-making enterprises or to any project receiving aid from other government sources, however, limited its effectiveness. With the Special Areas Reconstruction Association, established in 1936 to provide loans to small businesses in the Special Areas, and a £2 million trust established by Lord Nuffield such undertakings were designed to partly fill the gap; and by 1937 the Special Areas Amendment Act enabled the Treasury to give loans to larger firms, the development of trading estates was supported, and special tax incentives introduced.

The 1940 Report of the Royal Commission on the Distribution of the Industrial Population, recommended that the distribution of industry and population should be influenced centrally, with the object of redeveloping overcrowded urban areas, decentralizing and achieving a regional balance of diversified industry, and encouraging development in certain areas before depression occurred. Most of the Commission supported a central, independent authority with powers to control industrial expansion in London and the South East, while a minority thought a government department should have that responsibility. The war delayed any action, but the report did form the basis of the Distribution of Industry Act 1945, and many of its ideas were incorporated in the more active regional industrial policy of the 1960s, which subsequently interested Brown.

The 1945 Act, which was to determine regional industrial policy for the next 15 years, was also linked to the 1944 White Paper on Employment Policy whereby the UK government accepted, in a Keynesian manner, responsibility for maintaining a high and stable level of employment.[6] To achieve this, it would influence industrial location, facilitating labor mobility and increasing the international competitiveness of basic industries. The Special Areas were extended to include major towns and cities within them—they had previously been excluded—and renamed them Development Areas. The title is indicative of actions to develop troubled areas rather than just treating immediate problems of unemployment.

The initial success of the policy in the immediate post-war period of reconstruction, however, led to it receiving a lower priority thereafter. There was the prosperity of the traditional industries such as coal mining, shipbuilding, and steelmaking, which would profit from buoyant national and international demand until the mid-1950s. After 1956, deflationary policies, combined with a nadir in the global trade cycle, forced many previously prosperous industries to cut back production. Unemployment in the regions began to rise, although it was still very low compared with pre-World War II levels, and the higher rates were not confined to the Development Areas. The UK's regional problems were, as Brown later put it, thus essentially "rooted in structural differences, and in so far as growth has been slow, so that structure has not had a chance to change fast and painlessly, policy has necessarily been a continuing aid to the adjustment rather than a quick cure" (1976b: 147).

The government's response was the Distribution of Industry (Industrial Finance) Act 1958 that increased the coverage of the Development Areas by adding smaller areas based on their unemployment levels rather than development potential. In 1960, the Local Employment Act gave the Board of Trade the power to designate or de-schedule the now Development Districts without recourse to Parliament. These Districts were based on smaller Local Employment Exchange Areas and chosen strictly on threshold unemployment criteria. Two of the problems with this were that its flexibility led to uncertainty among industrialists in the making of investment plans, and that no consideration was given to the economic potential for development in the areas; policy was entirely reactive. By 1966 the Districts covered 16.8 percent of the UK's population and included most of the earlier Development Areas plus most of Cornwall, North Devon, the Highlands and Islands, and rural northwest Wales.

The main forms of assistance between 1960 and 1966 were factory building and loans, the criteria for which had been relaxed in 1960. A limited number of grants were also awarded, but these, together with the loans, were only given after consultation (often extensive) with the Board of Trade, and thus their value could not be known in advance, reducing the effectiveness of the incentive.

The 1960 Act did, however, introduce grants of 25 percent for firms to build factories in the Development Districts, and after simplification in 1963, these became a major incentive and by 1966 accounted for 40 percent of regional assistance. Grants of 10 percent of the capital cost of new plant and machinery for projects creating employment in the Development Districts were introduced in 1963. In addition, the Finance Act of that year provided for "accelerated depreciation" whereby manufacturing industry could write off the cost of new plant and machinery against profits at any rate it chose.

By 1966 the emphasis of UK regional policy was shifted towards the wider advantages of balanced growth and development throughout the country. The Industrial Development Act 1966 replaced Districts with wider continuous Development Areas selected "with consideration given to all the circumstances, actual and expected, including the state of employment, population changes, migration and the objectives of regional policies." The idea was that, although the Areas could be altered, the wider set of criteria ensured that the rapid changes of the Development Districts were avoided, and the larger continuous Areas enabled industry to choose the most suitable locations for development in a region rather than unemployment black spots.

Incentives systems were also modified and the accelerated depreciation and the plant and machinery grants abolished to be replaced by automatic investment grants towards the cost of plant and machinery. These were available nationally but at a higher rate of 45 percent in Development Areas and 25 percent elsewhere applied in 1967 and 1968. The system of building grants was extended to the new Areas, and discretionary loans and grants towards the cost of transferring or setting up business in them continued. The incentives, excepting investment grants, were linked to the employment generated by a project. The Board of Trade continued to build factories for rent or sale on favorable terms. In 1967, the Regional Employment Premium (REP), a labor subsidy of £1.50 per week for adult male employees in manufacturing, was introduced in the Development Areas, with lower rates for adult women and young people. An additional Selective Employment Tax (SET) was payable at the current rate of £0.375 between 1967 and 1970, while Industrial Development Certificate (IDC) controls on factory building were applied vigorously outside the Areas, with a parallel system of controls on office development in the prosperous locations introduced in 1965 (Armstrong and Taylor, 2000).

THE HUNT COMMITTEE

In 1967 the UK government, besides other things, appointed a joint committee of civil servants and outside experts under the chairmanship of Sir Joseph Hunt. Its remit was:

> to examine, in relation to the economic welfare of the country as a whole and the needs of the Development Areas, the situation in other areas where the rate of economic growth gave cause (or might give cause) for concern (later called intermediate or grey areas), and to suggest whether revised policies to influence economic growth in such areas are desirable and, if so, what measures should be adopted. (Department of Economic Affairs, 1969: 1)

Brown, besides being a full member of the committee also, "undertook a number of special studies on our behalf which added considerably to our understanding of the problems we were facing" (p. 3).

This initiative was part of a broader review and of public discussions in the late 1960s regarding both the overall macroeconomic performance of the UK and the distribution of economic activity and welfare. In the context of regional policy, it represented the first comprehensive review of the British regions since the Barlow Commission's report in 1939. The debate was really initiated when, in 1967, the Department of Economic Affairs and the UK Treasury issued a Green (discussion) Paper on the implications of introducing the regional employment premium.[7] As Brown et al. (1967: 26) said at the time, this was a precedent in that it both put out for public consideration a budgetary measure prior to its introduction and provided a "brief and lucid analysis of the problem of the Development Areas as a background for the proposals that it develops."

Having said that, Brown and his colleagues questioned some of the proposals, or at least some of the rational advanced in support of them. The importance of focusing on manufacturing employment was looked at in some detail. The REP was only to support manufacturing workers, the sector considered important for exporting. Brown and his colleagues, well ahead of their time given the role of services in the UK economy now, questioned this on several grounds. They were not, excluding a few pockets of tourism, large employment generators in the Development Areas; but the "exporting" service industries were the fastest growing nationally, and a shortage of jobs in the Development Areas in such industries could result in migration of specialized labor to other areas. Added to this, it might be cheaper and easier to shift some types of footloose service employment in such fields as insurance and mail-order rather than manufacturing employment, into the Development Areas. Finally, the duration of the REP needed further consideration; a longer duration over the forecast five years (it was ultimately ended in 1977) would be more likely to attract investment. Overall, the argument went that:

> Service industries would, under the proposed scheme, be doubly discriminated against: in relation to local manufacturing (the main competitor with them for labour) they would be at a disadvantage to the extent both of exiting selective employment tax and of the new premium. Moreover, the increases in local prosperity due to the new subsidy would do less to help a local industry the greater the proportion of that industry's markets which came from beyond the development area. (Brown et al., 1967: 32)

A major problem in both assessing the implications of previous spatial economic policies and, perhaps of more importance, in under-standing the economics of UK regions in the late 1960s was the paucity of regional data, and especially information on the openness of the various regional economies. Brown's work in the war, much of which had involved looking at the resource bases of the Allied and Axis Powers, had made him aware of both the limitations of defining policy in the light of inadequate information and of the sorts of data required for assessing economic capability and ways of using it. There were reasons he carried a slide-rule with him: he appreciated that exactitude was impossible, but that a good idea of quantitative broad trends and comparisons is possible and needed.

Brown earlier contributed to improving the situation and showing how data can be better used, in his critique of the Green Paper, and in the use of, what was then, rather basic shift-share analysis. This technique develops indices that separate the economic growth of, say, a region's GDP from national trends, and then separates that per the industrial mix of the region. For example, he found when comparing different periods that, "By virtue of their structure alone the growth prospects of the [development] areas are thus shown to be only about half those of the country as a whole. For manufacturing industry by itself, the areas' prospects are relatively rather better than this" (Brown et al., 1967: 26). He also found that, as far as policy goes:

> In general, the growing industries have grown less fast, and the declining ones have declined faster in the regions containing development areas than elsewhere. If industries in the areas grew at the relevant *regional* rates of 1953–63, the areas' total gain of employment would be less than four-fifths of that which would result from industries growing at 1953–63 *national* rates. (Brown et al., 1967: 26, italics in original)

These general findings add support to the main diagnoses in the Green Paper that the Development Areas would continue to experience historical difficulties that contrast with trends in the rest of the country. Equally, it is clear from Brown's work that policy measures had not done a great deal to offset these difficulties. Where Brown differs is in terms of policy prescriptions. He was not convinced that the REP would meet its job and export creation objectives, mainly because of its adverse effects on the service industries.[8] But perhaps more directly relevant to his role on the Hunt Committee, he argued that the Green Paper had given only limited consideration to the dynamics of regional policy.

The discussions over the Green Paper, as with the early deliberations of the Hunt Committee, were overtaken to some extent as economic conditions deteriorated in 1967 and 1968, and there were concerns about the implications of this for the regions. Table 8.1 provides but one metric of the situation—differentials in regional male employment rates. Interim measures were introduced to help reduce local variations in economic performance within regions. In 1967, in certain areas within the Development Areas where colliery closures were expected to cause high and persistent unemployment, further financial assistance over and above that given elsewhere in the Areas was made available for new undertakings to set up there for the first time. Some colliery closures were also postponed and some new road construction initiated. These Special Development Areas were in Scotland, South Wales, and the Northern region of England.

Table 8.1   *Regional unemployment relatives in Great Britain, indexed on the national male unemployment rate*

	1964		1967		1969	
	June	December	June	December	June	December
London and South East	64.2	65.6	78.3	75.9	74.1	70.6
East and South	68.8	68.2	80.4	75.2	75.3	70.6
South West	89.0	102.0	112.0	101.8	103.2	101.4
Midlands	54.9	49.7	78.6	79.4	84.5	80.3
Yorkshire and Humberside	77.5	76.2	84.4	97.2	111.1	106.8
North West	130.1	127.2	101.4	105.7	102.2	105.7
North	199.4	188.7	171.0	173.8	185.8	196.4
Scotland	213.3	213.2	153.6	152.1	143.4	148.4
Wales	132.4	155.0	161.6	151.9	151.3	151.9
Great Britain	100	100	100	100	100	100

Note: Adjustments are made to reflect changes in regional boundaries.

Source: Employment and Productivity Gazette.

The Hunt Committee's report, *The Intermediate Areas* (Department of Economic Affairs, 1969), finally emerged after taking over two years to complete. Its findings reflected a shift from the more traditional reactive approach to regional economic problems to a more proactive one seeking to put in train measures to smooth out economic transition as signs of trouble emerged. It found, for example, that the Yorkshire and Humberside region was economically vulnerable as it was too dependent on industries which were shedding manpower, growth was slow and earnings low, and there was lack of alternative employment, particularly in view of the considerable unemployment expected to arise from the rundown in mining in the Yorkshire coalfield area. Moreover, much of the region had a poor physical environment because of dereliction from coal mining.

The Hunt Report considered that in the case of the North West it was of paramount importance to evolve a coherent and balanced policy by introducing policies to unify and stimulate the whole region: here too were the problems of declining traditional industries, slow growth, and industrial dereliction, as well as poor amenities and a lot of sub-standard housing. The report recommended the extension of regional assistance to both it and Yorkshire and Humberside, but that Merseyside should lose its Development Area status and be treated on a par with the rest of the North West.

Brown was not particularly happy with some of the policy recommendations of the Committee, although he did feel the specific recommendations on the Intermediate Areas "are generally helpful" (Department of Economic Affairs, 1969: 155). In particular, he was skeptical that measures such as tax relief would be sufficient to stave off potential economic decline in the Intermediate Areas, and even if they had that potential were too slow acting to be of any real use. The reasons for this were articulated in a "Note of Dissent" to the Report (Brown, 1969a).[9] In the subsequent critiques of the Report by academics, the most substantive ones—notably those by Harry Richardson (then a professor at the University of Kent at Canterbury, but subsequently Professor of Economics and Planning at the University of Southern California), the geographer, Derek Diamond (Reader in Regional Planning in the University of London), and Charles Carter (the founding vice-chancellor of Lancaster University)—devoted a disproportionate amount of space to Brown's dissenting voice. The preponderance of economists among the reviewers may partly account for this, but Brown's comments provided a powerful critique of the main thrust of the report.

The Hunt Report proposed that the whole of Yorkshire and Humberside and the North West should qualify for a new form of assistance, a 25 percent building grant for new projects without any attempt to link them with the creation of new jobs in "selected growth zones", and within these regions there should be government industrial estates and factory building with supported investment, including link roads. For these regions—and for Nottingham, Derbyshire, and North Staffordshire (sub-divisions of the East and West Midlands)—there should be an 85 percent grant for land clearance, as existed in the Development Areas. Control over the issue of IDCs should be relaxed throughout nationally by raising the exemption from 5,000 to 10,000 square feet. We have already mentioned that it was recommended that the Merseyside development area be rescheduled and put on the same basis for incentives as was being proposed for the rest of the North West region.

While commission reports are often accompanied by numerous dissenting minority reports, in this case Brown's was a significant one. As Alan Obder (1970: 205) put it, "There are two main problems in writing a review . . . The first is that it has already been done by Professor A.J. Brown in a note of dissent which combines brevity with comprehensiveness." One of Brown's main strategic focuses was on questioning the notion that large growth centers should be developed where possible in the Intermediate Areas to create significant agglomeration economies and, especially, to potential economies of infrastructure expenditure. He questioned the logic of this in Yorkshire and Lancashire, which had significant infrastructure, skilled labor, and industrial linkages, and where a more efficient approach would seem to be a multi-nodal development approach that would mini-mize transaction costs, let alone the social disruption of large-scale labor movements. Odber (1970), however, makes the point that there are real savings in grouping new infrastructure, and that existing opposition to traveling to work was declining—as was the stigma attached to notions such as "dormitory towns."

He also is not convinced that Liverpool should be rescheduled as an Intermediate rather than a Development Area, seemingly on the basis that this would harm Merseyside and do little for the surrounding Intermediate region it would be tied in with given the levels of inducement that would be offered.[10] The problem with Brown's position was that, following Charles Carter (1969: 253), "he appears not to have observed that the present policy is a nonsense." The problem Carter isolated was the land constraints around Merseyside that, unless "green belt" policies for the area between Merseyside and the mid-Lancashire towns were changed, doing the latter would mean losing good agricultural land and be expensive in terms of providing the necessary public infrastructure. Given the high birth rate in Merseyside and existing planned development, Carter argued for policies to disperse the population. In most other respects, Carter was, though, in broad agreement with the Dissenting Note.

Brown was not only critical of the proposed growth zones, but also of the strength of the set of policy instruments proposed to bring them about, and particularly the report's emphasis on the importance of infrastructure investment, arguing that "fiscal inducements, assisted by administrative action, are the most important element in any economical system for influencing industrial action" (Brown, 1969a). Infrastructure investment, he argued, could lead to investment in facilities that would be less utilized than elsewhere and are not a major drawer of industry. Regarding road infrastructure, for example, this involves great initial expenditures that produce only relatively small reductions in an already small component of the delivered costs of the products of less attractive regions. Given the challenges of defining counterfactuals and of establishing the iso-lated effects of road infrastructure investments, empirical verification of Brown's position is difficult to assess. Retrospective analysis of Brown's work by Kenneth Gwilliam (1979: 260) does suggest, however, that:

> the relevant areas of pure theory give no unambiguous guidance on the likely effect of transport improvements. Second, such propositions as can be derived from simplified theory cannot be subject to proper empirical testing. Third,

given these limitations, the sparse evidence available supports rather than undermines Brown's judgement that transport investment has limited impact on regional policy.[11]

Regarding financial incentives, Richardson (1970), while in general agreement with Brown on this, does suggest that Brown may be overstating the case in treating investment subsidies as a transfer payment without taking into account any of the opportunity costs involved, but equally points to the lack of any statistical evidence of the magnitude in this.[12] This latter problem is also highlighted by Diamond (1969: 321) when he makes the more general point that neither Brown's dissent nor the main report provides compelling arguments for their positions, and really miss the opportunity of picking up the baton and running with the idea of setting out ways for closing the gap in our knowledge concerning what actually motivates industrialists in their location decisions. In a way, Diamond could be interpreted as suggesting establishing something akin to Hubert Henderson's Oxford Economists' Research Group, in which Brown had worked in the 1930s, with its engagement of businessmen when analyzing matters of industrial organization.

He combines this concern with strength of incentives with that of having only two levels of assisted area. And specifically, after looking at the operation of Industrial Development Certificates, he argues that the non-Development Areas are far from homogeneous and that there is a stronger case to move out of some locations than from the Intermediate Regions. The solution he proposes is four classes of region. The Development Areas would be retained with similar inducement as then existed, the intermediate areas with fewer incentives, neutral areas with no incentives, and congested regions with additional taxation, specifically a Pigouvian "congestion tax," to reflect their external costs on the rest of the country. The practical problem, of course, is in defining the regions and fine-tuning the various incentive packages, and without very clear objectives this would be challenging.[13] As Richardson (1970: 58) says, "Yet, I doubt the wisdom of having both many different categories of area *and* several different types of incentive" (italics in original). Basically, Brown's ideas may be too complicated for industrial decision-makers to be able to weigh up all the relevant costs of alternative locations. The aim, however, harks back to Brown's *Great Inflation* in that by evening out the pressure of demand across the country, inflationary pressures could be contained.

Furthermore, Brown was not convinced the balance of labor and capital incentives, irrespective of their details, were balanced but rather excessively favored subsidizing capital costs. This was a problem because it was leading in the 1960s, per Brown's calculations, to capital-intensive industry concentrating in areas with abundant labor while labor-intensive industries were left in areas where labor was relatively scarce. The problem was compounded by the fact that lump-sum capital grants were more attractive than ongoing labor subsidies like the REP. He suggests some ways this could be rectified but, given that difficulty in assessing the impacts of various packages *ex ante*, these are inevitably rather speculative.

While not in principle disagreeing with Brown's empirical analysis, Richardson (1970: 56–7) does suggest the conclusion from his empirical work be tempered by the fact that Development Areas have an above average share of capital-intensive industry anyway because of their natural advantages. He also goes further, and questions whether capital-intensity is such a bad thing in any case. While in static analysis of the type used by Brown it is clear capital-intensity is, Richardson argues, in a more dynamic context, it may not be. He cites the case where capital-intensive industries had been growing faster since the mid-1960s than labor-intensive industries, and in doing so had on aggregate created more jobs. He also considers the possibility that the employment multipliers may be greater for capital-intensive industries and that this outweighs any disadvantage in terms of the jobs linked to the initial multiplicand.

The official reception to the report was mixed, but not very enthusiastic where it mattered.[14] The Prime Minister later reflected: "The Hunt Committee had made some new and imaginative recommendations," but that "Our examination of the Report and its thoroughly factual presentation led us to disagree both with the delineation of the areas recommended for action and with the particular choice of assistance proposed" (Wilson 1971: 840). Merseyside (where Harold Wilson's constituency was located), and following Brown's dissenting view, was not to be descheduled because it was considered highly vulnerable to sudden adverse economic shocks and had continued immigration from Ireland requiring adequate job opportunities.[15]

Largely on the basis that aid should not be spread too thinly, especially at a time of severe budget constraints, the Intermediate Areas that were established were smaller than Hunt recommended—embracing the Yorkshire coalfields, parts of Derbyshire and Humberside, the main industrial area of north-east Lancashire, a considerable part of south-east Wales, Leith, and Plymouth. These then received most of the benefits of Local Employment Areas, with some parts qualifying for 75 percent derelict land clearance grants. The Intermediate Areas would also receive priority for Industrial Development Certificates. These financial and administrative actions, to paraphrase Brown, were largely in line with his thinking, although equally, additional selective spending on, for example, roads was more in tune with the recommendations put forward in the main report than his Note of Dissent.

Regarding Brown's minority view, in the debate over the report in the House of Commons, Sir Keith Joseph, Member of Parliament for Leeds North East at the time, and the Opposition's spokesman on Trade, explicitly asked on 25 June 1969, "did the Government consider, as Professor Brown in his minority report suggested, cutting the investment grant to those capital-intensive projects which are disproportionate in their yield of new jobs?" Peter Shore, the Secretary of State for Economic Affairs, responded:

> I note what the right hon. Gentleman said about the removal of S.E.P. Obviously, I also considered the alternative possibility of making savings by other means, including the suggestion made by Professor Brown, but the conclusion to which I came was that, taking into account all the circumstances, the right thing to do was to remove the additional selective employment payment of 7s. 6d. a week. The total saving to be derived from this is £25 million a year.

Diamond (1969: 319) perhaps summed up the problems with the report and the subsequent government actions, but perhaps even more the general difficulties of formulating regional policy in the UK during the late 1960s:

> These contributions display yet again the two characteristics which have dogged past policies and the debate about their efficacy. Because the objectives of regional policy are expressed in very general terms, because the availability of suitable data is extremely limited, and because the impact of regional policy cannot be fully disentangled from other effects, there can at present be no adequate measurement of the outcome of previous regional policy. Consequently, any new proposals rely more on judgment than on rigorous evidence and thus disagreement within the Committee or between the Committee and the Government must remain largely unresolved.

THE FRAMEWORK OF REGIONAL ECONOMICS IN THE UNITED KINGDOM

Prior to serving on the Hunt Committee, Brown had been pursuing his own research work on regional economics funded by the Department of Economic Affairs, under the auspices of the National Institute of Economic Affairs. The remit was:

> to build up a theoretical and empirical framework for the analysis of regional economic development and the consideration of regional policy in the United Kingdom, especially in relation to the problems of national economic development.

Brown returned to this after 1969 with the resultant production of a large tome on the subject, *The Framework of Regional Economics in the United Kingdom* (Brown, 1969e), and a series of studies that appeared around the time Hunt reported and over a short period thereafter (e.g. Brown, 1970). His analysis of policy is, not surprisingly, that of an economist, despite the somewhat broad remit from the Department and an increased interest in the wider socio-political effects of policies in the 1970s. His problem was not so much that he wanted to ignore wider aspects of regional problems, and was certainly cognizant of them given his frequent referrals, but, as James Sundquist (1973: 278) explained in a subsequent review, and more directly than perhaps Brown would have done:

> Repeatedly, Professor Brown mentions the importance of social and politi-
> cal considerations to a policy judgment but then is forced to stop for lack of
> data ... it may be argued that the other disciplines were not ready, and to
> harness the advanced science of economics with the laggard disciplines of soci-
> ology and political science would only impair the former's contribution without
> getting much that was worthwhile from the latter.

Despite these challenges, the appearance of his book was especially timely, coming after a period of reflection by governments on the Hunt Report and at a time following a decade of yo-yoing policies. As the House of Commons Expenditure Committee put it in 1972 regarding the UK's regional programs, "There must be few areas of Government expenditure in which so much is spent but so little known about the success of the policy." *The Framework* added to what was known at the time using what is largely a demand-driven approach and, in doing so, provides intellectual support both for the need to move work to workers (rather than vice versa) and for approaching the short-term problems of regions rather differently to approaches relevant for producing long-term economic growth.

His focus in this work, and in line with his broader political economy view of regional economics, was "the presumption that, with a given volume of output, the satisfaction that it provides is capable of being increased so long as there is scope for reducing the inequality of distribu-tion between consumers" (Brown, 1972: 82). The study can be taken as essentially a Keynesian testing of the effectiveness of the UK's regional policies, and to this end, for example, he makes considerable use of regional multipliers.[16]

This approach, involving distributional matters as it did, was very much in line with that espoused by Ian Little (1957) in his discussion of welfare economics, and differs from the alternative position of seeking to enhance national income by transferring production from less to more efficient regions. This later alternative, which Brown gives less weight to, he also summarizes: "is so far as there are different rewards for comparable units of factors of production in different regions, the implication may be that those factors are imperfectly distributed and that the volume of national production is therefore smaller than it might be given total national resources" (p. 82). But he also highlights that "the benefits of interregional equalisation are small in comparison with the benefits of complete equalization of incomes" (p. 83), citing the fact that inter-industry differences in the UK are as much as three times inter-regional differences.

The book initially provides a near-comprehensive description of the regional economies of the UK, and a more general description of the performances in the 1960s. Given, as discussed above, the quality of the data available at the time there is no doubt that this was no trivial task. The early sections also look at moving away a little from conventional regional income accounting and social differences—including such things as mortality, housing stock, and education—and moves to consider more normative questions about such things as whether regional inequality matters, including less tangibles factors like local pride, but the results are admitted to be "vulnerable."

Looking at regional growth theory, Brown (along with most) argues that explaining why some regions' economies grow faster than others is a complicated matter. He decides "rather arbitrarily" to adopt the classic model of growth based upon James Meade's (1961) single-product growth analysis, and to focus on the supply-side but to modify the analysis as needed: for example, adding reality by including more products with differential availability of inputs between regions' spatial variations in demand. The degree of factor mobility is also a consideration, as, in the long term, are local population growth and regional migration. Perhaps because when the work was done at a time when free movement of labor was not an element of European policy, little is said about foreign immigration. But, overall, the focus is to add the demand dimension to the more conventional factor supply growth framework.

The core of the book, however, is its empirical analysis. Brown made use of many of the established tools of analysis then available in regional economics, together with some innovations that had emerged as part of the wider National Institute initiative. The latter was particularly used when isolating the components of differentials in regions' income and employment growth. Brown made extensive use of a variant of shift-share analysis in his work to separate out the various components that differentiate regions in terms of their economic growth potential.[17] This met with some subsequent criticism.

The traditional form of shift-share analysis examines changes in an economic variable under review, usually employment or income, between two periods (Dunn, 1960). Changes are calculated both regionally and nationally for each industry in the analysis. Each regional change is decomposed, as explained algebraically in Brown (1972: 131–2) into:

- A national growth effect (the share), which is the portion of the change attributed to the growth of the national economy. It equals the theoretical change that would have occurred in the regional variable if it changed by the same percentage as the national economy.
- An industry mix effect, which is the portion of the change attributed to the performance of the specific economic industry. This equals the theoretical change in the regional variable had it increased by the same percentage as the industry nationally, minus the national growth effect.
- The local share effect (differential effect), which is the portion of the change attributed to regional influences, and is the component of primary concern to most regional economists. It represents the change in the regional variable less the national growth and industry mix effects.

The problem with this is that it offers no way of testing the statistical significance of components. Thus, Brown adopts an analysis of variance approach to tease out the relevant variances. Specifically, he uses a method developed by Weeden (later published as Weeden, 1974) to provide regional and residual components in addition to the combined national area structural ones. This allows Brown to assess whether a region has a statistically significant regional element in its growth; conventional shift-share analysis does not allow this because it coalesces the regional and residual components.[18]

Brown's use of the analysis of variance approach was later explicitly criticized by Fothergill and Gudgin. They suggest that any additional rigor that it brings may turn out to be spurious in practice unless the processes modeled conform reasonably well to those in real life.

> To sum up, it is asserted that it is inappropriate to use analysis of variance as a substitute for shift-share in regional analyses using aggregated data, the main reason is that too many different location and growth processes are intermixed, while the state of both current knowledge and data availability are too crude to make separation of these processes a simple matter. (Fothergill and Gudgin, 1979: 209)

Additionally, shift-share analysis is, however, something of a misnomer. As David Houston (1967) points out in a critique, the technique is an exercise in index manipulation of data rather than an analysis in the sense of providing any explanation for the magnitude of the three components. The index numbers obtained are also sensitive to the level of aggregation used.[19] The more disaggregate the data set in the sense of having a large number of industrial categories, the more any region will deviate from the national average; its share will be smaller. These problems were known at the time Brown was writing *The Framework*, and he makes it clear exactly what data are being used and its level of aggregation, and he does seek to explain the variations found in terms of external variables. Nevertheless, the possible lack of robustness in the indices still poses problems.

From a practical perspective, while shift-share analysis, even with the caveats that must accompany it, can shed some light on the factors affecting differences in regional economic performance, what it is very poor at is separating out the changes in such differences over those that are due to market factors and those associated with public policies. Stuart Holland (1976) puts it this way: the last chapter of *The Framework* provides a careful separation of what appear to be policy effects from market effects, but because of the high levels of correlation involved, much of the rest of the quantitative analysis in the book therefore is "ambiguity."

Concerns that outmigration from depressed economic regions would have adverse effects by further depressing local expenditures Brown found to be unwarranted. The first-round effects tend to be neutral, involving either the unemployed migrating or the emigrants yielding their jobs to the local unemployed. There are secondary multiplier effects due to the loss of expenditures by migrating unemployed, but these are in practice relatively small. In quantitative terms, there are unlikely to be more than 18 to 30 jobs lost for every 100 unemployed out-migrants.

The empirical analysis produces a range of results. First, Brown finds that regional policy works, or at least does so in terms of the comparative static analysis of unemployment. Comparing a phase of weak policy (1953–59) with a stronger policy period (1961–66), Brown found that 72,000 new jobs per annum in the Development Areas could not be explained by either growth or structural change; unemployment there would have been 1 to 1.5 percentage points higher, and in the nation 0.5 points higher. Furthermore, the migration flow to the South of England would have been twice as high, and the loss of national output would have exceeded £200 million a year. But put another way, whether these results were worth the rather high budgetary costs of the programs, he saw as a matter for judgment. There was no genuine dynamic analysis in the assessment, and the negative multiplier effects of diverting resources from market were not considered in detail.

In his review of *The Framework*, Sundquist (1973) laments that Brown, mainly because of data limitations, says little about the effectiveness of specific regional policies, other than that in aggregate the programs appeared appropriate. This may be a little harsh even given the data available. For example, along with most analysts doing work roughly contemporaneously with him (e.g. Moore and Rhodes, 1973; Buck and Lowe, 1972), Brown dismisses the role of differential infrastructure policies. He argues that infrastructure needs to be good enough to permit industry to be established—industry may be repelled by a community that is notably unattractive. But making the infrastructure "extra-good" is an expensive way to add very little inducement when most industry of the day did not move in search of amenities or a pleasant environment. Brown, however, went against much of the conventional wisdom when he found that the free depreciation and tax allowances of the Local Employment Act of 1963 were less effective than the investment grants introduced in the Industrial Development Act of 1966.

In terms of broad strategy, he found, and emphasized, that moving the jobs to the workers is a more efficient way of correcting regional employment disparities than moving the workers to the jobs. The latter pumps additional demand into a region that has an excess of it already; hence it is inflationary. Further, in the absence of regional policy, jobs will not move automatically to areas of high unemployment. The resistance of wages, in the presence of a Keynesian money illusion, to downward adjustment, and the tendency toward national uniformity in pay scales as the result of the collective bargaining structure, prevents the economy from operating in a self-correcting manner. Furthermore, the widely-accepted notion of the time that concentration of industry and population in large aggregations increases productivity because of agglomeration economies is shown to be unlikely. What looks like higher productivity, Brown finds, is often no more than a higher-priced output, reflecting the higher costs of operation in large complexes. Reflecting this fact, the trend in individual industries, and independent of the effects of government policy, he found to have been toward geographical dispersion rather than greater concentration.

Finally, he showed that Britain's depressed regions do not suffer from inherent disadvantages that will make the UK economy significantly less productive if national policy succeeds in locating a greater share of industry there. Scotland, South Wales, and the North of England declined not because they were basically bad locations but simply because they happened to have concentrations of declining industries.

The degree to which *The Framework of Regional Economics in the United Kingdom* impacted on British regional economic policy is difficult to judge. The UK joined the European Community in 1973, and with it came an engagement in a much larger geography and an involvement in developing a much wider set of regional policies. In terms of funding, the

UK now had access (and contributed through its national taxes) to the financial instruments of the European Coal and Steel Community, the European Investment Bank, the European Social Fund, and the European Agricultural Guidance and Guarantee Fund. But, set against this, it had to adhere to the Community's Competition Policy that set limits on investment subsidies to central regions of the Community (including the Intermediate Areas) and put a question mark over the legitimacy of the Regional Employment Premium. Independent of this, in 1974 the UK did put additional resources into training under the 1973 Employment and Training Act, despite the uncertainties of EEC rules, doubled the REP, and, in 1975, passed the Industry Act that established the National Enterprise Board with funding to help firms establish themselves in depressed regions. All the latter initiatives are broadly in line with Brown's findings regarding useful policy, but the joining of the European Community tended to dominate thinking regarding regional policy by the late 1970s.

Domestically, and in part because of the longer experiences in Europe and the US, the UK economy was also changing. The reforms of the higher education system in the 1960s—with its large expansion in the number of universities following the Robbins Report in 1963 and the establishment of the Open University in 1969 as a distance-learning university—began to change the shape of the national labor forces, with a significant up-scaling in the overall skill base. Added to this, and running parallel to the university expansion policy, the creation of more polytechnics from 1966 was in part designed, despite central oversight by the Council for National Academic Awards, to meet the specific labor requirements of regional markets. The "Polys" initially focused on applied education for professionals, with a concentration on diplomas and degrees in advanced engineering and applied science (Department of Education and Science, 1966). The implications of these educational developments, however, took time to work their way through the economy and were hardly beginning to be felt in 1972.

SUBSEQUENT WORK ON REGIONAL ECONOMIC ISSUES

As we saw earlier, a major concern of Brown's since his early encounter with regional matters was the relatively poor quality of the data available. While the subject is alluded to in some detail in *The Framework* and, to some extent, in his earlier survey paper in the *Economic Journal* (Brown, 1969d), he waited until 1976 to address a particularly difficult issue in detail. This was the problem of the how to treat the UK-published data on regional unemployment and vacancies, and especially in the context of imperfect labor markets. Given the data available and the fact that in many parts of the country, and for some periods, unemployment and vacancies are far from equal, it is difficult to estimate when they would achieve inequality.[20] The relevant functions can only be estimated far from this point, and the reliability of their extrapolation is uncertain. Brown (1976a) points to periods when the unemployment and vacancies (UV) curve seemed to have moved in, most notably in the decade after World War II, and to the movement out after 1966, and that ideas of excess demand in the former case seem an inadequate explanation. Brown favored a hoarding explanation, not unlike that of Walter Oi (1962), that labor had become a quasi-fixed factor of production.

But equally, by the mid-1960s this hoarding habit had changed with the so-called labor shake-out that occurred. The underlying reason for the hoarding, Brown suggests (and in line with Oi), is that there are costs to labor hiring, and hence an in-house reserve is kept for contingencies. But if all companies shed labor this provides an external pool that can be drawn upon and increases the unemployment rate; basically there are external effects. The result was that in the mid-1960s this is what may have occurred, with both more vacancies and more unemployed. Brown only puts this forward as a suggestion, arguing that the prevailing ideas of prolonged unemployment were the result of greater public support for those not working, and that mismatches of skills and vacancies were inadequate to explain what had happened. What is not explained is why the shakeout, for example, occurred when it did; it remains an unexplained external shock in the analysis.

In 1977 Brown, along with Michael Burrows (a Nuffield Foundation Fellow at Leeds), revisited the matter of regional problems, albeit in a wider geographical scope than in *The Framework*. The work was much less technical in its orientation than *The Framework*; as the Preface says: "In our presentation we have aimed at readability rather than either scholarly and detailed attribution throughout the text to the numerous sources to which we are indebted, or the provision of a statistical base from which further analysis might proceed." Its publication was also very timely given the gradual emergence of a specific European Communities' regional economic strategy. The agriculture and social cohesion policies, although manifestly spatial in their implications, but not so labeled, had been a key element in the Treaty of Rome, and 20 years later they were to the fore again.

The European Commission had adopted a first Communication in 1965, followed by the creation of the Directorate-General for Regional Policy in 1968. As Jean Rey, President of the EC from 1967 to 1970, stated:

We believe there is still a great deal to do in the Community in the field of regional policy. The possibilities have perhaps not been properly realised or acted on. In particular, we need to give a fresh impetus to regional policy formulated at the same level of the Community and, I should point out, with regular cooperation by Member States' governments, which is essential if it is to succeed.[21]

In 1972, the Heads of State and Government adopted conclusions in Paris that described Regional Policy as "an essential factor in strengthening the Community." The 1973 Thompson Report, published by the Commission of the European Communities (1973), concluded that, "although the objective of continuous expansion set in the Treaty has been achieved, its balanced and harmonious nature has not been achieved." Thus, the European Development Fund was established in 1975 for a three-year period, with the objectives of correcting regional imbalances due to the predominance of agriculture, industrial change, and structural unemployment. The Fund could finance investments in small enterprises creating at least ten new jobs; in infrastructure related to this; and in infrastructure in mountainous areas, which had to be eligible under the agriculture guidance fund. Eligibility was for up to 50 percent of public expenditure, preferably to be carried out in national state aid areas. The academic interest was to decide whether this sort of approach was a productive way of handling regional economic disparities across a range of countries, and whether the definitions of the regions themselves were sensible.

The Brown and Burrows volume was certainly timely in this sense, although its spatial coverage exceeded that of the European Community to embrace (at least in 1977) non-European country case studies, as well as the United States. While *The Framework* was largely focused on the UK, this book is comparative in nature and the analysis is at a more general level, although it does provide a relatively detailed account of why regional problems occur. In doing this it separates out the specific economic problems of agricultural, coal mining, old textile, and congested regions and the impacts regional policies, and especially those components of policy that seek to move jobs to workers, had on reducing spatial disparities. In doing this, the amount of space devoted to cutting-edge analysis is limited, and subsequent reviews (for example Chisholm, 1978; Carter, 1979; Hewing, 1979) see it, as the authors seem to have intended, more as a useful advanced teaching aid, supplementing the more technical material then coming onto the market. As the Preface says regarding the available literature, "Books on these techniques are already in good supply." Indeed, Michael Chisholm commends it for "eschewing all formal statistical notation" and, in that way, does not circumvent Sundquist's earlier criticism of

The Framework for its lack of any broader appreciation of the role of other social sciences in regional analysis.

The Framework's obvious strength, especially given its US and European coverage, was its timeliness. It appeared at a time the European Community was developing its portfolio of regional policy instruments and during the decade of its first expansion, with Ireland, Denmark and the UK joining in 1973 when broader issues of integration came to the fore. Taking some notice of happenings in a large, mature, federal economy like the US offered potentially useful insights. But the lessons seem to be limited. Brown and Burrows find that while a structural explanation may be relevant in explaining the regional unemployment disparities within the European countries examined, the dominant problem they find in Europe are the geographical concentrations of declining industries such as coal mining and textiles— something that reflected the failures of the 1951 Treaty of Paris and of its instrument, the European Coal and Steel Community, to rationalize basic industries. One can, in retrospect, question whether they have subsequently been major issues across Europe when many of the then declining industries have ceased to have a significant role in European economies and as, even more recently, new and, notably, service sector industries have emerged. As Christopher Carter (1979) says in his review of the book, it does not offer any genuine dynamics of the regional economics problem.

NOTES

1. Later, in Brown and Burrows (1977: 13), he adopts a definition akin to Jacob Viner's, recalled by his pupil Kenneth Boulding—that "Economics is what economists do"— when he describes regional economic problems as "economic problems with a spatial bias of the particular kind that we normally call 'regional.'"
2. This use of these types of technique was popularized by the likes of Robert Barro and Xavier Sala-i-Martin (1991) some 30 years after Brown's work on regional analysis, although the underpinnings of the methodology can certainly be traced back to the ideas of Frank Ramsey (1928).
3. The UK Office for National Statistics (ONS) now produces regular overviews of regional accounts. For the methods used, see www.ons.gov.uk/methodology (last accessed 17 July 2017).
4. See Richard Stone (1961). US regional accounting, largely because of the greater needs for this sort of data within a federal system, was somewhat in advance at the time compared to the UK (for example, see Hirsch, 1966).
5. Although published before Brown's main body of work, Brown does not mention Nicholas Kaldor's (1970) offering of a clear outline of this argument when reviewing regional growth theory in his later *The Framework of Regional Economics in the United Kingdom*. More recently, and for slightly different reasons, Lucas and Romer have developed the endogenous theory of growth where neo-classic ideas of economies of scale have been supplemented by the ability of wealthier regions to reinvest in technology and conduct R&D; see Button (2011) for a survey.
6. Beveridge (1944b) provides a more economics-based argument for the policy.

7. The REP was the first attempt by any country to use direct subsidies as a job-creation instrument. It involved a labor subsidy given per worker in developing areas. In 1969, it was supplemented by the Selective Employment Tax, a payroll tax intended to help exports by subsidizing manufacturing industry from the proceeds of the services industries.

8. Basically, he argued that the multiplier effects of labor on employment depend on how it is spent. They may be used to reduce consumer prices while wages stay constant; labor unions may bid up money wages, leaving the level of employment unchanged; or they may be absorbed into profits, leaving wages and output unchanged. Each will have different multiplier implications.

9. He also provided technical Appendices (Brown, 1969b, c).

10. In a later talk entitled 'Thoughts on the Hunt Report' to the Regional Science Association Conference in May 1969, Brown also noted that, "the descheduling of Merseyside . . . although it was never put that way, did just happen to pay for pretty well all the others."

11. The role of infrastructure investment re-emerged in the 1980s when some macro studies found a correlation between public infrastructure expenditure and national productivity. Subsequent work, however, raises several technical issues involving, for example, causality and aggregation bias. The broad conclusion of the subsequent debate was that at the investment level there was no clear picture and the impacts of investment varied widely—for a survey see Clifford Winston (1991).

12. The report does note that, of the firms refused development certificates in the West Midlands and the South East, more than 80 percent undertook investment elsewhere.

13. In his review, Alan Odber (1970) supports Brown's idea of more levels of regional and offers some thoughts of his own on how to go about this.

14. Both Roy Jenkins (the then Chancellor of the Exchequer) and Tony Benn (Minister of Technology) were totally opposed to the findings of the report. The secretariat also decided it "would involve spreading resources too thinly," as well as being "expensive . . . and the effects . . . long term and uncertain" (Cabinet Office Papers, 134/3211, 1969).

15. Wilson (1971: 841) saw subsequent justification for this in the merger of factories after the report's publication, as well as crises in the docks.

16. For this he draws on the methodology developed in an earlier National Institute paper with Bowers and Lind (Brown et al., 1967). Liew (1974), when reviewing *The Framework*, while not critical of regional multipliers in themselves, highlights the questionable specifications Brown deployed due to data inadequacies.

17. J.H. Jones is generally considered to be the pioneer of shift-share analysis, in an Appendix to the Barlow Report (Royal Commission on the Distribution of Industrial Population, 1939). Pioneering empirical work in the UK was conducted by Leser (1951), who joined Brown at Leeds University in the 1960s.

18. At about the time Brown's book was published, Joan-María Esteban-Marquillas (1972) also produced a paper showing how the regional share effect can be decomposed isolating a regional shift component that is not correlated to the industrial mix.

19. A defense of standard shift-share, when used with circumspection, is offered by Stephen Fothergill and Graham Gudgin (1979).

20. As Brown had found in his empirical work for *The Framework*, good estimates of vacancies may well also be more important in understanding inflation than are employment data: "It is, however, noteworthy that it proves in some respects easier to explain changes of earnings in terms of unfilled vacancies than of unemployment. . . . It may thus be claimed that the 'Phillips' type relation is less overshadowed by other influences if it is formulated in terms of vacancy rates rather than unemployment rates" (1972: 240).

21. http://ec.europa.eu/regional_policy/archive/policy/history/index_en.htm (last accessed July 2017).

9. Brown's later activities

AN OVERVIEW

Following the publication of *The Framework of Regional Economics*, when he was not engaged in senior management at Leeds University, Brown became engaged academically in both refining some narrower aspects of his analysis of spatial regional analysis and in a continuation of his more direct interest in policy applications. He also set about updating and expanding his earlier analysis of inflation. But in addition to his pure academic interest, as in the past, he continued to be engaged in work on this for international bodies as advisor and as a committee member, and in contributing to the ongoing economic debates of the time.

This was a period of considerable change in terms of the state of many countries' economic performance. Deploying the words of the subsequent UK Chancellor of the Exchequer, Iain Macleod, in a 1965 speech to Parliament, "We now have the worst of both worlds—not just inflation on the one side or stagnation on the other, but both together. We have a sort of 'stagflation' situation. And history, in modern terms, is indeed being made." This is not a situation that Brown had not foreseen as a possibility earlier in 1958, as we have recorded, but he did so without introducing the neologism.

While the magnitude of the economic challenges took time to be appreciated, by the late 1970s the nature of political economics had switched, and on both sides of the Atlantic, from the demand-side Keynesian thinking to the supply-side approaches of Margaret Thatcher and Ronald Reagan.[1] Brown remained the applied economist and continued to look at the data and information at hand to address some of the new economic problems that were perceived to be arising, but setting them in the broader framework of experience. He both served on several bodies addressing the issues of the day—including staying on the UTC until 1978 over a very difficult time for university funding—and produced a flow of academic writing. But he also took on additional, senior managerial responsibilities at Leeds.

These later years also saw reflections and updating of his previous work. Brown was certainly not dogmatic in his approach. His inclination as an applied economist was very much that of Maynard Keynes, who reputedly, although it may well be apocryphal, said something along the lines of, "When my information changes, I alter my conclusions. What do you do, sir?" In some cases, as with inflation, the world had moved on considerably since the 1950s—as had econometric procedures, as well as the quality and quantity of data sources. Hence, he re-examined his prior work on the subject, as well as that of Phillips, in the late 1980s. But this needs to be set in the context of his other commitments at the time.

PRO-VICE-CHANCELLOR

Besides Brown's role within the Economics Department at Leeds, we have already seen he was engaged in various activities. One should add, for completeness, if a little distant from his strict contribution to applied economics, that Brown made another, wider major contribution to his institution. Brown's involvement at Leeds University, besides that of activities in the Economic Department (later School) and serving on a *potpourri* of university committees, was two years as pro-vice-chancellor. Under the UK system of the day, universities had faculty who served periods in the higher level of management. The titles varied, as did the functions performed. A pro-vice-chancellor (or sometimes deputy vice-chancellor) might oversee areas such as administration, research students, or education affairs.

At Leeds, the pro-vice-chancellor substituted for the vice-chancellor in both ceremonial and executive functions when he or she was absent from the university, and chaired specific committees. Brown was pro-vice-chancellor at Leeds between 1975 and 1977 and, amongst other things, he presided over changes in the handling of annual promotions, the constitutional future of Computer Science and Computer Studies, and the location of the School of English. His contribution in some of these latter activities was highlighted in a motion moved by the vice-chancellor at the University's Senate on Brown's retirement: "As Chairman of Academic Staff Committee, Professor Brown introduced or presided over some important changes in the handling of the annual promotions exercise, and his own sure footedness did much to ease the steps of his colleagues."[2]

THE EUROPEAN UNION

In terms of research, Brown's later interests in regional economics extended to include looking at the interactions of mega-regions, and particularly the economic ties between the mega-regions of the European Economic

Community. Brown became involved in 1977 with an EEC Commission Study Group to look at the challenges of further economic integration in Europe. This was at a time when there was something of a push for greater integration in Europe after Britain, Denmark, and Ireland had joined the EEC in 1973. This enlargement brought into the Community states that differed somewhat from the existing six members in terms of their economic interests that had traditionally been less oriented towards the core of Europe and that they were more market oriented than most of the founding states. The Community had also become somewhat moribund at that time, with very limited progress in their genuine economic integration.

Donald MacDougall chaired the Commission. He had been educated at Balliol College, Oxford, reading mathematics and PPE; and, like Arthur Brown, he graduated in 1936, but did not gain a first. Again, like Brown, he won Junior and Senior George Webb Medley prizes allowing him to study international trade under Roy Harrod. He held fellowships at Nuffield College and Wadham College, was a Reader in International Economics at Oxford from 1950 to 1952, a professorial fellow from 1952, and first bursar of Nuffield from 1958 to 1964. MacDougall took up a lectureship in economics at Leeds in 1936, but with the outbreak of hostilities served Churchill in the office of First Lord of the Admiralty and then the prime minister's statistical branches until 1945, and at the beginning of Churchill's 1951 premiership. He was at the National Economic Development Office and the Department of Economic Affairs under George Brown, working on a "national plan" as director general. From 1969 for five years he headed the Government Economic Service at the Treasury and was chief economic adviser to Chancellors Jenkins, MacLeod, and Anthony Barber. At the end of his government service he became Chief Economic Adviser to the Confederation of British Industry (CBI) and a director of the Organisation for European Economic Co-operation (OEEC) in Paris. His *Guardian* obituary on 24 March 2004 sums him up as "a London 'special adviser', a mover and shaker in Whitehall and Westminster." [3]

The Commission asked a group of independent economists under MacDougall—that, besides Brown, included Professors Dieter Biehl (Technische University, Berlin), Francesco Forte (University of Turin), Yves Fréville, and Theo Peeters (Catholic University of Leuven), and Martin O'Donoghue, who had just become Irish Minister for Economic Planning and Development—to examine the future role of public finance at the Community level in the general context of European economic integration. Brown's inclusion was obviously partly due to his considerable abilities and experience in applied economics; but also many of the issues to be considered were akin to those that had cropped up in assessing UK regional economic policies.

The timing of the Commission was ideal for Arthur Brown. He was winding down his full-time academic career, his work on UK regional policy had been completed, and the subject of economic integration harked back to his early government work on Africa. He had known MacDougall for some time, with their overlapping at Oxford and in the civil service. Brown, in broad terms, was largely sympathetic to MacDougall's largely anti-EEC position—MacDougall had been active in 1973 in the campaign against UK membership. Indeed, Brown (1968) had, in one of his few ventures into the media in the late 1960s, questioned the benefits of joining the Community. Reviewing the "British disease of slow growth," he felt that "the Common Market dose of salts is clearly contra-indicted." Importantly, Brown gets to the nub of the essential question posed in the 2016 referendum on continued UK membership of the European Union: "Where does economics end and politics begin?"

> People often ask: "Can we afford to stand by ourselves in competition, increasingly, with very large market areas?" In many ways, this is a political rather than an economic question; the role of a great power clearly depends on size, and the question whether we should function independently as a middle-sized power, or should associate ourselves at some sacrifice of independence with a bloc of other States is an important one politically. But even if it is decided that, politically, we ought to ally ourselves in some exclusive way with western Europe is a proposition which I, for one, would want to examine critically. It does not in the least follow that this either demands or entails the kind of economic relation with Europe that EEC membership involves. (Brown, 1968)

The 73-page, typed report—the Commission's documents of the day went more for substance than visual presentation (Commission of the European Community, 1977a)—was backed up by a second volume of research (1977b). The latter has Brown's piece on the UK. The report's conclusions, supported by the independent economists as well as six Commission officials, argue that without boosting the Community's budget to at least 5–7 percent of gross domestic product (GDP), a currency union would be impossible to sustain. Full federalism would require a Community budget of 25 percent of the Community's GDP. By way of context, in 1977 the Community's budget was about 0.7 percent of GDP; today it has grown to slightly over 1 percent of the EU's GDP. The longer-term objective of this was to provide "a limited budget equalization scheme for extremely weak member states to bring their fiscal capacity to, say, 65 percent of the Community average and so ensure their welfare and public service standards are not far below the main body of the Community."

The central argument supporting this view is that to combine economies as divergent as Belgium, Germany, France, Italy, Luxembourg, the

Netherlands, Denmark, Ireland, and the United Kingdom checks would need not only national spending and wage developments, but also a budget that could make up for inter-regional differences in competitiveness. "The danger [is] that, as economic integration proceeds, there will be increasing pressure from wage-earners for real earnings equal to those in the richer member countries, regardless of the remaining international differences in productivity." The report warned: "This is a danger, which could weaken the competitive power of the poorer countries and/or promote rapid infla-tion in them." In some ways, this may be seen as a foreseeing of the under-pinnings of the economic crises that confronted Greece, Italy, Spain, and several other EU countries after 2008.

Since there were no notes of dissent to the report, one must assume that Brown generally went along with these interpretations, which was not that surprising since they echo words from 22 years earlier in *The Great Inflation*, albeit that those were at the regional level in the United Kingdom.

His own chapter to the report focused on the UK situation, looking at the experiences there regarding the impact of regional income transfers on economic stability. This was used as a proxy microcosm of transfers at the national level within a large geographical region such as the EEC. Being a largely empirical exercise, the work was hampered somewhat by the paucity of good regional data, and particularly so in terms of regional public expenditure, inter-regional trade, and the international trade of regions (except for Northern Ireland).[4] Despite these challenges, and making the best assumptions he felt reasonable, Brown provides estimates of the impact of external shocks on regional economies; for example a 1 percent fall in demand for a particular national factor would have an impact of about 3.6 percent on any producing region. Public finance, he finds, acts as a buffer to assist the lower-income parts of the UK, with Southeast England and the West Midlands contributing between 7 and 8 percent of their GDP (some 3–3.5 percent of national GDP) to the other regions. Considering other factors reduces this somewhat, but Brown's (1977: 24) general conclusion is, "At all events., it is clear that the public sector plays an important part in financing regional current account balances, notably those of the peripheral regions."

The underlying policy focus, and very much following Brown's line, was thus to be on income redistribution at times of inflationary crisis as opposed to tight monetary policy; in other words, neo-Keynesian fiscal policy was the key to stability and not monetary policy. This was enmeshed with notions of fiscal federalism and more coordinated and targeted demand management across the member states. The data amassed by the Commission showed that:

> As well as redistributing income regionally on a continuing basis, public finance in existing economic unions plays a major role in cushioning short term and cyclical fluctuations . . . there is no such mechanism in operation on any significant scale between member countries, and that is an important reason why in present circumstances monetary union is impractical. (Commission of the European Community, 1977a: 12)

One vehicle for pan-European redistribution that the MacDougall group suggested was a "community unemployment fund." Workers across Europe would pay part of their unemployment insurance into the European budget and in turn Brussels would finance part of their benefits if they lost their jobs.[5] The fund could not only help cushion regional recessions, but could also create an emotional tie with the European institutions, the report argues. The idea, however, never gained political favor, although Brown and the Commission members may not have been too surprised: "It is most unlikely that the Community will be anything like so fully integrated in the field of public finance for many years to come as the existing economic unions we have studied" (Commission of the European Community, 1977a: 11).

The MacDougall Commission's findings also ran very much against those of a similar committee set up by the Organisation for Economic Co-operation and Development (OECD) and reporting at the same time: the McCracken Committee (McCracken, 1977). This also had a distinguished chair—Paul McCracken had been, amongst other things, chairman of the Council of Economic Advisers for President Nixon – and involved several leading economists.[6] This Committee, albeit taking a global and not only a European perspective and focusing on overcoming stagflation, concluded, as with MacDougall, that there was a need for better use of fiscal and monetary instruments, but took the line that monetary policy should be at the core. Fiscal policy should only be used cautiously, to avoid dangers in adversely affecting business confidence, and fiscal fine-tuning, abandoned monetary policy, and budgetary neutrality once full employment had been achieved.[7]

The MacDougall Commission Report had little impact at the time, in part because the more conventional arguments for handling inflation and slow growth were overtaken by supply-side thinking, the reunification of Germany, and enlargement. The conventional wisdom had swung more to the neo-liberal views expounded by McCracken. Ultimately, the Maastricht Agreement adopted the latter's position that a small budget would do. The official line was that, despite the copious empirical evidence presented by MacDougall, the principle of subsidiarity was being applied rigorously and no more centralized action was needed; that the creation of a central bank would be sufficient to prevent recessions, and indeed a common fiscal policy would stymie the ability of countries to pursue individual monetary policies; and that there were national automatic fiscal shock mechanisms in place in each country. Added to all this, the proposals contained in the report were inevitably going to have some short-term adverse consequences for the overall economic performance of the Community when it had already been performing badly since 1973.

Brown in a book chapter in 1983 did return, albeit in a rather tangential way, to the topic of the MacDougall Report and offered some reflections on budgetary issues involving the European Community, perhaps ironically, at a time just after Greece had joined.[8] Little had changed by then in terms of the scale of the EEC budget as a percentage of the overall Community income; he estimated it at 0.8 percent, which he compares to the 45 percent or so that European nations' governments were spending nationally of their GDPs.

He articulates rather more clearly than did the MacDougall Report the need for a larger fiscal regime to diminish welfare and income differences, not only between countries but also between states or regions, highlighting that if further economic integration, and possibly monetary union, are to be achieved then the poorer regions will need convincing of their benefits to them. Probably only correctly, however, when he surmised that "It does ... seem broadly the case in Europe that the more prosper members of the EC are more in favour of closer union, while some, at least of the less prosperous, more peripheral members are more doubtful" (Brown, 1983: 309).[9] Subsequent events suggest that the UK is an exception when it comes to the "more prosperous members."

His focus in the piece, however, moves from the importance of fiscal policy in the Community for fostering union to ways to enhance its fiscal efficiency. In that domain Brown questions the use of the value-added tax (VAT) as being too complicated and of the Commission collecting a proportion of each country's VAT revenue as its main income, preferring a proportion of a country's GDP. As he puts it, "The real difference is that a contribution calculated from GDP, perhaps in such a way as to provide a degree of progressiveness, has more chance of being recognised as equitable than has the yield of a hypothetical VAT, or indeed, any other practical tax" (Brown, 1983: 313). What he, and most others at the time, did not really consider was the practical issue of dealing with the creative accountancy at the national level that became manifest later with the introduction of the Euro.

But the MacDougall Report did emerge and get dusted off in later debates about the debt crisis in Europe after the 2007–2008 Great Recession. Gabriele Steinhauser (2012) in the *Wall Street Journal*, for example, suggests senior European bureaucrats should "take [a] stroll in the commission's historical archives . . . and walk all the way to the section for 1977." She also quotes from a *Real Time Brussels* interview with Horst Reichenbach, a Community civil servant involved with the Commission, who by 2012 had become head of the Task Force for Greece: "A lot of what is happening today was clear to us then, just not quite this dramatically." In a recent, more academic work, William Mitchell (2015) suggests "A close reading of the MacDougall Report will leave one wondering why the Eurozone was ever created. The major issues they [*sic*] highlighted were clearly still relevant in the 1990s."

The MacDougall Report did not address directly the matter of a single currency, although it was not being ignored in Brussels at the time. The idea of monetary union for Europe was not new in the 1970s. In 1970 an expert group chaired by Luxembourg's Prime Minister and Finance Minister, Pierre Werner, presented a commonly agreed blueprint to create an economic and monetary union in three stages (Werner Plan). The project experienced serious setbacks from the crises arising from the non-convertibility of the US dollar into gold in August 1971, and the de facto collapse of the Bretton Woods System, and from rising oil prices in 1972. An attempt was made in 1972 to limit fluctuation of EEC currencies, using a snake in the tunnel whereby most of the EEC countries agreed to maintain stable exchange rates by preventing fluctuations of more than 2.25 percent, but this was only adopted by a limited number of members.

Brown, while not directly writing on the actualities of the attempts at European monetary union, despite his experiences with such things in the African Unions, in reviewing Max Corden's *Inflation, Exchange Rates, and the World Economy*, does comment on Corden's suggestion that a Friedmanian policy of a steady rate of money supply increase across Europe may be desirable given variations in the natural rates of inflation (Friedman, 1968; Phelps, 1967). Brown's (1978: 1964) position is to ponder over:

> . . . whether, even in a world of vertical Phillips curves, a common currency might not promote demands for uniformity of nominal wage-levels to an extent that could only be reconciled with differences in national situations, and with national aspirations to share in the Community's prosperity, by restoring the switching device of variable exchange rates.

A RE-EXAMINATION OF INFLATION

By the mid-1980s, economic data had increased in its coverage and in its quality, and computing hardware and software had evolved considerably since the 1950s. Brown decided it was time to look again at some of the issues that had underlain the inflation debates of 30 years earlier. The timing was also important, flowing as it did into the stagflation of the 1970s and early 1980s that was accompanied by a shift in macroeconomic policy emphasis away from a Keynesian focus to an emphasis of supply-side factors. Added to this, the levels of inflation during this period of stagflation were, at least in the UK, much higher than in the early 1950s, the subject of Brown's earlier book. For example, whereas in 1951 the consumer price index rose by 9.1 percent and by 9.2 percent the following year, in 1974 inflation was 16.0 percent, in 1975, 24.2 percent, and in 1976, 16.5 percent, but rising again to 18 percent in 1980. The inflation problem was, therefore, of a different order of magnitude.

Much of the industrial deregulation that accompanied the last two years of the Carter administration in the United States and then the policies of Ronald Reagan were largely based upon the idea that inflationary pressures were at least partly driven by cost factors brought about by excessive, dated regulation of industry. The Thatcher government's policies in the UK followed similar reasoning. Even though tight monetary policy was the main inflation policy instrument, prices were also seen as being pushed up by limits to both static and dynamic competition in many highly regulated markets, including energy, transportation, and telecommunications.[10] The underlying question was just how much of the inflationary problem was cost oriented.

Brown had largely moved away from mainstream work on inflation by the 1980s, his focus being on regional economics; but, as he puts it, "More recently, pure curiosity has led back to an attempt to make sense of the last thirty years' experience of inflation by an international comparative study to see how well or badly my insights of 1955 survive."[11]

In 1985 Brown, with the help of Jane Darby, revisited the issue of global inflation in *World Inflation Since 1950: An International Comparative Study*. As might be expected with the advances that had taken place in computing and econometrics, this study offers a much more technical examination of the topic than his work of 30 years earlier, and, to quote from the Preface, "The present work is an attempt to make sense of the greater inflation which has occurred since." The book was written after the experiences of several decades of relative peace, with the availability of better data, and the hard- and software to provide a more rigorous analysis of it, and with a maturing of thinking about the debates over the Phillips Curve in the late 1950s and early 1960s. Importantly, a range of new minds had enjoyed the opportunity to mull over the underlying causes of inflation.

Despite the developments since 1955, Brown and Darby still pinpointed the major and ongoing challenges in conducting work on wage-change:

There are, of course, plenty of other factors which may be expected to have influenced wage inflation [since 1950]. Given the monopolistic character of much of wage bargaining, changes in the relative bargaining power of employees and employers, insofar as it is not already represented by the level of unemployment or the state of price expectations, might be considered to take it into account. The trouble is that it is not easily measured. (Brown with Darby, 1985: 252)

The findings contained in *World Inflation* are not radically different to those of *The Great Inflation*. They remain primarily Keynesian in that the predominant source of inflation was found to be rises in costs. The transmission mechanism involves prices of manufactured goods being determined by costs plus a mark-up: *viz*, "Most finished goods. especially in the advanced market economies, were priced mainly by a mark-up over cost, the mark-up being relatively insensitive to pressure of demand" (Brown with Darby, 1985: 377). The costs in this case include wages set by a bilateral monopoly of employers and unions, market-determined materials prices, and administered oil prices. Put another way, and in terms of justifying economic deregulation, there was considerable X-inefficiency in economies that tempered the powers of competition as a force to keep prices down. Money supply was largely elastic, and accommodated the level of costs.

A sample of 13 countries—including the six major nations (USA, UK, Japan, West Germany, France, and Italy), five smaller OECD countries, and India and Brazil—serves as the database for the analysis of the process of inflation between the early 1950s and, mainly, 1981. They largely used the work of Angus Maddison (1964) to define economic cycles. The analysis features four kinds of inflationary and disinflationary impulses. Distinguished annually in the 11 OECD countries, inflationary impulses are defined as: wage-push-rates of increases of hourly earnings rise causing profit's-share of value-added in manufacturing to fall; expenditure-pull-rate of increase in money GDP rises and profit-share of value-added in manufacturing rises; cost-push from non-labor inputs-rate of change of import prices weighted by import share of GDP rises by more than 1 percent; and money injection-rate of increase of broad money rises; and the rate of increase of velocity falls.

Disinflationary impulses were negative versions of the four inflationary impulses. Each acceleration and each deceleration of inflation is treated as a separate episode. Over the 29-year period Brown and Darby studied, there are 76 episodes of accelerating inflation and 70 disinflationary episodes of somewhat longer duration, so in only 46 percent of the time did the sample experience accelerating inflation. Of the 588 impulses, 312 are designated as inflationary. The ambiguous cases identified by Brown and

Darby are attributed to changes in productivity when rates of growth of nominal expenditure and hourly earnings increase without a change in profit-share. The main conclusion from this is that the incidence of money injection was counter-inflationary, that of wage and import-price push was inflationary, and expenditure pull was associated with accelerating output growth much more so than with rising inflation.

Each of the inflationary impulses is then examined in turn, of which the longest chapter in the book is devoted to wages and the labor market. In a chapter on price formation in national economies, markets for final goods and services are found to have mostly passed on costs of factor inputs; the impact of change in demand has been mainly on output rather than prices, whereas in world foodstuffs and raw materials markets, changes in supply and demand have had drastic price effects. The labor market in many countries is found to have exerted almost continuous upward pressure on costs, strongly affected by various institutional circumstances. Chapters on the effects of inflation on welfare and growth, on the post-1979 recession, summarily show that Brown believed, on balance, that inflation was no scourge and efforts to contain it were misguided. In sum, the study finds that "Inflation in a given industrial country therefore varied with the tightness of its labour market and (through the channels both of raw material and labour markets) with the relative growth rates of monetary demand in them" (Brown with Darby 1985: 377).

The book, while more rigorous in its econometrics, is somewhat less strong in its institutional basis than the 1955 book. Although Brown clearly understood that the basic inflation rate was much lower in the period before the late 1960s than in subsequent years, the book nowhere considers the possibility that the behavior of the reserve-currency country under the Bretton Woods system might have accounted for the difference, or whether international channels of transmission of inflation might differ depending on the monetary regime. It is debatable whether it is accurate to describe the period after 1953, the starting point after the Korean War for most statistical measures in the book, as one of continuous inflation as Brown and Darby imply. It is now generally accepted that there was no inflation in the United States until 1966, since measured price increases until then could well have reflected inadequate allowance for quality changes in goods and services. This comment applies also to other countries with basic inflation rates of under 15 percent in the first period.

Defining the monetary injection impulse, as Brown and Darby do, would also seem to bias downward their findings of inflationary impulses from that source. A less objectionable definition would have been a rise in the ratio of money stock per unit of output. There is an asymmetry in the role assigned to money. Increases in money growth are accommodating, with no independent expansionary effects. Decreases in money growth, however, are not accommodating; they have contractionary effects. Portraying money growth as dependent on demand for loans is a throwback to an older idea of the "pushing of a string" notion of the impotence of monetary policy. Bank investments create money as surely as their lending does. The argument that an increase in money growth owing to an increase in lending is self-limiting because "new money penetrates to those who use it to repay debt to banks" (Brown with Darby, 1985: 181) ignores the incentive of the banks to maintain their interest-earning assets, whether loans or investments. Extinction of a given loan does not bring to a halt the expansion of bank liabilities to the public, provided the central bank is not engaging in open market sales or other contradictory actions.

Explicitly in terms of the Phillips Curve, the authors emphasize the ordinal nature of their findings: "The simple Phillips relation between the tightness of the market and the *rate of change* of hourly earnings remains as a persistent, though not universal, constituent of wage equation" (italics as in original); and, regarding the larger matter of inflation, "Institutional and political changes contribute heavily to the complicated story of wage push (Brown with Darby, 1985: 382).

The book did not attract the level of attention of Brown's earlier work.[12] A lot of water had flowed under the bridge since then, and the literature on inflation had grown considerably, as can be seen in the Martin Bronfenbrenner and Franklyn Holzman (1963) survey published only eight years after *The Great Inflation*. There was also the works of others to compete with, and especially those of a strong monetarist persuasion or with an interest in the role of institutions (Baumol, 1978). But *World Inflation* did not go unnoticed, although not all assessments were entirely positive.

In reviewing *World Inflation Since 1950* in the *Economic History Review*, Anna Schwartz (1986: 670), for example, finds that the book is certainly a well-written and well-organized study of a wide-ranging collection of data across a sample of countries—but that it provides little enlightenment on the central question to which it is addressed. The main limitation of the study, from her monetarist view is seen in its lack of context. Schwartz argues there is no indication that inflationary impulses are in any way affected by the nature of the international monetary system which was one of its main themes. Was inflation a home-grown cost phenomenon in the late 1960s in countries experiencing massive dollar reserve inflows that they could not sterilize? Would not constraints on the impulses differ under an international gold standard, under the Bretton Woods system, or under managed floating?

At a more detailed level, she points out, that following Milton Friedman:

permanent income is now generally accepted as the variable to which private consumption responds. Suspicion of thrift as a negative influence on the macro-economy seems a far cry from the current need for increased saving in many industrialized and less developed countries to make possible increased investment in both tangible and knowledge-related capital.

And further that:

There is no indication that inflationary impulses are in any way affected by the nature of the international monetary system . . . he nowhere considers the possibility that the behaviour of the reserve-currency country under the Bretton Woods system might have accounted for the difference, or whether international channels of transmission of inflation might differ depending on the monetary regime. (Schwartz, 1986: 671)

Brown followed up on *World Inflation* with a paper in the *National Institute Economic Review* offering a somewhat tighter examination of how prices moved during major recessions over the preceding century, and covering more economies (Brown, 1988b). To do this he took 16 countries and examined their economic cycles since 1870.[13] Some of his findings were in retrospect hardly surprising, for example that the world depression from 1979 was the "biggest of the last 120 years except for the great depression of the 1930s (and the reconversion depressions immediately following the world wars)."

In terms of inflation, the post-1979 economic depression was also exceptional in that it was not accompanied by falling prices until there had been a significant period of high unemployment: six years of 7.5 percent unemployment in OECD countries. The explanation he finds partly in that the depression was initiated by a supply-side shock stemming from the second oil crisis following the Iranian Revolution, leading to price rises that produced policy reactions resulting in a wage–price spiral. The situation, he found, to have been worsened by the bias in labor markets from the 1950s that saw wages rising in the absence of external cost shocks when national economies were highly active. Overall, however, the picture Brown (1988b: 78) summarized thus: "So long as receivers of wages and profit margins can and do take measures to defend their real incomes, it carries the implication that any change in the terms of trade against the non-primary sector will lead to a world price-wage spiral as the two oil shocks did." In other words, he again finds that cost factors combined with market inflexibilities are a major force in causing world inflations.

RETIREMENT AND HONORS

Brown retired from Leeds University in 1979 and took up an emeritus professorship. This allowed him to retain his links with the institution and make use of its facilities. He made good use of this, and certainly, as we have seen, did not rest on his laurels after his retirement. Not only did he continue to contribute to the academic literature and discourse, but he also contributed to public affairs and produced reflective work on the history of economic thought and ideas (Brown, 1988a), including that of his own involvement (Brown, 1997a). He also inevitably had more time for his own hobbies of gardening and walking.[14]

Brown obviously had a very diverse and successful career. But for the academic community, he also demonstrated the importance of applied economics to decision-making. His professional life and work illustrated that economics can, conducted carefully, provide important, generally quantitative insights to help decision-makers. While he recognized the importance of other disciplines and the limitations of applied economics, he still thought that given a very imperfect world—with limited information and, often, somewhat biased ideas—the information good applied economics can offer is an invaluable aid to making better decisions. This in turn ultimately enhances welfare.

Brown lived at a time of transition. He was born at the beginning of World War I; his upbringing was during the Great Depression; he saw the consequences of World War II, the end of British colonialism, the emergence of the Cold War, radical changes in the British higher education system, the decline of the Soviet Union, and the development of the European Union. In terms of economics, not only was there the acceptance of many of the ideas of Maynard Keynes, but also significant, albeit ultimately unsuccessful, were innovations in central planning theory and in microeconomics, with a movement away from the often restrictive abstraction of Alfred Marshall. Technology changed considerably, vastly more and better data becoming available as the world moved into the information age and the ability to manipulate the numbers as they emerged.

This all combined and resulted in an invigoration of interest in economics and the emergence of new debates about how the world functioned and the degree to which it could, or indeed should, be manipulated. In this Brown was a man of his generation. He took up the ideas of John Maynard Keynes whilst still a student, explored several of the new approaches to the quantification of some of the key concepts of Keynesian economics, and became actively involved in trying to apply these to the formulation of economic policy. However, as with most top-flight applied economists he left no major legacy of new theory, although (as we saw earlier) the likes of

Bernard Corry and Anthony Thirlwall would probably contest this regarding the unemployment–inflation relationship. Nor is there any school of thought or specific methodology associated with him.

What we do find are significant works, as well as the establishment of a leading economics department, that focus on making use of the economic knowledge that we do have, tweaking this knowledge when helpful, and, where possible, putting broad numbers on the key parameters. In this latter sense, his sympathies regarding excessive quantification, while not totally adverse, were broadly in line with the skepticisms of Maynard Keynes—regressions should be treated with care. But Brown's roots were still in Oxford and not Cambridge, and his higher education under the tutelage of the likes of Hitch and Marschak, provided for a somewhat more eclectic approach to economic issues involving a significant degree of pragmatism compared to those more directly engaged in the *The Years of High Theory*, to deploy Shackle's description. This was something reflected not only in his methodology but also in the subject matters he chose to study. They involved major topics of the day rather than some larger vision of how a multifaceted economic system works.

Brown deviated significantly in his career compared to many of his contemporaries by neither staying in the civil service nor following a path in the well-established, large economics departments that existed after the war. Part of this would seem to reflect a manifest love of the northern part of England, with its specific character and rugged scenic beauty; but it must also have been influenced by a rare opportunity to build up a major economics department within an established university, and to do so at a period in his life when he was still very active in his research and heavily engaged in public service. One can speculate on what his career would have brought had he stayed in government services or taken an academic position either in Oxbridge or London, where there was an established concentration of economic activity and where most of the major academic figures of the period resided. But going to Leeds is likely to have kept him more grounded in the state of the British economy outside of the south of the country, without significantly encumbering his foreign ventures or London-based activities too much.

His overall approach to economics—whether it be research, advising, or educating—was one of a pragmatist rather than being heavily overloaded with ideology. He certainly had a Keynesian bias to his thinking, perhaps an inevitable consequence of his background and the sway of economic ideas during his years at Oxford; but he was no hard-core disciple. While he did bring several prominent Keynesians to the Department of Economics at Leeds, the overall pattern was more diverse, and quality was the diktat rather than belief. His broad approach to economics was that of problem solving within a longer established Anglo-Saxon tradition. He largely believed in market forces, with interventions when it was demonstrable both that there were market failures and that government actions would produce superior results. Simply intervening when markets are imperfect, along the Continental tradition of economics, was not his way. Careful empirical analysis is required to assess the wider pros and cons of potential government actions before they are adopted. This is clear in the advice he offered to the various committees he served on, and in his studies of regional economies and economic unions.

Brown was also one of an almost extinct band of applied economists who "analyzed" using a significant amount of intuition entwined with more technical evaluation. At the same time, he also appreciated the inexactitudes of the science of economics, and his empirical papers seldom, at best, took results beyond one decimal place. Economics is about human behavior and, while evidence had been growing over his life-time about the factors determining many aspects of this behavior, it was still far from complete and he was reluctant to just become a speculator about the unknown. This led him to seek to improve not only analytical methods, but also the databases upon which empirical economics relies.

By the time of his retirement, he had been honored by being elected a Fellow of the British Academy for the Advancement of Science in 1972 and President of the Royal Economics Society; he was also made a Commander of the Order of the British Empire 1974, and received honorary doctorates from four universities—Bradford (a D.Litt.) in 1975, Aberdeen (a D.Litt.) in 1978, Sheffield (a Litt.D.) in 1979, and Kent (a D.Litt.) in 1979. He had been involved in the formation of two of these institutions, and was obviously respected by the others.

The recognition in the statements accompanying the awards of the doctorates serves to summarize some of Brown's achievements. Perhaps the most apposite is from the University of Sheffield's graduate speech on the conferment of his degree:

> But it is even more fitting that we should honour today the unity of this wise man with his work. The open-minded honesty of his empirical approach is matched with a total mastery of his discipline. He transmutes the compromises involved in the formulations of state policy into a cross-fertilisation between academic and public need. He is a giant of uniquely English modesty and one of the most distinguished economists of our time.[15]

Arthur Brown died on 28 February 2003 aged 88.

NOTES

1. William Niskanen (1988) provides an account of both the particularities of supply-side economics and its rise to prominence in economic policy making in the late 1970s and 1980s.
2. *Pro-Vice-Chancellor: Professor Brown*, Baron Boyle of Handsworth to University of Leeds Senate (20 October 1977, AJB C&P).
3. His memoires, *Don and Mandarin,* offer more flesh to this long career than there is space available here. (MacDougall, 1987). In addition, at the same time as Brown (1951a, b) was publishing his work on currency depreciation and trade, MacDougall had produced a series of four papers published in 1951 and 1952 in the *Economic Journal* on British and American exports. These were later brought together in his collected economics paper (MacDougall, 1975: 5–68).
4. The issue of the quality of regional economic data had been addressed previously by Brown and Woodward (1969: 346). To give a flavor of the limitations of the official statistics at that time, "Regional estimates of GDP by the production method are still not possible, but from 1964 one can produce reasonably reliable estimates of total GDP (by adding together factor incomes) and total regional expenditure to show the major regional economic differences in the United Kingdom. Even for 1964, parts of the estimates are based on rather shaky data. The weakest point is the regional distribution of manufacturing investment in plant and machinery."
5. The details of this were presented in Biehl's chapter in the report.
6. These were Guido Carli, Herbert Giersch, Robert Marjolin, Robin Matthews, Attila Karaosmanoglu, Ryutaro Komiya, and Assar Lindbeck.
7. David Felix (1979) provides a critique.
8. Brown saw the main budgetary issue at the time as one of collecting and dispersing revenues. It was difficult to devise a tax system based upon any criterion of ability to pay, and hence the main way of redistribution was through *ad hoc* compensation mechanisms such as the European Regional Development Fund. While the Community's income remained small this could be handled; but looking forward it would become impractical.
9. Germane to the recent history of the EU, he also observes (1983: 310), "A country joining an economic or monetary union with little supranational public finance would have to rely for cushioning on its ability to borrow, either from its partners in the union or outside."
10. The contributions to Kenneth Button and Denis Swann (1989) provide details of the situation.
11. http://prabook.com/web/person-view.html?profileId=953241# (last accessed 18 July 2017).
12. It was reviewed for example in *New York University Journal of International Law and Politics*, 1987, 19: 532–3.
13. The study mainly used data from prior analysis by Angus Maddison (1982) supplemented by data from the OECD.
14. These prospects were well summarized in a note of thanks from the University of Leeds Senate: "The Senate wishes Arthur Brown a happy retirement. There will be work to be done in the hillside garden that Joan Brown and he have created; walks on higher hills; and work projected at the National Institute on another steady climber, the rate of inflation." *Letter from University of Leeds Senate to Brown* (20 October 1979, AJB C&P).
15. Speech on Brown's award of Doctor of Literature by the University of Sheffield in 1979 (no date, AJB C&P).

References

Unpublished letters and other documents relating to Brown are from Arthur Brown's correspondence and papers; Brotherton Library, University of Leeds. These are denoted in footnotes as AJB C&P. Where they are mimeos, they are presented as a full reference when first used, and just by title thereafter.

Adler, J.H. (1945) United States import demand during the interwar period, *American Economic Review*, **35**, 418–30.

Advisory Commission on the Review of the Constitution of Rhodesia and Nyasaland (1960) *Report*, Cmnd 1148, HMSO, London.

Allan, L. (2008) Why have economists done so well in the British civil service?, *Oxonmics*, **3**, 26–9.

Amid-Hozour, E., Dick, D.T., and Lucier, R.L. (1971) Sultan schedule and Philips Curve: An historical note, *Economica*, **38**, 319–20.

Annan, N. (1999) *The Dons: Mentors, Eccentrics and Geniuses*, University of Chicago Press, Chicago.

Armstrong, H.W. and Taylor, J. (2000) *Regional Economics and Policy* (3rd ed.), Wiley-Blackwell, Hoboken.

Backhouse, R.E. and Biddle, J. (2000) The concept of applied economics: A history of ambiguity and multiple meanings, *History of Political Economy*, Supplement, **32**, 1–24.

Barr, N. (2000) The history of the Phillips machine, in A.R. Leeson (ed.) *A.W.H. Phillips: Collected Works in Contemporary Perspective*, Cambridge University Press, Cambridge, pp. 89–114.

Barro, R.J. and Sala-I-Martin, X. (1991) Convergence across states and regions. *Brookings Papers on Economic Activity*, **1**, 107–82.

Baumol, W.J. (1978) On the stochastic unemployment distribution model and the long-run Phillips curve, in A.R. Bergstrom, A.J.L. Catt, M.H. Peston, and B.D.J. Silverstone (eds.) *Stability and Inflation: A Volume of Essays to Honour the Memory of A.W.H. Phillips*, Wiley, Chichester, pp. 3–20.

Beloff, M. (1968) *The Plateglass Universities*, Secker & Warburg, London.

Benham, F.C. (1938) *Economics: A General Introduction*, Pitman, London.

Bergstrom, A.R., Catt, A.J.L., Peston, M.H., and Silverstone, B.D.J. (eds.) (1978) *Stability and Inflation: A Volume of Essays to Honour the Memory of A.W.H. Phillips*, Wiley, Chichester.

Besomi, D. (1998) Roy Harrod and the Oxford Economists' Research Group's inquiry on prices and interest, 1936–39, *Oxford Economic Papers*, **50**, 534–62.

Beveridge, W.H. (1942) *Social Insurance and Allied Services (Beveridge Report)*, Cmd 6404, HMSO, London.

Beveridge, W.H. (1944a) *Full Employment in a Free Society*, Allen & Unwin, London.

Beveridge, W.H. (1944b) The government's employment policy, *Economic Journal*, **54**, 161–76.

Blyth, C.A. (1975) A.W.H. Phillips, MBE: 1914–1975, *Economic Record*, **51**, 303–7.

Bollard, A.E. (2011) Man, money and machines: The contribution of A.W. Phillips, *Economica*, **78**, 1–9.

Borts, G.H. (1981) Report of the managing editor: *American Economic Review, American Economic Review, Papers and Proceedings*, **71**, 452–64.

Bowers, J.K. (ed.) (1979) *Inflation Development and Integration: Essays in Honour of A.J. Brown*, Leeds University Press, Leeds.

Bowers, J.K. (2003) Professor Arthur Brown: Applied economist who used his slide-rule to devastating effect, *The Independent*, 6 March.

Boyle, E. (1979) The economist in government, in J.K. Bowers (ed.) *Inflation Development and Integration: Essays in Honour of A.J. Brown*, Leeds University Press, Leeds, pp. 1–23.

Bronfenbrenner, M. (1955) Review of "The Great Inflation 1939–1951", *Journal of Economic History*, **15**, 304.

Bronfenbrenner, M. and Holzman, F.D. (1963) Survey of inflation theory, *American Economic Review*, **53**, 594–661.

Brothwell, J.F. (1972) An alternative theoretical explanation of the Phillips Curve relationship, *Bulletin of Economic Research*, **24**, 57–64.

Brown, A.J. (1938) The liquidity-preference schedules of the London clearing banks, *Oxford Economic Papers*, **1**, 49–82.

Brown, A.J. (1939a) Interest, prices, and the demand schedule for idle money, *Oxford Economics Papers*, **2**, 46–69.

Brown, A.J. (1939b) German mineral supplies II: Oil, *Bulletin of International News*, **16**, 1307–11.

Brown, A.J. (1939c) German mineral supplies III: Iron, nickel, and copper, *Bulletin of International News*, **16**, 1366–70.

Brown, A.J. (1940a) The use of advisory bodies by the Treasury, in R.V. Vernon and N. Mansergh (eds.) *Advisory Bodies: A Study of their Uses in Relation to Central Government, 1919–1939*, Allen & Unwin, London.

Brown, A.J. (1940b) World sources of petroleum, *Bulletin of International News*, **17**, 769–76.

Brown, A.J. (1940c) The economic prospects of Latin America, *Bulletin of International News*, **17**, 1148–52.

Brown, A.J. (1940d) The economic prospects of Latin America, *Bulletin of International News*, **17**, 1211–15.

Brown, A.J. (1940e) German exploitation of occupied countries I, *Bulletin of International News*, **17**, 1607–13.

Brown, A.J. (1940f) German exploitation of occupied countries II, *Bulletin of International News*, **17**, 1671–78.

Brown, A.J. (1941a) *The Arsenal of Democracy*, Oxford University Press, Oxford.

Brown, A.J. (1941b) Japan's strength and weakness, *Bulletin of International News*, **18**, 255–9.

Brown, A.J. (1941c) Canada's war effort, *Bulletin of International News*, **18**, 679–84.

Brown, A.J. (1941d) Italy's economic weakness, *Bulletin of International News*, **18**, 1802–6.

Brown, A.J. (1941e) Prices in some German occupied countries, *Bulletin of International News*, **18**, 1870–72.

Brown, A.J. (1942a) Trade balances and exchange stability, *Oxford Economics Papers*, **6**, 57–75.

Brown, A.J. (1942b) The United States War economy I, *Bulletin of International News*, **19**, 43–7.

Brown, A.J. (1942c) The United States War economy II, *Bulletin of International News*, **19**, 83–97.

Brown, A.J. (1942d) Review of "League of Nations: World Economic Survey, 1939–41", *Economic Journal*, **52**, 234–7.

Brown, A.J. (1943a) *Industrialization and Trade: The Changing World Pattern and the Problem for Britain*, Royal Institute for Economic Affairs, London.

Brown, A.J. (1943b) Some implications of synthetic rubber supply, *Bulletin of International News*, **20**, 194–200.

Brown, A.J. (1945a) War-time inflation I: What is inflation? *Bulletin of International News*, **22**, 11–15.

Brown, A.J. (1945b) War-time inflation II: Some outline case studies, *Bulletin of International News*, **22**, 102–9.

Brown, A.J. (1945c) Coal and cotton, *Bulletin of International News*, **22**, 474–81.

Brown, A.J. (1947) *Applied Economics: Aspects of the World Economy in War and Peace*, Allen & Unwin, London.

Brown, A.J. (1948) *Applied Economics: Aspects of the World Economy in War and Peace*, Allen & Unwin, London.

Brown, A.J. (1949a) Inflation and the flight from cash, *Yorkshire Bulletin of Economic and Social Research*, **1**, 33–42.

Brown, A.J. (1949b) *The American Economy and World Trade*, Institute of Bankers, London.

Brown, A.J. (1949c) Review of "Economics: An Introductory Analysis", *Nature*, **164**, 464 5.

Brown, A.J. (1951a) The fundamental elasticities in international trade, in T. Wilson and P.W.S. Andrews (eds.) *Oxford Studies in the Price Mechanism*, Oxford University Press, Oxford.

Brown, A.J. (1951b) Some aspects of international trade changes since devaluation, *Yorkshire Bulletin of Economic and Social Research*, **3**, 151–63.

Brown, A.J. (1951c) Review of "The Foundations of Economic History and Theory in the Analysis of Economic Reality", *International Affairs*, **27**, 488–9.

Brown, A.J. (1954) Should commodity prices be stabilised?, *District Bank Review*, December, 3–17.

Brown, A.J. (1955) *The Great Inflation, 1939–1951*, Oxford University Press, Oxford.

Brown, A.J. (1956) How to cure inflation: A new approach, *The Listener*, **60**, 783–84.

Brown, A.J. (1957) Professor Leontief on the pattern of world trade, *Yorkshire Bulletin of Economic and Social Research*, **9**, 63–75.

Brown, A.J. (1958) Inflation and the British economy. *Economic Journal*, **68**, 449–63.

Brown, A.J. (1959a) *Introduction to the World Economy*, Allen & Unwin, London.

Brown, A.J. (1959b) Memorandum of Evidence Submitted by Professor A.J. Brown, in Committee on the Working of the Monetary System, *Report*, Cmnd 827, HMSO London, pp. 48–50.

Brown, A.J. (1959c) Minutes of Evidence Before the Committee on the Working of the Monetary System *Report*, Cmnd 827, HMSO, London, pp. 591–5.

Brown, A.J. (1960) Review of "The Theory of Wage Determination: Proceedings of a Conference held by the International Economics Association", *Economica*, **27**, 78–80.

Brown, A.J. (1961a) Economic separatism versus a common market in developing countries, *Yorkshire Bulletin of Economic and Social Research*, **13**, 33–40.

Brown, A.J. (1961b) Customs union versus economic separatism in developing countries, Part II, *Yorkshire Bulletin of Economic and Social Research*, **13**, 88–96.

Brown, A.J. (1962a) Should African countries form an economic union? Paper presented to the Nyasaland Economic Symposium, Lilongwe.

Brown, A.J. (1962b) *The Economics of Disarmament*, United Nations Association, London.

Brown, A.J. (1964) *The Economic Consequences of Disarmament*, David Davies Memorial Institute of International Studies, London.

Brown, A.J. (1965) Britain and the world economy, *Yorkshire Bulletin of Economic and Social Research*, **17**, 46–60.

Brown, A.J. (1966) Review of "The German Inflation, 1918–1923", *Economica*, **33**, 362–4.

Brown, A.J. (1967) The effect of disarmament on the balance of payments of the United Kingdom, in E. Benoit with N.P. Gleditsch (eds.) *Disarmament and World Economic Interdependence*, Columbia University Press, New York, pp. 115–38.

Brown, A.J. (1968) Some myths about the Six, *Yorkshire Post*, 4 March.

Brown, A.J. (1969a) Note of dissent: Impact of investment grants on capital intensive industries, in J. Hunt, *The Intermediate Areas: Report of a Committee under the Chairmanship of Sir Joseph Hunt*. Cmnd 3998, HMSO, London, pp. 155–65.

Brown, A.J. (1969b) Appendix H: Economic structure and employment, in J. Hunt, *The Intermediate Areas: Report of a Committee under the Chairmanship of Sir Joseph Hunt*. Cmnd 3998, HMSO, London, pp. 229–31.

Brown, A.J. (1969c) Appendix J: Impact of investment grants on capital-intensive industry, in J. Hunt, *The Intermediate Areas: Report of a Committee under the Chairmanship of Sir Joseph Hunt*. Cmnd 3998, HMSO, London, pp. 237–8.

Brown, A.J. (1969d) Survey in applied economics: Regional economics, *Economic Journal*, **68**, 761–96.

Brown, A.J. (1969e) Some English thoughts on the Scottish economy, *Scottish Journal of Political Economy*, **16**, 233–47.

Brown, A.J. (1970) Criteria of regional economic policy, *Yorkshire Bulletin of Economic and Social Research*, **22**, 45–53.

Brown, A.J. (1972) *The Framework of Regional Economics in the United Kingdom*, Cambridge University Press, Cambridge.

Brown, A.J. (1976a) UV analysis, in G.D.N Worswick (ed.) *The Concept and Measurement of Involuntary Unemployment*, Allen & Unwin, London, pp. 134–45.

Brown, A.J. (1976b) Review of "Public Policy and Regional Development: The Experience of Nine Western Countries", *Economic Journal*, **86**, 145–7.

Brown, A.J. (1977) United Kingdom, in Commission of the European

Community, *Report of the Study Group on the Role of Public Finance in European Integration Volume II: Individual Contributions and Working Papers*, EEC, Brussels, pp. 11–28.

Brown, A.J. (1978) Review of "Inflation, Exchange Rates, and the World Economy", *Economic Journal*, **88**, 163–4.

Brown, A.J. (1979) Inflation and the British sickness, *Economic Journal*, **89**, 1–12.

Brown, A.J. (1980) Some library costs and options, *Journal of Librarianship and Information Science*, **12**, 211–16.

Brown, A.J. (1983) The General Budget, in A. El-Agraa (ed.) *The Economics of the European Community*, Philip Allan, Oxford, pp. 301–13.

Brown, A.J. (1988a) A worm's eye view of the Keynesian Revolution, in J. Hillard (ed.) *J.M. Keynes in Retrospect*, Edward Elgar Publishing, Aldershot, UK and Brookfield, VT, USA, pp. 18–44.

Brown, A.J. (1988b) World depression and the price level, *National Institute Economic Review*, **123**, 65–79.

Brown, A.J. (1997a) Arthur Brown, in K. Tribe (ed.) *Economic Careers: Economics and Economists in Britain, 1930–1970*, Routledge, London, pp. 138–44.

Brown, A.J. (1997b) The inflationary dimension, in G.C. Harcourt and P.A. Riach (eds.), *A Second Edition of The General Theory: Volume 2 Overview, Extensions, Method and New Development*, Routledge, London, pp. 41–60.

Brown, A.J. (2000) Foreword, in A.R. Leeson (ed.) *A.W.H. Phillips: Collected Works in Contemporary Perspective*, Cambridge University Press, Cambridge, pp. xii–xvi.

Brown, A.J. and Burrows, E.M. (1977) *Regional Economic Problems: Comparative Experiences of Some Market Economies*, Allen & Unwin, London.

Brown, A.J. and Woodward, V H (1969) Regional social accounts for the United Kingdom, *Review of Income and Wealth*, **15**, 335–47.

Brown, A.J. with Darby, J. (1985) *World Inflation Since 1950: An International Comparative Study*, Cambridge University Press, Cambridge.

Brown, A.J., Bowers, J.K. and Lind, H. (1967) "The Green Paper on Development Areas", *National Institute Economic Review*, **40**, 26–33.

Brown, A.J., Bowers, J.K., Cheshire, P.C., Lind, H., and Woodward, V.H. (1968) Regional problems and regional policy, *National Institute Economic Review*, **46**, 42–51.

Brown, J. (1998) *The Twentieth Century: The Oxford History of the British Empire Volume IV*, Oxford University Press, Oxford.

Brown, W.A. (2011) MONIAC: A brat's eye view, *Economia Politica*, **28**, 33–4.

Brunner, K. and Meltzer, A.H. (1963) Predicting velocity: Implications for theory and policy, *Journal of Finance*, **18**, 319–54.

Buck, T.W. and Lowe, J.F. (1972) Regional policy and the distribution of investment, *Scottish Journal of Political Economy*, **19**, 253–71.

Butler, R.E. (1971) *Art of the Possible: Memoirs of Lord Butler*, Hamish Hamilton, London.

Button, K.J. (2011) The economist's perspective on regional endogenous development, in R. Stimson and R. Stough (eds.) *Regional Endogenous Development*, Edward Elgar Publishing, Cheltenham, UK and Northampton, MA, USA, pp. 20–38.

Button, K.J. (2018) A.J. Brown, Phillips' curve, and economic networks in the 1950s, *Journal of the History of Economic Thought*, **25** (forthcoming).

Button, K.J. and Pearce, D.W. (1977) What British economists think of their journals, *International Journal of Social Economics*, **4**, 151–8.

Button, K.J. and Swann, D. (eds.) (1989) *The Age of Regulatory Reform*, Oxford University Press, Oxford.

Cagan, P. (1955) Review of "The Great Inflation 1939–1951", *Journal of Political Economy*, **63**, 539.

Carter, C.F. (1969) The Hunt Report, *Scottish Journal of Political Economy*, **16**, 248–55.

Carter, C. (1979) Review of "Regional Economic Problems: Comparative Experiences of Some Market Economies", *Town Planning Review*, **50**, 102–3.

Champernowne, D.G. (1936) Unemployment, basic and monetary: The Classical analysis and the Keynesian, *Review of Economic Studies*, **3**, 201–16.

Chandavarkar, A. (2001) Sir (Abraham) Jeremy Raisman, Finance Member, Government of India (1939–45), *Economic and Political Weekly*, **36**, 2641–55.

Chang, T.C. (1948) A statistical note on the world demand for exports, *Review of Economics and Statistics*, **30**, 106–16.

Chester, N. (1986) *Economics, Politics and Social Science in Oxford, 1900–85*, Macmillan, London.

Chisholm, M.D.I. (1978) Review of "Regional Economic Problems: Comparative Experiences of Some Market Economies", *Environment and Planning A*, **10**, 111–22.

Clough, S.B. (1949) Review of, "Applied Economics; Aspects of the World Economy in War and Peace", *Journal of Economic History*, **9**, 112–13.

Coase, R.H. (1982) Economics at LSE in the 1930s: A personal view, *Atlantic Economic Journal*, **10**, 31–4.

Coase, R.H. (2006) The conduct of economics: The example of Fisher

Body and General Motors, *Journal of Economics and Management Strategy*, **15**, 255–78.

Coats, A.W. (1968) The origins and early development of the Royal Economic Society, *Economic Journal*, **68**, 349–71.

Coats, A.W. (1982) The distinctive LSE ethos in the inter-war years, *Atlantic Economic Journal*, **10**, 18 30.

Commission of the European Communities (1973) *Report on the Regional Problems of the Enlarged Community*, COM (73) 550 Final, Brussels.

Commission of the European Community (1977a) *Report of the Study Group on the Role of Public Finance in European Integration Volume I: General Report* (MacDougall Report), EEC, Brussels.

Commission of the European Community (1977b) *Report of the Study Group on the Role of Public Finance in European Integration Volume II: Individual Contributions and Working Papers*. EEC, Brussels.

Committee on Finance and Industry (1931) *Report of the Committee*, Cmnd 3897, HMSO, London.

Committee on Higher Education (1963) *Higher Education: Report of the Committee Appointed by the Prime Minister under the Chairmanship of Lord Robbins 1961–63*, Cmnd 2154, HMSO, London.

Committee on the Working of the Monetary System (1959a) *Minutes*, Cmnd 827, HMSO, London.

Committee on the Working of the Monetary System (Radcliffe Report) (1959b) *Report*, Cmnd 827, HMSO, London.

Corry, B. (2001) Some myths about Phillips's curve, in P. Arestis, M. Desai, and S. Dow (eds.), *Money, Macroeconomics and Keynes: Essays in Honour of Victoria Chick, Volume 1*, Routledge, London, pp. 161–72.

Craver, E. (1986) Patronage and directions of research in economics: The Rockefeller Foundation in Europe, 1924–1938, *Minerva*, **24**, 205–22.

Dalton, H. (1923) *Public Finance*, Routledge, London.

Daniels, G.W. (1930) Economic and commercial studies in the Owens College and the University, *The Manchester School*, **1**, 3–9.

Department of Economic Affairs (1969) *The Intermediate Areas: Report of a Committee under the Chairmanship of Sir Joseph Hunt*, Cmnd 3998, HMSO, London.

Department of Education and Science (1966) *A Plan for Polytechnics and Other Colleges*, Cmnd 3006, HMSO, London.

Desai, M. (1975) The Phillips curve: A revisionist interpretation, *Economica*, **42**, 1–19.

Diamond, D.R. (1969) Regional development: The Intermediate Areas, *Political Quarterly*, **40**, 319–22.

Dicks-Mireaux, L.A. and Dow, J.C.R. (1959) Determinants of wage inflation, 1946–56, *Journal of the Royal Statistical Society*, **122**, 145–84.

Donner, A. and McCollum, J.F. (1972) The Phillips Curve: An historical note, *Economica*, **39**, 323–4.

Dow, A., Dow, S., and Hutton, A. (2000) Applied economics in a political economy tradition: The case of Scotland from the 1890s to the 1950s, *History of Political Economy*, **32**, 177–98.

Dunn, E.S. (1960) A statistical and analytical technique for regional analysis, *Papers of the Regional Science Association*, **6**, 97–112.

Durbin, J. and Watson, G.S. (1950) Testing for serial correlation in least squares regression, I, *Biometrika*, **37**, 409–28.

Durbin, J. and Watson, G.S. (1951) Testing for serial correlation in least squares regression, II, *Biometrika*, **38**, 159–79.

East Africa Economic and Fiscal Commission (1961) *East Africa: Report of Economic and Fiscal Commission (Chairman, Sir Jeremy Raisman)* Cmnd 1279, HMSO, London.

Economist Intelligent Unit (1963) *The Economic Effects of Disarmament*, Economist Intelligent Unit, London.

Ellsworth, P.T. (1954) The structure of American foreign trade: A new view examined, *Review of Economics and Statistics*, **36**, 279–85.

Esteban-Marquillas, J.M. (1972) A reinterpretation of shift-share analysis, *Regional and Urban Economics*, **2**, 249–61.

Felix, D. (1979) Review of "Towards Full Employment and Price Stability: A Report to the OECD by a Group of Independent Experts", *Economic Development and Cultural Change*, **27**, 804–89.

Fisher, I. (1926) A statistical relation between unemployment and price changes, *International Labour Review*, **13**, 785–92.

Fisher, I. (1930) *Theory of Interest, as Determined by Impatience to Spend Income and Opportunity to Invest It*, Macmillan, New York.

Fisher, I. (1973) I discovered the Phillips Curve, *Journal of Political Economy*, **81**, 496–502.

Forder, J. (2010) Friedman's Nobel Lecture and the Phillips Curve myth, *Journal of the History of Economic Thought*, **32**, 329–48.

Forder, J. (2014) *Macroeconomics and the Phillips Curve Myth*, Oxford University Press, Oxford.

Forder, J. (2015) Textbooks on the Phillips Curve, *History of Political Economy*, **47**, 207–40.

Fothergill, S. and Gudgin, G. (1979) In defense of shift-share, *Urban Studies*, **17**, 193–210.

Friedman, M. (1968) The role of monetary economics, *American Economic Review*, **58**, 1–17.

Friedman, M. (1977) Nobel Lecture: Inflation and unemployment, *Journal of Political Economy*, **85**, 451–72.

Frisch, R.A.K. (1933) Propagation problems and impulse problems in dynamic economics, in A.M. Kelley (ed.) *Economics Essays in Honour of Gustav Cassel*, Frank Cass, London, pp. 171–206.

Frisch, R.A.K. (1934) *Statistical Confluence Analysis by Means of Complete Regression Systems*, Universitets Økonomiske Institutt, Oslo.

Galbraith, J.K. (1952) *A Theory of Price Control*, Harvard University Press, Cambridge M.A.

Ghai, D.F. (1964) Territorial distribution of benefits and costs of the East African Common Market, *Eastern African Economic Review*, 11, 29–40.

Goodwin, R.M. (1953) The problem of trend and cycle, *Bulletin of Economic Research*, **5**, 89–97.

Gordon, R.J. (2011) The history of the Phillips curve: consensus and bifurcation, *Economica*, **78**, 10–50.

Granger, C.W.J. and Jeon, Y. (2011) The evolution of the Phillips Curve: A modern time series viewpoint, *Economica*, **78**, 51–66.

Gray, A.L. (1962) Review of "Economic and Social Consequences of Disarmament", *American Economic Review*, **52**, 906–8.

Grier, L. (1926) Review of "The Economics of Private Enterprise", *Economic Journal*, **36**, 610–13.

Griffon, K. (1962) A note on wages, prices and unemployment, *Bulletin of the Oxford Institute of Economics and Statistics*, **24**, 379–85.

Gurley, J.G. (1956) Review of "The Great Inflation 1939–1951", *American Economic Review*, **46**, 188–90.

Gwilliam, K.M. (1979) Transport infrastructure and investments and regional development, in J.K. Bowers (ed.) *Inflation Development and Integration: Essays in Honour of A.J. Brown*, Leeds University Press, Leeds, pp. 241–62.

Hall, R.L. and Hitch, C.L. (1939) Price theory and business behavior, *Oxford Economic Papers*, **2**, 12–45.

Hall, T.E. and Hart, W.R. (2012) The Samuelson-Solow Phillips curve and the great inflation, *History of Economics Review*, **55**, 62–72.

Hancock, K. and Isaac, J.E. (1998) Sir Henry Phelps Brown, 1906–1994, *Economic Journal*, **108**, 757–78.

Harberger, A. (1950) Currency depreciation, income, and the balance of trade, *Journal of Political Economy*, **58**, 47–60.

Harrod, R.F. (1936) *The Trade Cycle: An Essay*, Clarendon, Oxford.

Harrod, R.F. (1937a) Mr. Keynes and traditional theory, *Econometrica*, **5**, 74–86.

Harrod, R.F. (1937b) L'Université d'Oxford, in *L'Enseignement Économique en France et à l'Étranger: Cinquantenaire de la Revue d'Économie Politique*, Librairie du Recueil Sirey, Paris, pp. 79–90.

Harrod, R.F. (1949) Wesley C. Mitchell at Oxford, *Economic Journal*, **59**, 459–60.

Harrod, R.F. (1953) The pre-war faculty, *Oxford Economic Papers*, Supplement, **5**, 59–64.

Hazlewood, A. (1966) The East African Common Market: Importance and effects, *Bulletin of the Oxford University Institute of Economics and Statistics*, **28**, 1–18.

Hazlewood, A. (1967) Economic integration in East Africa, in A. Hazlewood (ed.) *African Integration and Disintegration: Case Studies in Economic and Political Union*, Oxford University Press, London.

Hazlewood, A. and Henderson, P.D. (1960) Nyasaland: The economics of federation, *Bulletin of the Oxford University Institute of Economics and Statistics*, **22**, 1–91.

Henderson, H.D. (1932) *Supply and Demand*, Cambridge University Press, Cambridge.

Henderson, H.D. (1939) The significance of the rate of interest, *Oxford Economic Papers*, **1**, 1–13.

Henderson, P.D. (1961) The use of economists in British administration, *Oxford Economic Papers*, **13**, 5–26.

Hendry, D.F. and Morgan, M.S. (1989) A re-analysis of confluence analysis, *Oxford Economic Papers*, **41**, 35–52.

Hewing, G. (1979) Review of "Regional Economic Problems: Comparative Experiences of Some Market Economies", *Journal of the American Planning Association*, **45**, 352–3.

Hicks, J.R. (1932) *The Theory of Wages*, Macmillan, London.

Hicks, J.R. (1937) Mr Keynes and the Classics: A suggested interpretation, *Econometrica*, **5**, 147–59.

Hicks, J.R. (1939) *Value and Capital: An Inquiry into Some Fundamental Principles of Economic Theory*. Oxford: Clarendon.

Hicks, J.R. and Allen, R.G.D. (1934) A reconsideration of the theory of value: Part I, *Economica*, **1**, 52–75.

Hirsch, W.Z. (eds.) (1966) *Regional Accounts for Policy Decisions*, Johns Hopkins University Press, Baltimore.

Holland, S. (1976) *Capital versus the Regions*, Macmillan, Harmondsworth.

Horesh, E. (1966) Review of "Introduction to the World Economy", *Economica*, **33**, 379.

Houston, D.B. (1967) The shift and share analysis of regional growth: A critique, *Southern Economic Journal*, **33**, 577–81.

Howson, S. and Winch, D. (1977*)* *The Economic Advisory Council,*

1930–1939: A Study in Economic Advice during Depression and Recovery, Cambridge University Press, Cambridge.

Humphrey, T.M. (1985) The early history of the Phillips Curve, *Federal Reserve Bank of Richmond Economic Review*, September, 17–24.

Irvine, A.G. (1959) *The Balance of Payments of Rhodesia and Nyasaland, 1945–1954*, Oxford University Press, Oxford.

Johnson, H.G. (1956) Review of "The Great Inflation 1939–1951", *Economic Journal*, **66**, 121–3.

Jones, J.H. (1926) *The Economics of Private Enterprise*, Pitman, London.

Joy, S. (1973) *The Train that Ran Away*, Ian Allan, London.

Junz, H. and Rhomberg, R. (1965) Prices and export performances of industrial countries, *IMF Staff Papers*, **12**, 224–71.

Kahn, R.F. (1984) *The Making of Keynes' General Theory*, Cambridge University Press, Cambridge.

Kaldor, N. (1970) The case for regional policies, *Scottish Journal of Economics*, **17**, 337–47.

Katz, S.I. (1959) *Radcliffe Report: Monetary Policy and Debt Management Reconciled*, Federal Reserve System, Washington DC.

Keynes, J.M. (1913) *Indian Currency and Finance*, Macmillan, London.

Keynes, J.M. (1924) Alfred Marshall: 1842–1924, *Economic Journal*, **34**, 311–72.

Keynes, J.M. (1929) The German transfer problem, *Economic Journal*, **39**, 1–7.

Keynes, J.M. (1930) *A Treatise on Money*, Macmillan, London.

Keynes, J.M. (1931) The Pure Theory of Money: A reply to Dr. Hayek, *Economica*, **34**, 387–97.

Keynes, J.M. (1936) *The General Theory of Employment, Interest and Money*, Macmillan, London.

Keynes, J.N. (1917) *The Scope and Method of Political Economy*, Macmillan, Cambridge.

Khan, A.A. (1962) Economic and social consequences of disarmament, *Pakistan Horizon*, **15**, 177–85.

Khusro, A.M. (1952) An investigation of liquidity preference, *Yorkshire Bulletin of Economic and Social Research*, **4**, 1–20.

Kubinski, A. (1950) The elasticity of substitution between sources of British imports, 1921–1938, *Yorkshire Bulletin of Economic and Social Research*, **2**, 17–29.

Kuh, E. (1967) A productivity theory of wage levels: An alternative to the Phillips Curve, *Review of Economic Studies*, **34**, 333–60.

Laidler, D. (1989) Radcliffe, the quantity theory and monetarism, in D. Cobham, R. Harrington, and G. Zis (eds.) *Money Trade and*

Payments: Essays in Honour of D.J. Coppock, Manchester University Press, Manchester, pp. 17–37.

Laidler, D. (2002) Phillips in retrospect, in W.J. Samuels and J.E. Biddle (eds.), *A Research Annual (Research in the History of Economic Thought and Methodology) (Vol. 20, Pt 1)*, Emerald, Bingley, pp. 223–35.

Lancaster, K.J. (1979) A.W. Phillips, in *International Encyclopedia of the Social Sciences, Vol. 18*, Free Press, New York.

Lee, F.S. (1981) The Oxford challenge to Marshallian supply and demand: The history of the Oxford Economist's Research Group, 1934–1952, *Oxford Economic Papers*, **33**, 339–51.

Lee, F.S. (1991) The history of the Oxford challenge to marginalism, 1934–1952, *PSL Quarterly Review*, **44**, 489–511.

Leeson, A.R. (1994a) A.W.H. Phillips M.B.E. (Military Division), *Economic Journal*, **104**, 605–18.

Leeson, A.R. (1994b) Some misunderstandings concerning the contributions made by A.W.H. Phillips and R.G. Lipsey to the inflation–unemployment literature, *History of Economics Review*, **22**, 71–82.

Leeson, A.R. (1995) Fisher and Phillips, *History of Economics Review*, **23**, 117–18.

Leeson, A.R. (1997) The trade-off interpretation of Phillips' dynamic stabilization exercise, *Economica*, **64**, 155–71.

Leeson, A.R. (ed.) (2000) *A.W.H. Phillips: Collected Works in Contemporary Perspective*, Cambridge University Press, Cambridge.

Lehfeldt, R.H. (1926) *Money*, Oxford University Press, Oxford.

Leontief, W.W. (1944) Output, employment, consumption, and investment, *Quarterly Journal of Economics*, **58**, 290–314.

Leontief, W.W. (1953) Domestic production and foreign trade: The American capital position re-examined, *Proceedings of American Philosophical Society*, **97**, 322–49.

Leontief, W.W. (1956) Factor proportions and the structure of American trade: Further theoretical and empirical analysis, *Review of Economics and Statistics*, **38**, 386–407.

Leontief, W.W. and Hoffenberg, M. (1961) The economic effects of disarmament, *Scientific American*, **204**, 47–55.

Lerner, A.P. (1951) *The Economics of Employment*, McGraw-Hill, New York.

Leser, C.E.V. (1951) *Some Aspects of the Industrial Structure of Scotland: An Analysis of the Industrial Distribution of Insured Persons in Scotland, Parts of Scotland and Regions of England and Wales in 1947*, Jackson, Glasgow.

Liew, C.K. (1974) Review of "The Framework of Regional Economics in the United Kingdom", *Annals of Regional Science*, **8**, 142.

Lipsey, R.G. (1960a) The theory of customs unions: A general survey, *Economic Journal*, **70**, 496–513.

Lipsey, R.G. (1960b) The relationship between unemployment and the rate of change of money wages in the United Kingdom 1862–1957: A further analysis, *Economica*, **27**, 1–31.

Lipsey, R.G. (1978) The place of the Phillips curve in macroeconomic models, in A.R. Bergstrom, A.J.L. Catt, M.H. Peston, and B.D.J. Silverstone (eds.), *Stability and Inflation: A Volume of Essays to Honour the Memory of A.W.H. Phillips*, Wiley, Chichester, pp. 49–76.

Lipsey, R.G. (2000) The famous Phillips Curve article, in A.R. Leeson (cd.), *A.W.H. Phillips: Collected Works in Contemporary Perspective*, Cambridge University Press, Cambridge, pp. 222–42.

Little, I.M.D. (1957) The economist in Whitehall, *Lloyds Bank Review*, April, 29–10.

Littlechild, S. (2008) Chairs of applied economics and economic theory, Presented at a conference in honor of the 65th birthday of Professor David M.G. Newbery, Cambridge, 13 September.

MacDougall, D. (1975) *Studies in Political Economy, Vol. II: International Trade and Domestic Economic Policy*, Macmillan, London, pp. 5–68.

MacDougall, D. (1987) *Don and Mandarin: Memoirs of an Economist*, John Murray, London.

MacFie, A.L. (1934) *Theories of the Trade Cycle*, Macmillan, London.

McCracken, P.W. (1977) *Towards Full Employment and Price Stability: A Report to the OECD by a Group of Independent Experts*, OECD, Paris.

McKinley, R.A. (1997) *The University of Bradford: The Early Years*, University of Bradford, Bradford.

Maddison, A. (1964) *Economic Growth in the West*, Allen & Unwin, London.

Maddison, A. (1982) *Phases in Capitalist Development*, Oxford University Press, Oxford.

Makower, H., Marschak, J., and Robinson, H.W. (1939) Studies in mobility of labour, part I, *Oxford Economic Papers*, **2**, 70–97.

Makower, H., Marschak, J., and Robinson, H.W. (1940) Studies in mobility of labour, part II, *Oxford Economic Papers*, **4**, 39–42.

Massell, B.F. (1963) *East African Economic Union: An Evaluation and Some Implications for Policy*, Memorandum RM-3880-RC, Rand Corporation, Santa Monica.

Mavroeidis, S., Plagborg-Møller, M., and Stock, J.H. (2004) Empirical evidence on inflation expectations in the New Keynesian Phillips Curve, *Journal of Economic Literature*, **52**, 124–88.

Meade, J.E. (1936) *Introduction to Economic Analysis and Policy*, Oxford University Press, Oxford.

Meade, J.E. (1937) A simplified model of Mr. Keynes' system, *Review of Economic Studies*, **4**, 98–107.

Meade, J.E. (1961) *A Neo-Classical Theory of Economic Growth*, Allan & Unwin, London.

Meade, J.E. (2000) The versatile genius, in A.R. Leeson (ed.) *A.W.H. Phillips: Collected Works in Contemporary Perspective*, Cambridge University Press, Cambridge, pp. 18–19.

Meade, J.E. and Andrews, P.W.S. (1937) Summary of replies to questions on effects of interest rates, *Oxford Economic Papers*, **1**, 14–31.

Meltzer, A.H. (1963) The demand for money: The evidence from the time series, *Journal of Political Economy*, **71**, 219–46.

Meyer, J.R. (1963) Regional economics: A survey, *American Economic Review*, **53**, 19–54.

Mitchell, W.F. (1999) *The Origins of the Phillips Curve*, Centre of Full Employment and Equity, Working Paper 99-02, Newcastle, NSW.

Mitchell, W.F. (2015) *Eurozone Dystopia: Groupthink and Denial on a Grand Scale*, Edward Elgar Publishing, Cheltenham, UK and Northampton, MA, USA.

Mitchell, W.F. and Muysken, J. (2008) *Full Employment Abandoned: Shifting Sands and Policy Failures*, Edward Elgar Publishing, Cheltenham, UK and Northampton, MA, USA.

Moggridge, D.E. (2010) *Keynes and the Wireless*, Palgrave Macmillan, Basingstoke.

Moore, B. and Rhodes, J. (1973) Evaluating the effects of British regional economic policy, *Economic Journal*, **83**, 87–110.

Morgan, E.V. (1955) Review of "The Great Inflation 1939–1951", *Economic History Review*, **8**, 253–5.

Morgan, E.V. (1959) Review of "Introduction to the World Economy", *Economic Journal*, **69**, 551–3.

Newlyn, W.T. (1950) The Phillips/Newlyn hydraulic model, *Yorkshire Bulletin of Economic and Social Research*, **2**, 111–27.

Newlyn, W.T. (1965) Gains and losses in the East African Common Market, *Yorkshire Bulletin of Economic and Social Research*, **17**, 130–38.

Newlyn, W.T. (2000) The origins of the machine in a personal context, in A.R. Leeson (ed.) *A.W.H. Phillips: Collected Works in Contemporary Perspective*, Cambridge University Press, Cambridge, pp. 31–8.

Niskanen, W.A. (1988) *Reaganomics: An Insider's Account of the Policies and the People*, Oxford University Press, Oxford.

Odber, A.J. (1970) Policy after Hunt, *Urban Studies*, **7**, 205–7.

Oi, W.Y. (1962) Labor as a quasi-fixed factor, *Journal of Political Economy*, **70**, 538–55.

Orwell, G. (1937) *The Road to Wigan Pier*, Gollancz, London.

Paish, F.W. (1962) *Studies in an Inflationary Economy: The United Kingdom, 1848–1961*, Macmillan, London.

Peston, M.H. (2006) The 364 were correct, in P. Booth (ed.) *Were 364 Economists All Wrong?* Institute of Economic Affairs, London, pp. 77–82.

Petridis, R. (1994) Review of "Oxford Economics and Oxford Economists", *History of Economics Review*, **21**, 145–7.

Phelps, E.S. (1967) Phillips Curves, expectations of inflation and optimal employment over time, *Economica*, **34**, 254–81.

Phelps Brown, E.H. (1996) Autobiographical notes: Henry Phelps Brown, *Review of Political Economy*, **8**, 129–39.

Phelps Brown, E.H. and Hopkins, S.V. (1950) The course of wage rates in five countries, 1860–1939, *Oxford Economic Papers*, **2**, 226–96.

Phelps Brown, E.H. and Shackle, G.L.S. (1938) An index of real turnover, 1919–36, *Oxford Economic Papers*, **1**, 32–48.

Phillips, A.W.H. (1950) Mechanical models in economic dynamics, *Economica*, **17**, 283–305.

Phillips, A.W.H. (1954) Stabilization policy in a closed economy, *Economic Journal*, **67**, 290–323.

Phillips, A.W.H. (1957) Stabilization policy and the time-forms of lagged responses, *Economic Journal*, **67**, 265–67.

Phillips, A.W.H. (1958) The relation between unemployment and the rate of change of money wage rates in the United Kingdom, 1861–1957, *Economica*, **25**, 283–99.

Phillips, A.W.H. (1959a) Discussion of Dicks-Mireaux and Dow's "The Determinants of Wage Inflation: United Kingdom, 1946–1956", *Journal of the Royal Statistical Society*, **122**, 176–77.

Phillips, A.W.H. (1959b) *Wage Changes and Unemployment in Australia, 1947–1958*, Economic Monograph No. 14, Economic Society of Australia and New Zealand.

Phillips, A.W.H. (1961) A simple model of employment, money and prices in a growing economy, *Economica*, **28**, 360–70.

Phillips, A.W.H. (1962) Employment, inflation and growth, *Economica*, **29**, 1–16.

Pigou, A.C. (1920) *Economics of Welfare*, Macmillan, London.

Pigou, A.C. (1927) *Industrial Fluctuations*, Macmillan, London.

Pigou, A.C. (1928) *Study in Public Finance*, Macmillan, London.

Pigou, A.C. (1945) *Lapses from Full Employment*, Macmillan, London.

Ramsey F.P. (1928) A mathematical theory of saving, *Economic Journal*, **38**, 543–59.

Reddaway, W.B. (1936) The General Theory of Employment, Interest and Money, *Economic Record*, **12**, 28–36.

Reid, G. (1981) *The Kinked Demand Curve Analysis of Oligopoly: Theory and Evidence*. Edinburgh University Press, Edinburgh.

Renfro, C.G. (2004) Econometric software: The first fifty years in perspective, *Journal of Economic and Social Measurement*, **29**, 9–107.

Richardson, H.W. (1970) The Hunt Report, *Yorkshire Bulletin of Economic and Social Research*, **22**, 54–64.

Robbins, L.C. (1932) *An Essay on the Nature and Significance of Economic Science*, Macmillan, London.

Robbins, L.C. (1971) *Autobiography of an Economist*, Macmillan, London.

Robbins, L.C., Medema, S.G., and Samuels, W.J. (1998) *A History of Economic Thought: The LSE Lectures*, Princeton University Press, Princeton.

Robinson, E.A.G. (1939) "Oxford Economic Papers", numbers 1 and 2, *Economic Journal*, **49**, 538–43.

Robinson, E.A.G. (1985) Hubert Douglas Henderson, 1890–1952, *Proceedings of the British Academy*, **70**, 439–50.

Robinson, J.V. (1933a) *Economics of Imperfect Competition*, Macmillan, London.

Robinson, J.V. (1933b) The foreign exchanges, in J.V. Robinson (ed.) *Essays in the Theory of Employment*, Blackwell, Oxford, pp. 188–94.

Robinson, M.E. (1922) *Public Finance*, Cambridge University Press, Cambridge.

Robson, P. (1968) *Economic Integration in Africa*, Allen & Unwin, London.

Rosenberg, S. and Weisskopf, T.E. (1981) A conflict theory approach to inflation in the postwar U.S. economy, *American Economic Review*, **71**, 42–7.

Routh, G. (1959) The relation between unemployment and the rate of change of money wages: A comment, *Economica*, **21**, 303–8.

Royal Commission on the Distribution of Industrial Population (1939) *Report*, Cmnd 6153, HMSO, London.

Royal Commission on Local Government in England (1969) *Local Government Reform*, Cmnd 4039, HMSO, London.

Safarian, A.E. (1957) Review of "The Great Inflation 1939–1951", *Canadian Journal of Economics and Political Science*, **23**, 447–9.

Samuelson, P.A. (1947) *Foundations of Economic Analysis*, Harvard University Press, Cambridge, MA.

Samuelson, P.A. (1948) *Economics: An Introductory Analysis*, McGraw-Hill, London.

Samuelson, P.A. and Solow, R. (1960) Analytical aspects of anti-inflation policy, *American Economic Review*, **50**, 177–204.

Santomero, A.M. and Seater, J.J. (1978) The inflation-unemployment trade-off: A critique of the literature, *Journal of Economic Literature*, **16**, 499–544.

Sargan, D. (1964) Wages and prices in the United Kingdom: A study in econometric methodology, in P. Hart, G. Mills, and J.K. Whitaker (eds.) *Econometric Analysis for National Economic Planning*, Butterworth, London, pp. 25–63.

Sawyer, M.C. (1989) The political economy of the Phillips Curve, in P. Arestis and Y. Kitromilides (eds.) *Theory and Policy in Political Economy*, Edward Elgar Publishing, Aldershot, UK and Brookfield, VT, USA, pp. 100–129.

Sayers, R.S. (1940) Business men and terms of borrowing, *Oxford Economics Papers*, **3**, 23–31.

Schumpeter, J.A. (1954) *History of Economic Analysis*, Allen & Unwin, London.

Schwartz, A.J. (1986) Review of A.J. Brown, "World Inflation Since 1950: An International Comparative Study", *Economic History Review*, **39**, 670–72.

Schwarzer, J.A. (2012) A.W. Phillips and his curve: Stabilisation policies, inflation expectations and the "menu of choice", *European Journal of the History of Economic Thought*, **19**, 976–1003.

Schwarzer, J.A. (2013) Samuelson and Solow on the Phillips Curve and the "menu of choice": A retrospective, *Oeconomia*, **3-3**, 359–88.

Schwier, A.S. (2000) Playing around with some data, in A.R. Leeson (ed.) *A.W.H. Phillips: Collected Works in Contemporary Perspective*, Cambridge University Press, Cambridge, pp. 24–5.

Scott, D.A. (1981) *Ambassador in Black and White: Thirty Years of Changing Africa*, Weidenfeld & Nicolson, London.

Shackle, G.L.S. (1967) *The Years of High Theory: Invention and Tradition in Economic Thought 1926–1939*, Cambridge University Press, London.

Skidelsky, R. (1992) *John Maynard Keynes: Volume Two—The Economist as Saviour, 1920–1937*, Macmillan, London.

Sleeman, A.G. (2010) "Bill" Phillips war and his notorious pass degree, *Economic Record*, **86**, 414–20.

Sleeman, A.G. (2011) Retrospectives: The Phillips Curve: a rushed job? *Journal of Economic Perspectives*, **25**, 223–38.

Smith, A. (1759) *The Theory of Moral Sentiments*, A. Millar, London.

Smith, A. (1776) *An Inquiry into the Nature and Causes of the Wealth of Nations*, Oxford University Press, Oxford (1997 ed.).

Stamp, J. (1922) *Wealth and Taxable Capacity*, King & Son, London.

Steil, B. (2013) *The Battle of Bretton Woods*, Princeton University Press, Princeton.

Stein, H. (1996) A successful accident: Recollections and speculations about the CEA, *Journal of Economic Perspectives*, **10**, 3–21.

Steinhauser, G. (2012) Back to the Future . . . of 1977, *Wall Street Journal*, 11 June.

Stewart, W.A.C. (1989) *Higher Education in Postwar Britain*, Macmillan, Basingstoke.

Stone, J.R. (1945) The analysis of market demand, *Journal of the Royal Statistical Society*, **108**, 286–391.

Stone, J.R. (1961) Social accounts at the regional level: A survey, in W. Issard and J.H. Cumberland (eds.), *Regional Economic Planning*, OECD, Paris, pp. 263–96.

Suits, D.B. (1957) Use of dummy variables in regression equations, *Journal of the American Statistical Association*, **52**, 548–51.

Sultan, P. (1957) *Labor Economics*, Holt, New York.

Sundquist, J.L. (1973) Review of "The Framework of Regional Economics in the United Kingdom", *Urban Studies*, **10**, 277–8.

Swerling, B. (1954) Capital shortage and labor surplus in the United States? *Review of Economics and Statistics*, **36**, 275–96.

Taussig, F.W. (1915) *Principles of Economics* (2nd ed.), Macmillan, New York.

Taussig, F.W. (1927) *International Trade*, Augustus M. Kelley, New York.

The Times (2003) Professor A.J. Brown, 9 April.

Theakston, K. (1995) *The Civil Service since 1945*, Blackwell, London.

Thirlwall, A.P. (1972) The Phillips Curve: An historical note, *Economica*, **39**, 325.

Thirlwall, A.P. (2003) Arthur Brown: Eminent economist who applied Keynesian theory to the regions, *The Guardian*, 12 March.

Tinbergen, J. (1946) Some measurements of elasticities of substitution, *Review of Economics and Statistics*, **29**, 109–14.

Tobin, (1947) Liquidity preference and monetary policy, *Review of Economics and Statistics*, **29**, 124–31.

Tobin, J. (1965) The monetary interpretation of history, *American Economic Review*, **55**, 464–85.

Tobin, J. (1972) Inflation and unemployment, *American Economic Review*, **62**, 1–18.

Tsiang, S.C. (1961) The role of money in trade-balance stability: Synthesis of the elasticity and absorption approaches, *American Economic Review*, **51**, 912–36.

Turvey, R. (1955) Review of "The Great Inflation 1939–1951", *Economica*, **22**, 261–2.

Twain, M. (1933) Letter to Anne Macy. Reprinted in N. Braddy, *Anne Sullivan Macy: The Story Behind Helen Keller*, Doubleday, Doran, and Co., Garden City.

United Nations (1962) *Economic and Social Consequences of Disarmament:*

Report to the Secretary-General Transmitting the Study and its Consultative Group, Department of Economic and Social Affairs, UN, New York.

United States Arms Control and Disarmament Agency (1962) *Economic Impacts of Disarmament*, United States Arms Control and Disarmament Agency, Washington DC.

University Grants Committee (1967) *Report of the Committee on Libraries (The Parry Report)*, HMSO, London.

University Grants Committee (1976) *Capital Provision for University Libraries: Report of a Working Party*, HMSO, London.

Valavanis-Vail, S. (1954) Leontief's scarce factor paradox, *Journal of Political Economy*, **62**, 523 28.

Viner, J. (1950) *The Customs Union Issue*, Carnegie Endowment for International Peace, New York.

Waller, C. (2013) Brown, Arthur J., in T. Cate (ed.) *An Encyclopedia of Keynesian Economics* (2nd ed.), Edward Elgar Publishing, Cheltenham, UK and Northampton, MA, USA, pp. 53–5.

Weeden, R. (1974) *Regional Rates of Growth of Employment: An Analysis of Variance Treatment*, Cambridge University Press, London.

Wicksell, K. (1901) *Lectures on Political Economy, Vol. 1*, translated by E. Classen, Routledge and Kegan Paul, London.

Wicksell, K. (1906) *Lectures on Political Economy, Vol. 2*, translated by E. Classen, Routledge and Kegan Paul, London.

Williamson, O.E. (2000) The new institutional economics: Taking stock, looking ahead, *Journal of Economic Literature*, **38**, 595–613.

Wilson, H. (1971) *The Labour Government 1964–70: A Personal Record*, Weidenfeld & Nicolson/Michael Joseph, London.

Winston, C.M. (1991) Efficient transportation infrastructure policy, *Journal of Economic Perspectives*, **5**, 113–27.

Worswick, G.D.N. (1979) The great inflation revisited, in J.K. Bowers (ed.) *Inflation Development and Integration: Essays in Honour of A.J. Brown*, Leeds University Press, Leeds, pp. 27–38.

Wright, P.G. (1915) Moore's economic cycles, *Quarterly Journal of Economics*, **29**, 631–41.

Wulwick, N.J. (1987) The Phillips Curve: Which? Whose? To do what? How? *Southern Journal of Economics*, **53**, 834–57.

Wulwick, N.J. (1989) Phillips' approximate regression, *Oxford Economic Papers*, **41**, 170–88.

Yamey, B.S. (2000) The famous Phillips Curve: A note on its publication, in A.R. Leeson (ed.) *A.W.H. Phillips: Collected Works in Contemporary Perspective*, Cambridge University Press, Cambridge, pp. 335–41.

Young, W. (1987) *Interpreting Mr. Keynes: The IS-LM Enigma*, Westview, Boulder, CO, USA.

Young, W. (1989) *Harrod and His Trade Cycle Group: The Origins and Development of the Growth Research Programme*, Macmillan, London.

Young, W. and Lee, F.S. (1993) *Oxford Economics and Oxford Economists*, Macmillan, London.

Index

.